Gary Rhodes

at the table

Gary Rhodes
at the table

Photographs by Sîan Irvine

BBC

To John, my father for many years,
thank you for introducing me to the table.

Acknowledgements

Writing and bringing together so many flavours takes time and effort, and without the help of the following it would not have been possible. Thank you to: Wayne Tapsfield and fellow chefs, Borra Garson, Lissanne Kenyon, Sue Fleming, Jo Pratt, Nicky Copeland, Khadija Manjlai, Sîan Irvine, Andrew Barron, along with Nick Vaughan-Barratt, Mandy Cooper, Maggie Elliott and the rest of the BBC production team. And thank you, of course, to my wife Jennie and sons Samuel and George for listening, helping and putting up with me for another long year.

This book is published to accompany the television series entitled *Gary Rhodes at the Table*, first broadcast in 2001. The series was produced by BBC Features and Events.

Executive Producer: Nick Vaughan-Barratt

Producer: Mandy Cooper

Published by BBC Worldwide Limited, Woodlands,
80 Wood Lane, London W12 0TT

First published 2000

ISBN 0 563 55180 1

Commissioning Editor: Nicky Copeland

Project Editor: Khadija Manjlai

Copy-editor: Deborah Savage

Art Editor: Lisa Pettibone

Designer: Andrew Barron & Collis Clements Associates

Styling by Sue Rowlands

Food prepared for photography by Gary Rhodes

Thanks to David Mellor, Divertementi, Habitat and Heal's for the loan of items for photography

Typeset in Officina Sans

Printed and bound in France by Imprimerie Pollina s.a. -n° L81457

Colour separations by Imprimerie Pollina s.a., France

Jacket printed by Pollina s.a., France

Previous page:

Pan-fried Sea Bass with Blackberry Shallots and Creamy Hollandaise Sauce

contents

fish

mains

gary rhodes

vegetables

savouries

basic recipes

menus

Introduction

Gary Rhodes at the Table is a compilation of courses and recipes, which will hopefully encourage more of us to be drawn back to this great, social eating place. Although we have been eating for ever, the way in which we eat now is a fairly recent development. The dividing up of a formal meal into separate, defined stages, with one dish chosen from a range at each stage, is so familiar to us that we could be forgiven for thinking this has been the established norm for centuries. Not so, though. It's really only in the last 200 years that our eating habits changed. The word 'menu' was itself a new acquisition to our culinary vocabulary, with different dishes being offered as separate courses.

During the many hundreds of years previous to this, menu in Britain was known as the 'bill of fare'. This list of dishes was once put on the kitchen wall to let the chef and his team know just what they had to prepare and produce. The lists would often consist of hundreds of dishes, especially during medieval times throughout Europe. These formal meals, particularly those enjoyed by the aristocracy and the wealthy, were more in line with what we now call feasts. They would have on the table in front of them a huge selection of foods available at one time, with more arriving as the food was prepared and cooked. The look of the table – with many decorative, usually inedible, pieces made of pastry, marzipan and, quite often, amazingly spun sugar and sweet sculptures – was always important, and became the main feature of the whole event. People would help themselves to whatever they liked in front of them, or get servants to offer them the chosen dishes from elsewhere on the table. Interestingly, the word 'banquet', which is now virtually synonymous with 'feast', was originally the name for the final episode of a feast,

usually consisting of sweet and/or savoury concoctions. These were often served in a separate dining room (perhaps it's from here that 'banqueting suites', usually attached to hotels, found their title). In general, this mode of formal eating was to last for centuries.

Balancing dishes wasn't really part of the structure of the meal. The whole idea was to impress the eaters with lots of over-elaborate dishes that would often excite them visually more than they did taste-wise. A big influence on the development of the menu as we know it today was the aftermath of the French Revolution. Following the collapse of the aristocracy in France at the end of the eighteenth century, chefs from the great houses were forced to seek work of a different kind. Many opened eating houses in Paris, while others fled to England.

Up until this time, the only establishments in France selling food were inns and *traiteurs* (caterers who sold mainly cooked meats and stews). In inns, travellers would sit at the host's table and eat a set meal, the *table d'hôte*. It wasn't long after this that eating houses or, as we know them today, restaurants, were being opened by the chefs, offering a choice of dishes to those with money and the inclination to eat away from home. Eating out for pleasure, as something that one chose to do, is a fairly new concept, in both France and Britain, which developed very quickly. It's said that in 1789 there were just 100 restaurants in Paris; fifteen years later there were over 500, reflecting a passion for eating across the world that certainly hasn't slowed down.

It is with restaurant menus in mind that this book has been structured, with each chapter representing a course – from appetizers, soups and fish through to main courses, desserts and savouries – and ends with suggestions for compiling menus, including a six-course 'gourmet' meal. Six courses are certainly not what I'm suggesting we should all try; quite the opposite in fact. I hope these courses will help you to find the dish(es) or menu(s) to suit you. Virtually all the appetizers will stand as perfect one-course meals, as will soups, fish, main courses and most of the savouries, which are very English. These are small items that are thought to provide a perfect finish to the meal and help aid digestion. The recipes featured in this chapter are not quite so small, and will stand as dessert alternatives or snacks. The menu compilation can begin at one-course meals, and be built up to two, three, four or more courses.

The cheese course (page 198) is the modern equivalent of the savoury course. In France (and quite often in England) the cheese course is served before the dessert. Its purpose is to cleanse the palate before the sweetness of a pudding, and at the same time finish off the wines still sitting on the table from the main course. However, one of the loves of the British people is to offer a good glass of port to finish off the meal, with cheese becoming its perfect accompaniment. With modern British menu-planning, dessert seems to take priority over its savoury friends. While the chapter order in this book follows this, the choice is totally yours, but I do hope that some of these little friends will be given a chance to prove themselves at almost any eating time.

With so many dishes and combinations to choose from and try, I've included some two-, three- and four-course menus, and a six-course gourmet menu, with brief explanations for the choice of dishes in each to help you with your menu-planning.

Food is one of the few wonderful resources that draws family and friends naturally to the table. I hope your choice of dishes will carry an *à la carte* feel, but will be presented in a *table d'hôte* fashion at the host's table in the comfort of your own home.

As Shakespeare's Guildford says in *Henry VIII*:

...a general welcome from his Grace
Salutes ye all; this night he dedicates
To fair content and you. None here, he
    hopes,
In all this noble bevy, has brought with her
One care abroad; he would have all as merry
As, first, good company, good wine, good
    welcome
Can make good people.

(Act I, Scene IV)

Previous page:
Twice-baked Cheese Soufflés
Below: Hotchpot

General information

1 Follow one of the measurements only; do not mix metric and imperial.

2 Eggs used are large.

3 Unsalted butter is mostly used because it gives greater control over the seasoning of a dish.

4 A tablespoon is 15 g (½ oz) for solids and 15 ml (½ fl oz) for liquids, a dessertspoon is 10 g for solids and 10 ml for liquids and a teaspoon is 5 g for solids and 5 ml for liquids. All spoon measurements are level.

5 Unless otherwise stated, 'season' or 'seasoning' simply means seasoning with salt and pepper – preferably freshly ground white.

6 There are a number of stock and sauce recipes throughout the book, but there are also many good bought alternatives (fresh, dried or cubed) available in supermarkets.

7 All soft herbs, such as tarragon, flatleaf parsley and basil, are best torn by hand to prevent them bruising and breaking the texture. If you substitute dried for fresh herbs, remember to use only half the amount specified.

8 Fine pin bones are found in round fish fillets, that is, red mullet, trout, salmon, cod and so on. The bones run down the centre of most of these fillets and are easily removed with fine pliers or tweezers. It's worth spending the time needed to remove them, as the fish then becomes more comfortable to eat.

9 Caul is the lacy lining of a pig's stomach. It is quite difficult to get hold of, but you should be able to order it through your butcher. It must be soaked in cold water for 24 hours first, which makes it easier to use, then drained. It's used almost like cling film, rolled around meat or a meaty mixture, to which it will cling. If caul is unavailable, cook without a covering or use buttered foil.

10 Many recipes advise soaking dried beans overnight before use because this helps to soften the bean. However, I prefer to cook the beans straight from the packet. Although a longer cooking time is necessary, the natural shape of the bean is maintained. Tinned varieties are, of course, ready to use and require no additional cooking time.

11 Powerful butane gas canisters can be used as a blow torch in the kitchen to give a crispy glaze to many desserts. They are available from almost any hardware store and can also be found in the kitchen sections of department stores. Follow the instructions and use carefully and, of course, keep away from children.

12 I use a selection of vinegars in this book. Red-wine vinegar is a favourite. Because many of those available are thin and not very red-wine-flavoured, I urge you to spend a little more and buy a vinegar that bears the hallmark of a good wine – a Bordeaux, say, or my current favourite, Cabernet Sauvignon.

appetizers

Grilled Asparagus with Champ Potato Sauce and Tarragon Oil

Serves 4–6 as a starter

5–6 asparagus spears per portion

olive oil, for brushing the grill

butter, for brushing

salt and pepper (coarse sea salt can also be used)

For the Champ

about 100 ml (3½ fl oz) single cream

about 100 ml (3½ fl oz) milk

50–75 g (2–3 oz) butter (100 g/4 oz for the ultimate finish)

450 g (1 lb) potatoes, preferably Maris Piper, peeled, cooked and mashed

knob of butter, melted

bunch of spring onions, thinly sliced

salt, white pepper and a pinch of freshly grated nutmeg (optional)

4 dessertspoons Tarragon Oil (page 207), to serve

Introduction British home-grown asparagus is only available between May and July, so should be taken advantage of during this short season. I really do believe that the British produce the best asparagus in the world. Steaming or poaching the spears will give a very natural flavour, but grilling does lend an extra bite, with a slightly bitter edge from the grill lines.

Champ is the famous Irish potato dish that was originally prepared for Hallowe'en, with the man of the house pounding the large pot of cooked potatoes with a wooden stick (known as a beetie), before spring onions, onions, chives or parsley were thrown in (see also page 23). I'm also adding single cream and milk to loosen the potatoes to a thick sauce stage, so that, once spooned on the plate, they'll start to spread. Butter is also added, not forgetting that it is one of the most important original ingredients. And, to contribute an extra flavour, I've trickled a little tarragon oil around the plate, the herb enriching the total finish.

Method The asparagus can be blanched in advance, keeping it refrigerated until needed. To prepare, trim the spiky/pointy 'ears' from along the stalks, also cutting away 2–4 cm (¾–½ in) of the grey/white base stalk, keeping the spears a uniform length. The asparagus can now be plunged into a large saucepan of rapidly boiling, salted water. Twelve spears is the maximum that should be cooked at one time: any more and the water will lose its temperature and begin to stew the asparagus.

Cook, with the lid off, for 1–2 minutes and lift from the pot, transferring to iced water to stop the cooking process immediately. Once cooled, the spears can be wiped dry and refrigerated until needed.

To make the champ potatoes, heat together the single cream, milk and butter. Once warm, add to the mashed potatoes, seasoning with salt, pepper and nutmeg, if you like. The champ potatoes should now have a thick soft 'sauce' consistency. To loosen, if needed, more milk and cream should be added.

The next stage is to melt the knob of butter in a saucepan and, once bubbling, add the spring onions. Cook the onions for a minute or two until tender before adding to the creamy potatoes. The champ is now ready to serve.

To finish the asparagus, heat the grill plate, if you have one, brushing with olive oil. The asparagus can now be placed on the grill, brushing with butter and cooking for 2–3 minutes, turning the spears to achieve a good overall colour and flavour. Season with salt and pepper.

To serve, spoon the champ on to plates, allowing it to spread slightly. Place the asparagus spears on top before drizzling with the tarragon oil. The appetizer is now ready to serve.

The table is the only place where the first hour is never dull.

Brillat-Savarin

Bacon and Beans

Serves 4–6

600–900 ml (1–1½ pints) cooking oil or pork fat (lard)

750 g (1½ lb) boned piece of smoked or unsmoked streaky bacon, rind removed and trimmed (save any trimmings to flavour the *jus*/gravy)

150 ml (5 fl oz) *jus* (page 203, optional), to serve

glass or two of red wine (optional)

For the Beans

100 g (4 oz) dried haricot, black-eyed or butter beans (400 g/14 oz tinned can also be used)

1 tablespoon olive oil

1 large onion, finely chopped

1 large garlic clove, crushed

100–150 ml (3½–5 fl oz) Chicken Stock (page 201) or alternative

4 tomatoes, blanched (page 209) and diced

1–2 teaspoons 'chopped' fresh flatleaf parsley

1 teaspoon 'chopped' fresh basil

knob of butter

salt and pepper

Introduction The simple title might make this recipe sound like a breakfast dish, but far from it. The bacon is cooked as a 'joint', and can just be roasted, but I prefer to *confit* (preserve) it. This offers a double bonus: you can prepare and cook it well ahead of time, and the meat and fat are tenderized, with all the sinews breaking down. *Confit* of bacon can be used in many different dishes, in salads and soup garnishes. Here it is served on top of haricot, black-eyed or butter beans in a warm tomato dressing, and makes a great starter.

Method To make the *confit* first pre-heat the oven to 180°C/350°F/Gas 4. In a small roasting pan deep enough to allow the joint to be immersed, spoon a drop of the cooking oil/fat and heat on top of the stove. This stage is not essential but does add an extra flavour to the bacon. Place the piece of bacon in the pan, fat-side down, and fry to a golden brown. Turn the bacon in the pan and pour on the remaining oil/fat to cover. Bring to a soft simmer. Cover and cook in the pan for about 1–1½ hours. After the hour, check the tenderness of the meat by piercing with a knife. It should feel soft and totally tender; if slightly firm, continue to cook for the remaining 30 minutes.

Once it's cooked, if you're serving it immediately, remove the bacon. The excess fat will drain off. If not using, transfer everything to a bowl and leave to set in the fat. It's important that the meat is totally covered and encased in the fat. This *confit* can now be refrigerated until needed. Whenever needed, lift from the fat, scraping away any excess. Place in a roasting tray and bake in a pre-heated oven (same temperature as when cooked), fat-side down, for 20–25 minutes. During this warming time the joint of bacon will be able to return to its former succulent glory.

The gravy is an optional extra, certainly not essential, but does add another bite to the dish. Roughly chop any bacon trimmings and fry to release any excess oils, until golden brown. Drain away the excess fat before adding the *jus* or gravy and simmering for 15–20 minutes, to lend the bacon flavour to the finished sauce. Another extra that can be included for a richer taste is to add a glass or two of red wine to the bacon once the fat has been poured away. Now boil and reduce until almost dry before adding the gravy.

Place the beans in a large saucepan of soft water. The soft water will help soften the actual bean. A pinch of bicarbonate of soda can be added if only hard water is available. It's important not to add any salt to the pan, as this will toughen rather than soften the beans. Bring to the boil and cook fairly rapidly for 5–10 minutes before reducing the heat to a gentle simmer and continuing to cook for anything between 1 and 3 hours until tender.

The cooking time very much depends on the age of the bean: the younger they are, the better and quicker they cook. Once tender, drain, and the beans are ready to add to the tomatoes.

While the beans are boiling, warm the olive oil in a saucepan. Add the chopped onion and cook on a medium heat, gently frying for 8–10 minutes, without letting it colour. Add the crushed garlic and continue to cook for a further minute or two. Loosen with 100 ml (3½ fl oz) of the chicken stock and bring to the simmer. Add the diced tomatoes and continue to simmer for a few minutes until the tomatoes are just beginning to soften. If the mixture is too thick, loosen with the remaining 50 ml (2 fl oz) of stock. Season with salt and pepper. Add the warm beans, checking the seasoning again. Just before serving, add the chopped flatleaf parsley and basil along with the knob of butter.

To serve the dish, spoon the beans between serving plates and drizzle around a little *jus*/gravy. Any extra gravy should be offered separately. Cut the bacon into six pieces and sit on top of or beside the beans. The bacon and beans are now ready to serve. This dish may seem to contain an awful lot of work for an appetizer, but thinking ahead makes it a very simple one to finish.

Notes: *Goose fat can be used instead of cooking oil or lard, giving a richer flavour, but this is an expensive item, not easily obtainable.*

The bacon glazes beautifully when topped with a little clear honey and caramelized under a hot grill just before serving.

When cooking the beans, the quantity can be doubled, freezing half once cooked. They will defrost very easily, saving even more time.

The beans can be boiled in advance and then refrigerated until needed. If so, to re-heat, simmer in water for a few minutes to soften.

Tinned beans should first be heated in their liquor before draining and adding to the tomatoes. It's not essential to present the 'bacon joint' on top of the beans. Setting them side by side looks equally attractive.

The bacon can be pre-soaked in cold water for 24 hours to reduce its quite strong flavour. This works particularly well if using the smoked variety.

Crispy Prawn Cocktail

Serves 4

1 small iceberg lettuce

16–20 large prawns, prepared as per introduction

seasoned flour, for dusting

oil, for deep-frying

salt and pepper

coarse sea salt (optional)

For the Cocktail Sauce

8 tablespoons Mayonnaise (page 207) or bought ready-made mayonnaise

3 tablespoons Tomato Ketchup (page 207) or bought ready-make ketchup

1 lemon, cut into 6 wedges

splash (or two) of brandy

salt and pepper

For the Batter

225 g (8 oz) self-raising flour, sifted

300 ml (10 fl oz) cold lager (maximum)

Introduction Prawn cocktail seems to have introduced itself to our palates in a big way during the 1960s and 1970s. I featured this infamous dish in *New British Classics*, but I introduced one or two other flavours, which gave it a new face and finished taste. This version is even simpler, with the prawns fried in crisp batter, providing a hot and crunchy finish to dip into the cocktail sauce. Normally only served as a starter, this type of prawn cocktail works wonderfully as canapés, part of a finger buffet, starter, fish or complete main course. The best prawns to use are king, or the even bigger tiger prawns. Both varieties can be bought frozen, cooked or raw. You can sometimes also be lucky enough to find them fresh, but the frozen raw variety is a good alternative. Once defrosted, the tails should be picked free of shell, leaving just the last centimetre of shell and fan tail. Three to four large prawns will be plenty as a starter portion, with five or six working well as a main course.

With this recipe I'm making mayonnaise along with home-made tomato ketchup to form the sauce, but a bought, ready-made cocktail sauce can also be offered (or simply make your own using bought mayonnaise and ketchup). An alternative method is given for the sauce at the end of this recipe.

Method First, make the cocktail sauce. Whisk together the mayonnaise and tomato ketchup, add a squeeze or two of lemon juice from one of the wedges and season with salt and pepper. The brandy can now be added, to lift and enrich the flavours and suit your personal taste. The sauce can now be kept, refrigerated, until needed.

Quarter and finely shred the iceberg lettuce, also refrigerating until needed.

The prawns, although shelled will also need to have the thin black 'gut line', which runs down the back of the tail, removed. Using a sharp knife, simply cut centrally along the back of the prawn, this will reveal the thin black line that can now be easily removed. The prawns, if preferred, can now be rinsed and dried.

To make the batter, whisk three-quarters of the lager into the sifted flour. At this point, check the consistency of the batter; it should be thick, almost too thick. If it appears to be over-gluey, whisk in a little more lager to loosen it slightly.

Pre-heat the oil for deep-frying to 190°C/350°F.

The prawns can now be seasoned with salt and pepper and squeezed with lemon juice before passing through the seasoned flour for dusting. Its important only to dust them lightly and not have too much flour attached to the prawns.

Each prawn can now be dipped, holding the fan tail, through the batter and gently placed in the hot oil. You will find that, as the tails are submerged in the oil, they will begin to float; this is when to release them. The prawns will fry without sticking to the base of the fryer.

While the prawns are frying, season the iceberg lettuce with a sprinkling of coarse sea salt, if using, a twist of pepper and a squeeze of lemon juice.

The prawns will take 7–9 minutes to fry and become a rich, crispy, golden brown. It's important to gently turn the tails halfway through their cooking time, to ensure an overall golden finish. Once removed from the fryer, rest for 30–60 seconds on kitchen paper to collect any excess oil, then season with a pinch of salt.

The prawns can now be served on plates, along with small individual dishes of cocktail sauce (or offer a jug of sauce separately), iceberg lettuce and a wedge of lemon. The dish is now complete.

Note: *Instead of frying the prawns individually, they can be held together with a cocktail stick or skewer. To achieve this, simply place the portion together (4–6 tails depending on which course it constitutes), holding all by the fan tail. The cocktail stick can now be pushed through all the tails to the last 1 cm (½ in) of shell. This creates a fan shape of prawns which can now be seasoned, floured and 'battered' before gently placing in the hot oil. As they are submerged, they will begin to rise and float while frying. The batter soufflés, creating an even larger fan shape, and you will now cook only four batches instead of 16–20 individual ones. Once cooked, garnish as described previously.*

Instant Cocktail Sauce

150 ml (5 fl oz) tomato juice, preferably passata (sieved tomatoes)

2–3 tablespoons Heinz tomato ketchup

splash or two of brandy

squeeze of lemon juice

8 tablespoons bought ready-made mayonnaise

salt and pepper

Bring the tomato juice (passata) to the boil and reduce by two-thirds to three-quarters. Leave to cool. This will increase the tomato flavour, helping to balance the bought ketchup. The reduced juice, 2 tablespoons of ketchup, brandy and lemon juice can now all be added to the mayonnaise, adding the remaining spoon of ketchup if you like. Season with salt and pepper and the sauce is ready to serve.

Warm Sole Salad *'Belle Vapeur'*

Serves 4

1 kg (2¼ lb) lemon sole, filleted and skinned

For the Pickled Mushrooms

12 button or chestnut mushrooms

250 ml (9 fl oz) water

90 ml (3¼ fl oz) olive oil

juice of 1 lemon

1 teaspoon balsamic vinegar

1 bay leaf

fresh thyme sprig

few black peppercorns and coriander seeds

pinch of salt

For the Salad

1 lemon, segmented, saving any juice

olive oil

2 tomatoes, preferably plum, blanched (page 209) and seeded

6–8 Jersey Royals (or other new potatoes), cooked (page 147)

50–75 g (2–3 oz) fine French beans

2 thick slices of white bread, crusts removed, crumbed

25 g (1 oz) butter

225–350 g (8–12 oz) mixed green salad leaves, washed

bunch of watercress, divided into sprigs

8 black olives, stoned, halved and cut into strips

salt and pepper

For the Dressing

1 heaped teaspoon chopped capers

8–10 tablespoons olive oil

6 fresh mint leaves, chopped

1 heaped teaspoon fresh chives, cut into 1 cm (½ in) sticks

salt and pepper

Introduction Many moons ago, during my years at catering college, it was predominantly the French classics we were taught. One was a sole dish called *sole belle meunière* ('the beautiful miller's wife'). The fish was floured, pan-fried in butter and garnished with a slice of peeled lemon, a quarter of peeled tomato flesh, a whole mushroom and pan-fried herring roe; it was finished with lemony nut-brown butter and parsley. It really was a lovely dish to cook and eat, so I decided to borrow the idea, using most of the basic ingredients – the sole, lemon, tomato and mushroom – and turning them into a salad. The result is fresh flavours that have found a new home within a salad, becoming a perfect start to a meal. Other flavours are here, too – black olives, warm Jersey Royal potatoes and French beans among them. The mushrooms I prefer to use, although not essential, are mildly pickled. These can be made weeks in advance, and are a treat to add to many other salads and dishes. Alternatively, fresh mushrooms can be simply quartered and quickly fried in butter.

Lemon soles are the fish I use, as they steam quite quickly and have a very tender, soft texture. Dover soles, among the kings of fish, are twice the price and don't suit this salad quite so well. I prefer to steam the fillets from a large 1 kg (2¼ lb) fish. These have a thicker texture than smaller fish.

The ingredients list may look a little long for a simple starter, but the main features are the lemons, tomatoes, mushrooms and lettuce leaves. The others do add more personality to the salad, but it's not essential to include them all.

Method First, make the pickled mushrooms. As mentioned in the introduction to this recipe, these can be pickled weeks in advance and then kept in an airtight jar, refrigerated, until needed. It's an advantage to do so because, as the pickling liquor impregnates the mushrooms, their flavour becomes stronger and fuller. Bring all of the ingredients, bar the mushrooms, to the simmer and allow to cook for a few minutes. The stalks of the mushrooms can be trimmed level with the mushroom base. I also prefer to wipe them clean rather than wash them. Once trimmed and cleaned, add the mushrooms to the pickling liquor. Return to the simmer and cook for 5–6 minutes. Remove from the heat and leave to cool. These can now be refrigerated until needed. When ready to use, either quarter or slice the mushrooms and place in a saucepan with a tablespoon or two of the liquor. These are now ready to re-heat quickly and season again before adding to the salad. The pickling liquor can be kept and used once more with fresh mushrooms.

The fish should now be divided into four separate fillets. These can each be separated in two with a long diagonal cut. Each strip can then be folded over, creating a looped cravat shape. Place the fillets on buttered, seasoned, greaseproof paper, preferably in individual, two-fillet portions, ready to be steamed over simmering water. Refrigerate until needed.

Now make the salad. Cut away all the lemon peel and pith, then divide the flesh into segments, or cut into four shorter pieces. These can now be quickly seared in a hot pan brushed with olive oil. This gives the lemon pieces a bitter-edged flavour. Cut the tomatoes into strips, allowing 5–6 pieces per portion. While the new potatoes are still warm, slice and sprinkle with any lemon juice saved while segmenting and a tablespoon or two of the olive oil; season with salt and pepper. Keep warm.

Top the French beans, leaving the spiky end on, and blanch in boiling, salted water for just a minute or two, until tender with a bite. Refresh in iced water. The beans can now be split lengthways, making them thinner and easier to eat in the salad. Fry the breadcrumbs in the butter until crispy and golden brown. Once at this stage, remove from the pan and season with salt. The crumbs, when sprinkled over the salad, create an extra crunch.

The dressing is very simple: just add the chopped capers to the olive oil and season with salt and pepper. Vinegar is not needed, due to the acidity from the capers themselves, the lemon pieces and pickled mushrooms already in the salad.

Now it's time to steam the sole and mix the salad. Place the fillets over a pot of simmering water and cover with a lid. I prefer not to have the water boiling rapidly because this cooks the fish too quickly and can shrink the fillets. Steaming the sole will take 4–6 minutes, depending on their size.

While the fish is cooking, the salad can be made. In a large bowl, mix the salad leaves with the watercress. Add the lemon pieces, olives, tomatoes, French beans, warmed mushrooms and new potatoes. The chopped mint and chives can now be added to the dressing. Sprinkle the crispy golden crumbs into the salad and spoon over half of the dressing. Gently turn and mix the salad together before dividing between four plates.

Remove the sole fillets from the steamer and place two per portion on top of each salad. The remaining dressing can now be drizzled over the soles or around the salad before serving. As you've noticed before, there are several jobs that can be completed in advance, leaving just a last-minute assembly of the complete salad.

Spicy Vegetarian Crispy-top Pie

Serves 4

350–450 g (12–16 oz) Puff Pastry (page 212) or bought ready-made puff pastry

1 egg, beaten

For the Vegetables

2 large globe artichokes or 3–4 small artichokes, or tinned artichoke hearts

juice of 1 lemon

1 teaspoon truffle or olive oil, plus 1 tablespoon olive oil for cooking

25 g (1 oz) butter

12 button onions, peeled and blanched for 1 minute in boiling water

12 button, small chestnut or wild mushrooms, wiped clean

4 baby turnips or 8 very small turnips, peeled

150 ml (5 fl oz) Vegetable Stock (page 204) or alternative

1 teaspoon picked fresh marjoram leaves

salt and pepper

For the Artichoke Cooking Liquor (this quantity will be enough for 6 artichokes)

1 carrot, peeled and cut into 5 mm (¼ in) thick slices

4 over-ripe tomatoes, quartered

300 ml (10 fl oz) water

1 teaspoon coriander seeds, optional

1 bay leaf (optional)

pinch of salt

For the Vichyssoise Sauce

knob of butter

1 small potato, finely diced

1 medium leek, finely diced

150 ml (5 fl oz) white wine

300 ml (10 fl oz) Vegetable Stock (page 204)

100 ml (3½ fl oz) single cream (50 ml/2 fl oz more can be added for a creamier finish; crème fraîche can also be used)

squeeze of lemon juice

salt and pepper

Introduction The crispy top for this pie is puff pastry, which rises almost like a soufflé. You break through the golden crunchy topping into the pie, when the flavourful steam from the vegetables begins to excite your tastebuds. A separate creamy vichyssoise sauce, made with leeks, potato and cream, is poured over the vegetables once the crust is broken, which adds another flavour and texture. This recipe is for four starter portions cooked in small individual copper pans. Small bowls or one larger pie dish can also be used.

Method To cook the artichokes, place all the ingredients for the liquor in a pan and bring to a simmer (if cooking just two artichokes, reduce the tomatoes to two and the coriander seeds, if using, to ½ teaspoon).

Remove the stalks from the artichokes and then cut across the base. This will reveal the artichoke bottom. It's important any green is thinly trimmed away as it carries a bitter taste. With the base revealed, cut around in a cylinder fashion, removing all outside leaves. Now cut across about 4 cm (1½ in) from the base and you will have a cleaned artichoke. The middle of the bottoms can now be scooped clean, using a spoon, removing the bristly centres. Rub well in the lemon juice before adding to the hot liquor, pouring in any excess lemon juice. Bring to the simmer and cook for 15–20 minutes, until tender. The cooked artichokes can now be left to cool in the liquor.

The carrot slices cooked with the artichokes can be removed and added to the pie filling. Also strain off 150 ml (5 fl oz) of the stock: this will be mixed with the vegetable stock in which the pie vegetables are cooked.

Roll the puff pastry large enough to provide four toppings (or one large) for the pie dish(es) chosen. For a good soufflé rise, it's best to keep it about 3 mm (⅛ in) thick. Cut the discs required, making sure they are 1 cm (½ in) larger in diameter than the dish(es). Refrigerate until needed. To guarantee the pastry stays on, re-roll the trimmings thinly and cut 1 cm (½ in) thick strips. Brush around the top edge of the pie dish(es) with beaten egg and lay the strips about 5mm (¼ in) thick around and over the lip of the dish(es). These pie dishes can now be lightly buttered before refrigerating until needed.

For the vegetables, heat a tablespoon of olive oil and a knob of the butter in a saucepan. Add the button onions and mushrooms and cook for 6–7 minutes allowing to colour and beginning to soften. Halve the turnips (keeping very small ones whole) and, after a further 2 minutes, add them, with the vegetable stock and reserved artichoke liquor. Bring to the simmer and cook until all have become tender (6–8 minutes).

Split the cooked artichokes in half and cut each into three thick slices. These can now be added to the vegetables, along with the cooked carrot slices, if using. Season with salt and pepper. Add the remaining butter and the marjoram leaves and leave to cool before dividing equally between the dish(es), dotting a little of the truffle or olive oil on top of each portion.

Brush the pastry edges of the pots with beaten egg before topping with the pre-rolled discs. Press well around the sides, trimming round for a neat finish. The tops can now be brushed with egg and the pies refrigerated until needed.

To bake the pies, pre-heat the oven to 220°C/425°F/Gas 7. Bake the individual pies for 20–25 minutes and the large one for 25–30 minutes. In this time, the pastry will have coloured well; if it is becoming too deeply brown after 15 minutes, cover lightly with foil. For a shiny topping, brush the lids with melted butter or a dot of olive oil.

To make the sauce, melt the knob of butter in a saucepan, adding the chopped potato and leek. Cook on a medium heat for 8–10 minutes, until softened, before adding the white wine. Bring to the boil and reduce by three-quarters, adding the vegetable stock. Return the stock to the simmer, allowing to cook for a further 3–4 minutes. Whisk in the cream and season with salt, pepper and lemon juice. The sauce must now be liquidized to a creamy sauce consistency, spreading the flavour of the leeks and potatoes. You now have a vichyssoise-style sauce to offer with the pies. For the smoothest of finishes, it's best to strain the sauce through a sieve, re-warming before serving.

The pies can now be presented, offering the vichyssoise sauce separately, ready to be poured into the pots once the crispy puff tops have been broken.

Note: *Kept in the stock and refrigerated, the cooked artichokes will keep for 5–6 days.*

Grilled Mackerel with Champ Potatoes and Black Pudding

Serves 4

4 mackerel fillets, preferably from 300–350 g (10–12 oz) fish, pin-boned (page 13)

4 × 50 g (2 oz) slices of large black pudding (6–7 cm/2½–3 in in diameter)

25 g (1 oz) butter, melted

cooking oil (optional)

salt and pepper

For the Champ Potatoes

450 g (1 lb) potatoes, preferably Maris Piper, peeled and quartered

75–100 g (3–4 oz) butter

100 ml (3½ fl oz) milk, or single cream for a richer flavour

100–175 g (4–6 oz) spring onions, finely shredded, including green tops

1 quantity Red-wine Dressing (page 204)

salt, pepper and freshly grated nutmeg

For the Lemon Oil (optional)

2–3 tablespoons olive oil

1 tablespoon lemon juice

salt and pepper

Introduction This dish has three main components – mackerel, potatoes and black pudding. The creamy, oniony potatoes work well with either of the other ingredients as a complete dish, but I have brought all three together, creating a rich but still well-balanced combination of flavours.

Champ is an Irish dish, and is, basically, mashed potato flavoured with spring onions (or, variously, mild onions, shallots, parsley, even nettle tops). It was traditionally eaten at Hallowe'en – often offered as a gift to the fairies – and was served with a pool of melted butter in the middle, into which you dipped your forkful of potato.

Mackerel is a meaty and flavourful fish, with a reasonably high oil content. It's this that has led to its traditional association with gooseberry or rhubarb sauces, their sharpness cutting the oiliness of the fish. I'm not using a fruit here, but, instead, a red-wine dressing with a touch of mustard. This has its own 'bite' that brings all three main flavours – the fish, the creamy potato and the spicy pudding – together. This dish is a wonderful starter but also works well as a fish course or complete supper dish.

Method To make the champ, follow the stage-one method for Mousseline Potatoes (page 142), using the ingredients listed left, reserving 25 g (1 oz) of butter for frying the spring onions.

Melt the reserved butter in a large saucepan and, once bubbling, add the shredded spring onions. Cook for a minute or two just gently softening and not frying. Add to the finished mashed potatoes, check for seasoning and the champ is ready to serve on the plates or separately in a bowl.

The red-wine dressing will be used to drizzle around the finished dish. Mix together the ingredients for the lemon oil, if using.

With the champ potatoes and dressings made, it's time to cook the mackerel fillets and black pudding slices. Both can either be pan-fried or, much simpler, cooked under a pre-heated grill.

To grill, brush the black-pudding discs and skin side of the mackerel fillets with butter, seasoning both with salt and pepper. Place on separate buttered and seasoned trays and place the black pudding under the grill, cooking for 2–3 minutes before turning the slices over and continuing to grill for a further 2 minutes. This tray can now be placed in the oven or one shelf below the grill to keep warm. Place the fish under the grill and cook for 4–6 minutes, until the skin has become crispy and golden brown. The cooking time will depend on the size and thickness of the fish fillets.

If pan-frying the fish while the black pudding is grilling, heat a frying pan with a tablespoon or two of cooking oil. Lightly flour the mackerel, skin-side only, before brushing with butter and seasoning. Place in the pan, skin-side down, and allow to fry for 4–5 minutes without shaking the pan or moving the fish. This will then retain the heat and leave a crisper finish. If the fillets begin to curl in the pan, press each down gently with a fish slice as they are cooking. Turn the fillets over and continue to fry for a further minute.

To serve, place the black pudding in the centre of the plate, spooning some of the potatoes on top. For a neat finish, mould the champ into oval shapes between two large serving/kitchen spoons. Drizzle the red-wine dressing over and around the dish, using a tablespoon or two per serving, before sitting the crispy mackerel fillet on top. If using the lemon oil, drizzle it around and over the fish. The dish is now complete and, dressed in this fashion, holds the pleasure of biting through all three main components together.

Note: *If offering the champ separately, make a dip in the centre of the potatoes and add a generous knob of butter, creating the classic finish to the dish. Any remaining champ potatoes can be offered separately, with extra dressing, if available. It's very rare that any champ is left over!*

Country Pâté

Makes enough to fill a 25 × 8 × 8 cm (10 × 3 × 3 in) earthenware terrine

12–16 rashers of unsmoked streaky bacon, rinded

675 g (1½ lb) pork belly or 575 g (1¼ lb) lean shoulder of pork, chilled, then minced or chopped

175 g (6 oz) pork fat (if using lean pork) chilled, then minced or chopped

175 g (6 oz) chicken livers, preferably soaked in milk for 24–48 hours

2 teaspoons salt

1–2 teaspoons black pepper

knob of butter

2 onions, very finely chopped

3 tablespoons brandy

3 tablespoons port

3 garlic cloves, crushed (optional)

1 teaspoon dried mixed herbs

good pinch of ground allspice

1 tablespoon chopped fresh parsley

2 tablespoons white breadcrumbs

1 egg

fresh thyme sprig (optional)

1 bay leaf (optional)

Introduction Generally speaking, pâté (the French word for 'paste') is a pounded mixture of meat or fish, cooked by itself, or in a dish lined with bacon or pork, or in pastry. Terrine is also a French term, the name of an earthenware dish and the food cooked in it. The word comes from the Latin *terra*, or 'earth', thus earthenware. In fact, there is little difference in concept between French pâté and British potted meat. Country pâté is known in France as *pâté de campagne*, or *pâté maison*, and is usually made with all pork, with the belly, back fat and liver. I've replaced the pork liver with chicken livers, which have a richer flavour. If pre-soaked in milk for 24–48 hours, they will carry little or no bitterness.

The texture and consistency of this dish is entirely up to you. The pork meats can be bought already coarsely or finely minced, but for the very best results, the meats should be finely chopped by hand. This ensures all their natural juices are kept, resulting in a moister finish. You must plan ahead when making pâtés and terrines, cooking them at least two to three days in advance of eating, which gives all the flavours time to amalgamate, mature and improve.

Method Pre-heat the oven to 180°C/350°F/ Gas 4.

First line the terrine with the streaky bacon, saving 4 rashers to cover the top. If using the pork belly, omit the pork fat as belly contains the right amount of fat. Once cut, mix the two together, chopping with a knife until they are almost one mass. Take the chicken livers from the milk and lightly dry. These can now also be hand chopped, but I prefer to blitz them to a smooth paste in a food processor. It's now best to work the pâté mix in a bowl over ice as maintaining the deep chill keeps a good, firm texture. Add the blitzed livers to the meat and season with the measured salt and pepper.

Melt the butter in a saucepan, adding the chopped onions. Cook for a few minutes without colouring until softened. Add the brandy and increase the heat, allowing the liquor to reduce until almost dry. The port can now also be added, repeating the reduction process. Leave to cool. Once cold, add to the meats, along with the crushed garlic, if using, mixed herbs, allspice, parsley, breadcrumbs and, lastly, the egg.

A spoonful of the pâté mix can now be pan-fried in butter, like a small burger, to test that the seasoning is right; it's important to remember that the seasoning will need to be quite generous at the uncooked stage; once the paté is served chilled, some of that flavour is lost. Once you are happy with the seasoning, spoon the mix into the lined terrine, laying the 4 reserved streaky bacon rashers on top along with the sprig of thyme and bay leaf, if using. Cover with the terrine lid. Sit the terrine in a deep roasting tray. Fill the tray with enough hot water to reach between half and three-quarters of the way up the side of the terrine. This can now be cooked in the pre-heated oven for 1½–1¾ hours.

To check the terrine is cooked, pierce the pâté with a thin skewer; hold for 10 seconds before removing and check its heat carefully. The skewer should be hot, not warm. At this point, the pâté is cooked. Remove from the oven and pour away the water from the roasting tin. The terrine can now be left to relax for 20–30 minutes.

Place a small piece of wood or plastic wrapped in cling film or foil on top of the pâté and sit another terrine or suitable container of similar weight on top of it. This will squeeze some of the juices out of the terrine: they may even pour over the sides. After 45 minutes to 1 hour of pressing,

remove the weight and pour back any lost juices. The terrine can now be topped with its lid and refrigerated for about 2–3 days before turning out. The pâté will have matured, with all its flavours getting to know one another.

Note: *This pâté eats well at almost all eating times, served with crusty bread, gherkins and capers. Another accompaniment featured within this book is Pumpkin and Date Chutney (page 214), which eats so well and gives the pâté such a homely feel.*

Game Sausage and Clapshot

Serves 8–10

For the Seasoning Mix

1 teaspoon fennel seeds

1 teaspoon black peppercorns

8 juniper berries

1 bay leaf

½ teaspoon ground mace

For the Sausages

at least 10 × 15 cm (6 in) lengths of sausage skin

350 g (12 oz) diced lean venison, preferably from the haunch (good venison trimmings will work just as well and be a lot cheaper to buy)

175 g (6 oz) pork belly with good fat content, diced

1 teaspoon salt

1 egg

3 slices of white bread, crusts removed, crumbed

butter, for test frying and pan-frying

2 tablespoons cooking oil, for pan-frying (optional)

For the Marinade

100–150 ml (3½–5 fl oz) red wine

1 measure of port (optional)

grated zest of ½ orange

2 garlic cloves, crushed until smooth

1 teaspoon chopped fresh thyme

For the Sauce

300 ml (10 fl oz) red wine

75 ml (3 fl oz) port

4–5 juniper berries, lightly crushed

few black peppercorns

1 garlic clove, chopped

1 bay leaf

2–3 orange zest strips, pith removed

fresh thyme sprig

300 ml (10 fl oz) Game *jus*/gravy (page 202) or alternative

25 g (1 oz) butter (optional)

To Serve

Clapshot (page 150)

Introduction Venison is the game featured in these sausages, with pork lending its fat content to moisten the rich meat. Venison carries a very distinctive flavour, which is not lost with the others working beside it. Hare or wild pigeon can substitute, both also holding their own strong flavours. The texture of the sausage is up to you. I prefer a finer, smoother finish, but game sausages do eat very well slightly coarser, the meats being passed through a medium mincer just once. If you do not have mincer attachments at your disposal, I suggest you ask your local butcher to help out, or opt for the finer texture, blitzing the mix in a food processor. For a starter, I suggest one sausage per portion.

To accompany the sausage, I've chosen Clapshot as the turnip, potato and chive flavours all work so well. The clapshot recipe makes 4–6 main-course portions, but there will be plenty for 8–10 portions when served as an accompaniment for a starter.

Method To make the seasoning mix, blitz all the ingredients in a coffee grinder to a fine powder.

The sausage skins will have been preserved in salt and need to be well soaked and rinsed in cold water. These can then be squeezed dry and cut into the required lengths. Tie a knot in one end, preparing the skins to be filled.

Marinating the sausage filling with the red wine and port, if using, is not essential but does offer a fuller-flavoured finish. Alternatively, the wine can be boiled with the orange zest to a syrupy consistency and, once cold, added to the finished sausage mix.

If you opt to marinate the filling, mix all the sausage ingredients together, excluding the egg, breadcrumbs and butter, including 2 teaspoons of seasoning mix (or more, if you prefer a spicier finish). Combine all the marinade ingredients and immerse the sausage filling for several hours, or overnight for a better flavour.

The mix can now be minced three times through a fine blade to give a smooth consistency, or blitzed in a food processor. For the ultimate smooth finish, push the meat through a sieve.

In a bowl over ice, to firm the mix, beat in the egg, followed by the breadcrumbs. A small 'burger' can now be pan-fried in a knob of butter for a few minutes, to check the seasoning flavours. If necessary, add more salt and seasoning mix.

Once you are happy with the flavour, the sausage skins can be filled. This can be done most simply using a piping bag and plain nozzle. Place the skin over the nozzle and pull to the knotted end. Pipe the sausage mix and, as you do so, the skin will fill and extend naturally. Leave up to 4 cm (1½ in) of excess sausage skin, which provides space for it to shrink during cooking. The open end can now be tied. The sausages are best left refrigerated to settle for an hour or two before cooking.

To cook, the sausages can be gently pan-fried in 2 tablespoons of cooking oil with a generous knob of butter until golden brown all around. This will take at least

15–20 minutes. Another alternative is to poach them first in water, just enough to cover them, allowing the water to reach only the gentlest, almost non-moving simmer. Poach the sausages for 15 minutes, leaving them to cool in the water. Once cooled, they can be pan-fried with or without their skins in butter to a golden brown colour on a medium heat until warmed through.

A last alternative is to refrigerate the sausages once poached and cooled. You can then gently pan-fry or grill them with or without their skins whenever needed.

To make the sauce, pour the red wine and port into a saucepan with all the flavouring ingredients and bring to the boil. Cook and reduce by half before adding the game *jus*. Bring to a gentle simmer and cook for 30 minutes. Loosen with water, if necessary, and strain through a fine sieve. The sauce is now ready to serve and can also be softened with the addition of 25 g (1 oz) of butter just before serving.

To serve, the clapshot can be shaped between two large oval spoons and placed towards the top of the plate, presenting the sausage in front with sauce trickled around.

Note: *The* Creamy Cabbage and Bacon *from* New British Classics *also makes a good accompaniment to this dish.*

Marinated Vegetables with Soft Cauliflower Cream

Serves 6

12–18 baby carrots, peeled, or large carrots, cut into baton sticks

9 baby turnips, peeled/scraped

9 baby onions, peeled

9 spring onions, trimmed

9 small new potatoes, cooked and halved

100 g (4 oz) small girolle mushrooms, trimmed and washed, or 200 g (7 oz) chestnut or button mushrooms

100 g (4 oz) shiitake mushrooms, trimmed and washed

olive oil and a knob of butter, for frying

For the *à la Grecque* Liquor

juice of 2 lemons

100 ml (3½ fl oz) white wine

450 ml (12 fl oz) water

2 bay leaves

12 black peppercorns, lightly crushed

1 teaspoon coriander seeds

fresh thyme sprig

pinch of saffron (optional)

150 ml (5 fl oz) olive oil (extra virgin is not necessary)

pinch of sea salt

dash of balsamic vinegar (optional)

For the Cauliflower Purée

25g (1 oz) butter

1 cauliflower, cut into florets

2 teaspoons lemon juice

300 ml (10 fl oz) milk

salt and ground white pepper

To Serve

1 teaspoon snipped fresh flatleaf parsley

1 teaspoon snipped fresh chervil or tarragon

6 French bread slices, about 1 cm (½ in) thick, toasted, to serve

Introduction This vegetarian starter, although it may sound very summery, can be eaten at any time of the year, making a fresh, lively start to a meal. The dish carries that much-sought-after bonus of being able to be totally prepared in advance, just ready for last-minute assembly. The vegetables are cooked in water before being steeped in an *à la Grecque* dressing-marinade. The choice of vegetables is almost unlimited, but I do not recommend green vegetables. The acidic marinade will discolour them, taking away from their fresh, bright green appearance. If you wanted to add asparagus, broccoli florets, mangetout or French beans, for instance, simply steam them separately and then mix with the marinated vegetables just before serving. Girolle and shiitake mushrooms have been included here, but they are not essential, and can be replaced by small chestnut or button mushrooms. The cauliflower purée is served cold, although it also eats well if just warm, providing a contrast with the cold vegetables.

Method To make the liquor, warm the lemon juice, white wine and water together in a saucepan, along with the bay leaves, peppercorns, coriander seeds and thyme (also add the saffron, if using). Add the olive oil and gently simmer for 6–7 minutes. Remove from the heat, seasoning with a pinch of salt, allowing the flavours to infuse. Once cold, add a dash of balsamic vinegar to taste, if using.

The carrots, turnips, baby and spring onions can now all be cooked individually in boiling, salted water until tender. Once cooked, remove from the pan and place directly in the liquor, so the warmth of the vegetables can absorb the rich flavour of the marinade. Add the new potatoes to the vegetables. The mushrooms can now be quickly fried in olive oil and butter, searing to create a golden colour, until just beginning to soften. Add them to the marinating liquor. These vegetables are now best left to infuse for several hours, or even refrigerated overnight. The longer the marinating, the stronger the flavour.

To make the cauliflower purée, melt the butter until bubbling in a saucepan. Add the cauliflower florets and lemon juice cooking on a low/medium heat until softening. Add the milk and bring to the boil. This can now cook until the cauliflower is at a pulp/purée stage. Transfer the cauliflower florets from the pan to a food processor and blitz to a smooth purée, adding any of the remaining milk if needed. Season with salt and pepper before pushing through a sieve (preferably a drum sieve) for the smoothest of finishes. Leave to cool.

To serve the dish, cut the carrots, turnips, baby onions and spring onion through the centre in half (baby carrots can be left whole), providing three pieces of each per portion. Sprinkle the marinated vegetables, potatoes and mushrooms around plates or bowls. Pour some of the liquor (any excess can be kept refrigerated for further use) into a separate bowl, adding the snipped herbs.

Scoop the cauliflower purée, using a tablespoon per portion, on to the French bread toasts. The tablespoon helps create a neat oval shape with the purée. Place the toasts in the centre of the plates before dressing the vegetables with the herb-flavoured liquor. This colourful plate is now ready to serve.

Marinated Vegetables with Soft Cauliflower Cream

Note: *The button onions, once cooked, can be halved and pan-fried in butter to a golden brown before marinating. This will give them a different colour and flavour to enhance the dish.*
Any leftover marinade can be used in another recipe: it will keep for up to two weeks if refrigerated.

Chicken Liver Pâté with Bramley Apple Jelly

Serves 4–6

350 g (12 oz) trimmed chicken livers, soaked for 24 hours in milk

100 g (4 oz) unsalted butter (maximum weight), softened

100 ml (4 fl oz) double cream

a splash of cognac, armagnac or port, to taste

salt, pepper and a pinch of freshly grated nutmeg

melted butter, for topping

For the Bramley Apple Jelly

2 Bramley apples, peeled and cored

juice of ½ lemon

600 ml (1 pint) apple juice

4 gelatine leaves, soaked in cold water

Introduction As Henry VIII once said when asked his thoughts on *pâté de foie gras* – 'Full of heavenly stuffs'.

Chicken liver pâté is a basic combination of cooked chicken livers and butter, but many more flavours and seasonings can be added. In most recipes, the quantity of butter used is equal to that of livers. Personally, I find this over-buttery, almost spoiling the rich liver flavour. And, once the pâté is refrigerated, it results in a firm, butter-like consistency, which means it's really only ready for eating once returned to room temperature. The quantity of butter to livers can actually be as little as a quarter, with the maximum standing at a third.

Whenever buying chicken livers (fresh are best ordered in advance), an ounce or two over the measured weight will be needed. This provides the extra to compensate for trimming the veins and green-tinged areas. Livers should also be soaked in milk for 24 hours. This will remove excess blood, leaving a less bitter flavour.

Method To poach the livers, remove them from the milk and poach in simmering salted water for 2–3 minutes until just beginning to firm, looking for a rare to medium touch. It's best to lift one from the water and check by pressing. Remove from the liquor and leave to rest for a few minutes.

If you prefer to pan-fry the livers, remove them from the milk and dry on kitchen paper. Use the ingredients listed, with the addition of 2 teaspoons of finely chopped shallots, a knob of butter and an extra 2 tablespoons of cognac or other spirit. Melt the knob of butter in a frying pan and, once bubbling, add the livers. Increase the heat and continue to pan-fry for 1–2 minutes before turning over and continuing to cook for another minute. Add the chopped shallots, along with the extra cognac or armagnac. Flambé and remove from the pan. Leave to cool slightly.

Transfer the livers to a food processor, along with the butter (at room temperature), double cream and cognac, or other spirit. Season with salt, pepper and nutmeg and blitz to a smooth purée. You will now have a pâté rich pink in colour. For the smoothest of finishes, simply push the pâté through a fine sieve. Check for seasoning before spooning and smoothing into one large dish or 4–6 individual ramekins. Now wrap the dish(es) in cling film and refrigerate to set: this will take 30–40 minutes.

Melt 25–50 g (1–2 oz) of butter and top each dish with just enough to give the thinnest of coatings. This can be done up to 48 hours in advance.

To make the apple jelly, cut each Bramley apple into small 5 mm (¼ in) dice. Toss in the lemon juice, coating all the pieces. Place the apple juice in a saucepan and bring to the boil. Add the apple dice and simmer for a minute, until just tender. Strain from the juice, re-boiling the liquor and reducing by half: this will increase the apple flavour. Remove from the heat, add the leaves of gelatine and strain through a fine sieve or muslin, if necessary, to remove any apple sediment. Leave to cool, replacing the diced apple before leaving to set in the fridge.

Notes: *Two or three black or soft green peppercorns can be placed in the centre of each dish, along with a small sprig of thyme or a bay leaf, while the butter coating is still soft.*

When serving the pâté, the jelly is best stirred to distribute the apple pieces equally. Now offer it separately along with thick pieces of toast, or for the perfect harmony of flavours, toasted brioche. This really is a very simple and really satisfying dish to offer and eat.

Pressed Rabbit Terrine with Sweet Sherry, Tea and Prune Dressing

Serves 10–12

Makes enough to fill a 25 × 8 × 8 cm (10 × 3 × 3 in) terrine

12–16 rashers of streaky bacon or 300–350 g (10–12 oz) pork backfat, thinly sliced

1 large (1.3 kg/3 lb) rabbit, completely boned

2 small garlic cloves, crushed

finely grated zest of 1 large lemon

1 teaspoon picked fresh thyme leaves

glass of white wine

175 g (6 oz) piece of streaky bacon

225 g (8 oz) shallots or button onions, peeled

225 g (8 oz) button mushrooms

salt and pepper

1 bay leaf

For the Dressing

125 ml (4 fl oz) water

2 Earl Grey teabags

25g (1 oz) sugar

50 g (2 oz) prunes, stoned

2 tablespoons sweet sherry

sesame oil

salt and pepper

Introduction 'Terrine' is basically a French term used to describe the dish a pâté or meat mixture is cooked in. The word is now accepted as a description of both the mould and the food cooked within it. Many textures and tastes can be created in a terrine, and here rabbit is working alongside many that would normally accompany it in a creamy stew. So I thought we'd take those classics and bring them together in a 'new' form. If you're not a huge rabbit fan, please don't be put off, as a large chicken will happily replace our jumpy character.

The terrine is best made 48 hours in advance, giving the flavours a chance to mature. This will also help your menu-planning work-load, having one dish complete, ready for the big day.

The dressing consists of quite powerful flavours – sherry, tea and prunes – with which rabbit has had many affairs, and they are still getting on very well. This dressing will last for days in the fridge.

Method Line the terrine mould with the bacon rashers or pork fat, saving some to cover the top. (If you are using pork backfat, this will need to be pre-ordered from your butcher, stipulating it is to be sliced thinly.) Refrigerate.

I'm sure your butcher will happily bone the rabbit. The meat can then be cut into strips equal to the size of the loin fillets, leaving these whole. Marinate the meat with the crushed garlic, lemon zest, thyme leaves and white wine for 3–4 hours or, preferably, for a stronger flavour, overnight.

Pre-heat the oven to 180°C/350°F/Gas 4.

Cut the piece of streaky bacon into 5 mm (¼ in) thick, long strips. Blanch these in boiling water for a few minutes, then remove and leave to cool, or quickly refresh in iced water.

The shallots or onions are best blanched twice, removing their basic raw texture and taste. Place in a pan of cold water and bring to the boil, refresh in cold water and repeat the same process.

Trim the stalks and wipe the button mushrooms and lightly poach in water until just beginning to tenderize. Refresh.

Strain the rabbit from the marinade, saving the wine. The rabbit, bacon, onions and mushrooms can now all be seasoned with salt and pepper before layering in the mould, keeping a quite rustic appearance. Pack well, overfilling the terrine. Pour the wine over the meat and fold over any excess bacon or pork fat, also using the remaining rashers, and tucking in the bay leaf. Cover the terrine in baking parchment (or cling film) and tin foil. Place in a suitable roasting tray of hot water and cook in the pre-heated oven for 1–1¼ hours. To test, it is best to pierce with a skewer or thin, sharp knife, checking the cooked texture and heat. Once hot right through, the terrine is cooked. Remove from the oven and roasting tin and rest for 30 minutes.

Remove the foil and parchment and cover with cling film. Another terrine or something of a similar shape can now be used as a weight to press the terrine. Once cold, refrigerate, still with the weight, leaving it to mature for at least 24 hours, preferably 48.

To make the dressing, boil the water and pour into a small saucepan over the teabags, sugar and prunes. Leave to stand for several hours or overnight.

After soaking, remove the teabags, squeezing out any excess juices and add the sherry. Bring to the boil and reduce by half to two-thirds. This can now be strained through a sieve, pressing out all the juices but not puréeing the prunes through the sieve. This is now the base of the dressing.

Smoked Haddock Scotch Eggs with Curried Mayonnaise

If it is very thin, it can be reduced to a slightly thicker consistency.

To finish, for every tablespoon of the prune base, 2 tablespoons of sesame oil should be added. A pinch of salt and twist of ground black pepper may be needed to lift the finished flavour.

When you are ready to turn out the rabbit terrine, dip the dish in hot water, invert on to a plate and slice. The terrine can simply be plated, with the dressing trickled around, or use the dressing to dress a salad garnish. If you decide to make a salad, one of watercress, rocket, curly endive, chopped eating apple with a little finely shredded spring onion works well.

Serves 4

4 eggs, at room temperature

For the Mousse

175 g (6 oz) white fish fillet e.g. plaice, hake or lemon sole

1 egg white

150 ml (5 fl oz) double cream

squeeze of lemon juice

100–175 g (4–6 oz) smoked haddock fillets, steamed or poached in milk

salt and ground white pepper

For the Coating

sifted flour, for dusting

2 eggs, beaten

100–175 g (4–6 oz) dried white or golden breadcrumbs

cooking oil, for deep-frying

For the Curried Mayonnaise

1 dessertspoon olive oil

½ small onion, finely chopped

1 tablespoon mild curry powder

juice of ½ lime or ¼ lemon

2 tablespoons soured cream or crème fraîche

150 ml (5 fl oz) Mayonnaise (page 207), or bought ready-made mayonnaise

1 tablespoon smooth mango chutney

salt, if necessary

Introduction I gave a recipe for the classic Scotch eggs in *New British Classics*, my last book. Although I have much respect for that dish, I just had to include this recipe after it was cooked for me not long ago. It's a sound idea that works very well. Smoked haddock and eggs have long been friends and fans of one another, so bringing them closer together was well overdue. The dish makes a wonderful starter that could become quite a talking point around your table. I've also included a recipe for curried mayonnaise that eats very well with the flavours of smoky fish and eggs.

Method Place the four eggs carefully in a saucepan of boiling water. It's best to make sure the eggs are at room temperature rather than refrigerated. If they are too cold, the sudden change of temperature causes the eggs to crack. Boil for 7 minutes before removing and refreshing under running water for 2 minutes. This will end the cooking. Now leave to cool before shelling.

For the mousse, roughly chop the white fish and place in a food processor with a good pinch of salt. Blitz to a purée before adding the egg white and blitzing once more. Now add 75–100 ml (2¾–3½ fl oz) of the double cream and blitz into the fish, creating a smooth paste. It's important the mousse is not too thin. It must be firm enough to hold the cooked smoked haddock and also hold its shape around the egg. If still too thick and heavy, add the remaining cream. Season with salt and pepper and a squeeze of lemon juice.

Flake the cooked smoked haddock and, when cold, mix with the fish mousse. Making sure the eggs are dry, divide the haddock mix into four portions. Roll each between two sheets of cling film. Remove the top sheet and place the egg on the mousse. Lift and twist the four corners of the cling film, wrapping the egg completely, and refrigerate to set firmly. Repeat the same process with the remaining three.

Once set and firm, remove the cling film and dust the eggs lightly with flour. Beat the remaining two raw eggs, pass the covered eggs through, then roll in the breadcrumbs. For a crispier finish, pass through the beaten eggs and crumbs once more. The coated eggs are now best refrigerated to set and relax the mix.

While they are resting, make the curried mayonnaise. This sauce/dip can be made several hours in advance or, better still, a day or two in advance to allow time for the curry flavour to develop. Warm the olive oil in a small saucepan and add the chopped onion, cooking for 6–7 minutes, without colouring. Add the curry powder and continue to cook on a low heat for a further 5 minutes. Remove from the heat and leave to cool. Once cooled, mix in the remaining ingredients, whisking well to spread the curried onion taste. Season with a pinch of salt if needed.

To cook the eggs, pre-heat the cooking oil to 180ºC/350ºF. Place the eggs – it's best to just cook two at a time – in the oil and fry until golden brown. This will take 7–8 minutes. Now repeat the same process for the last two.

These Scotch eggs are best served just warm: the eggs are then very moist surrounded by the soft smoked haddock mousse. However, they can also be eaten cold without losing any of their many flavours. Split the eggs in two, revealing the tasty fillings, and serve with the curried mayonnaise. For an optional extra I suggest garnishing each portion with a wedge of lemon or lime and a few salad leaves dressed in olive oil. Hopefully, a new classic is born and will be able to sit proud and comfortable next to the Scotch egg of old.

Smoked Haddock
Scotch Eggs with
Curried Mayonnaise

Notes: *Here are a few ideas for extra flavours that can be added to the mousse:*

- *1 teaspoon of chopped fresh parsley, tarragon or coriander.*
- *1 teaspoon of chopped fresh shallots or spring onions.*

Smoked Trout and Almond Tart with a Nut-brown Butter Dressing

Serves 6

butter, for greasing

50 g (2 oz) nibbed almonds

finely grated zest of 1 lemon

1 quantity Shortcrust Pastry (page 211)

For the Filling

knob of butter

100–175 g (4–6 oz) finely shredded leeks, preferably baby leeks

3 egg yolks or 1 whole egg plus 1 egg yolk

300 ml (10 fl oz) crème fraîche

2 teaspoons Dijon mustard or horseradish cream

squeeze of lemon juice

4 smoked trout fillets, skinned

1 teaspoon chopped fresh tarragon (optional)

1 heaped teaspoon chopped fresh parsley (optional)

salt and pepper

For the Dressing

50 g (2 oz) butter

4 tablespoons olive oil

4 tablespoons groundnut oil

1 teaspoon balsamic vinegar

squeeze of lemon juice

salt and pepper

For the Salad

50–75 g (2–3 oz) flaked almonds

bunch of watercress, picked into sprigs

100 g (4 oz) rocket washed

Introduction Pan-fried trout with almonds is a classic French dish, served with nut-brown butter, lemon and parsley. I wanted to take that idea and present it with a new, fresh flavour and form. Smoked trout is the first change, the smoky flavour holding its own very well in the cream and egg base. A nuttiness can be found in the pastry, with its addition of lightly toasted nibbed almonds, and this is echoed by the flaked almonds in the accompanying salad. In the cream filling, I've chosen crème fraîche for a lighter finish. Double cream has an average fat content of 48 per cent, whereas crème fraîche stands at just 30 per cent. There is now an even lighter alternative at 15 per cent, and that, too, will work very well in this dish. The nut-brown butter that's classically poured, sizzling, over the whole pan-fried trout is instead added to a dressing to sprinkle over the salad.

Method For this recipe, you need a 23 cm (9 in) fluted or plain tart tin, preferably loose-based, that is no more than 2.5 cm (1 in) deep. Grease with butter. If the nibbed almonds seem quite large, quickly break them down in a food processor or with a rolling pin. Now lightly toast and allow to cool. These, along with the lemon zest, can be stirred into the pastry mix before adding the egg and water. Continue as per recipe.

Once rested, roll out the pastry and line the buttered tart tin, leaving any excess hanging over the edge; this guarantees an even finish to the cooked case. Refrigerate for 30 minutes.

Pre-heat the oven to 200°C/400°C/ Gas 6. Line the pastry case with greaseproof paper and fill with baking beans or rice. Bake in the pre-heated oven for 20–25 minutes before removing the paper. Continue to bake for a further 5–6 minutes, until the base has set. Remove from the oven. Reduce the oven temperature to 180ºC/350ºF/Gas 4.

Now make the filling. Melt the butter in a saucepan and, once bubbling, add the leeks and cook for a few minutes until beginning to soften. Season with salt and pepper before removing from the pan and leaving to cool. Whisk the egg yolks with the crème fraîche and mustard (or horseradish). Add a squeeze of lemon juice and season with salt and pepper. The trout fillets can now be broken down and placed in the flan case, along with the cooked leeks, spreading them evenly. Add the chopped herbs, if using, to the crème fraîche mix and pour into the flan case. Bake in the pre-heated oven for 30–40 minutes or until just set and golden brown. Remove from the oven and leave to rest. The tart is best eaten warm: if too hot, the flavours don't relax and help one another.

While the tart is relaxing, the salad dressing can be made. Melt the butter in a warm frying pan and allow to bubble to a nutty golden brown. While the butter is melting, mix the oils, balsamic vinegar and lemon juice. Add and whisk in the nut brown butter, seasoning with salt and pepper to finish.

The flaked almonds can now be toasted to a golden brown. Mix the watercress with the rocket leaves, adding the almonds, with enough dressing to moisten.

To serve the dish, remove the tart from the flan case and divide into portions. Present on plates with the salad, drizzling a spoonful or two more of the dressing over and around.

Note: *The salad can take on more flavours: red onions, shredded fennel or spring onions all work very well. A bag of mixed green leaves can be used instead of the watercress and rocket.*

Poached Eggs Benedict and Seared Tunafish Benedict

Serves 4

For Poached Eggs Benedict

1 quantity Simple Hollandaise Sauce (page 206)

2 muffins, split

butter, for spreading

4 Poached Eggs (page 209)

4 slices of good-quality ham (2 mm/⅛ in thick)

salt and pepper

olive oil and lemon juice, to serve (optional)

For Seared Tunafish Benedict

1 quantity Sauce Béarnaise (page 205) or Simple Hollandaise Sauce (page 206)

4 × 100 g (4 oz) slices of tunafish fillet

butter, for spreading

cooking oil

2 muffins, split

50 g (2 oz) Tartare Butter (page 35)

4 Poached Eggs (page 209)

salt and pepper

Introduction Although there is a poached egg dish called *Bénédictine* in classical French cooking (eggs served on top of *brandade* of salt cod, flavoured with black truffles), eggs Benedict are thought to have been invented in New York as a breakfast dish. A toasted buttered muffin is topped with slices of ham or crispy bacon (sometimes tongue), followed by a poached egg and hollandaise sauce. This is the recipe I'm offering you here, but I also give you a variation that is an absolute delight to eat: seared tunafish Benedict. The toasted muffin is spread with tartare butter, followed by quickly seared fresh tunafish steaks, the poached egg and a béarnaise sauce for a tarragon-flavoured finish. Cutting through the thick sauce into the softly poached egg, with the yolk trickling on to the tuna and muffin, is an experience before even a mouthful is tasted. Both the ham and tuna versions make perfect starters, and are wonderful lunchtime dishes too, although, for the latter, I'd suggest serving two muffins per portion.

Method First make the hollandaise sauce; this can be kept warm for up to an hour.

For the Poached Eggs Benedict, brush the four muffin bases with butter, and toast until golden brown. While the muffins are toasting, the eggs can be re-heated for 1 minute in simmering water. The slices of ham can be folded and served cold but I prefer to sprinkle the four folded slices with water and re-heat on a plate, cling filmed, in a microwave oven for about 30 seconds. This then takes the chill out of the ham, leaving a warm, tender finish.
If overheated, the ham tends to become slightly tough.

Place the ham on the toasted muffins and top with the warmed, seasoned poached eggs. Present in bowls or on plates before spooning 2 tablespoons of hollandaise sauce over each egg. The dish is now ready to serve. A small trickle (½–1 teaspoon) of olive oil can be drizzled around the dish. If using the oil, a good squeeze of lemon juice can also be added to provide an extra bite to the finished flavour.

For the Seared Tunafish Benedict, béarnaise or hollandaise sauce is also the first component of this dish to be made. The sauce can be kept warm for up to 1 hour before serving. Warm, simmering water must also be ready to re-heat the poached eggs: these will take 1 minute.

Brush the tunafish fillets with butter on the presentation side only. Season with salt and pepper. Heat the cooking oil in a frying pan and, once it's very hot, place the tuna in the pan, butter-side down, and season once again. It's important not to move the fish in the pan – this will only reduce the heat. Tunafish of this size is approximately 1 cm (½ in) thick. To sear to a rare to medium stage will take only 1–1½ minutes on each side.

While the fish is cooking, the muffins can be toasted to a golden brown and the poached eggs re-heated.

To serve, spread each muffin with the Tartare Butter before placing in bowls or on plates. Place the tunafish on top, topping with the warm poached eggs before coating each egg with 2 tablespoons of the béarnaise or hollandaise sauce.

Notes*: A teaspoon of Dijon mustard can be added to the béarnaise or hollandaise, giving a warmer finished flavour.*

An extra finish for the seared tunafish version of the benedict is to spoon around a trickle of Tarragon Oil (page 207).

Tartare Butter

100 g (4 oz) butter

1 heaped teaspoon very finely chopped shallots or onions

1 heaped teaspoon very finely chopped gherkin

1 heaped teaspoon very finely chopped capers

finely grated zest of ½ lemon

1–2 teaspoons lemon juice (or juice of ½ lemon for extra acidity)

salt and pepper

Introduction This recipe is for 100 g (4 oz) of butter. Seared Tunafish Benedict requires only 50 g (2 oz); any remaining can be frozen, ready for the next time. A larger quantity can be achieved by doubling the recipe.

Method Mix all the ingredients together, seasoning with salt and pepper. This is now best rolled into a cylinder shape in cling film and frozen until needed. To use, cut the required quantity and defrost before spreading on the muffins.

Poached Ale 'Open Potted' Herrings

Serves 4

150 ml (5 fl oz) light ale

4 tablespoons cider vinegar

½ teaspoon demerara sugar

1 bay leaf

few allspice berries, roughly cracked

few black peppercorns

fresh thyme sprig

4 herrings (225–275 g/8–10 oz each), filleted

50 g (2 oz) butter

2 large onions, finely sliced

squeeze of lemon juice (optional)

1 tablespoon torn or chopped flatleaf parsley

salt and pepper

Introduction The term 'potted', when used of fish, can mean something quite different from its more common association of preserving meat under a layer of butter. For many years the generous use of spices would also provide the passport to this culinary term. The fish fillets were cooked in ale and vinegar, quite often far too much of the latter (becoming pickled) with spices galore and usually served straight from the pot once they were cooked. This dish will be moving along a very similar route, but once cooked, the liquor is boiled and reduced before finishing with butter to create an accompanying sauce. Hence the 'open potted': spices will be used, and the butter, instead of sealing in flavours and preserving, will be emulsifying a collection of everything used.

It's a very enjoyable starter, with the onions sautéd in butter to enrich their flavour, reminding me of the French classic herrings *à la lyonnaise*. Warm sliced new potatoes can also be added to the finished dish, along with salad leaves and lemon.

Method Mix together the ale, vinegar, sugar, bay leaf, allspice berries, black peppercorns and thyme. Bring to the simmer and cook for a few minutes. Remove from the heat, cover with a lid and leave to cool. This will allow the spices to infuse the liquor. Lay the herring fillets, flesh-side down, in a lightly buttered, ovenproof dish, seasoned with a pinch of salt. Re-boil the liquor and pour over the fish. Place the dish on the stove and bring to the simmer. Remove from the stove and cover with a lid.

Heat a frying pan with a knob of the butter. Once bubbling, fry the sliced onions for 7–8 minutes, until softened and golden brown. Season with salt and pepper.

Lift the herring fillets from the pan, cover and keep warm. Boil the liquor, reducing by half before straining through a sieve. Spoon 1–2 tablespoons on to the fried onions and mix in. Now whisk the remaining butter into the remaining liquor: this can also be blitzed with a hand blender, to help emulsify the sauce. Check for seasoning with salt and pepper. A squeeze of lemon juice added to the sauce may be needed to lift all the flavours.

Divide the onions between four plates, placing the herring fillets (two per portion) on top. Add the parsley to the liquor and spoon over and around the fish. The dish is now ready to serve.

Notes: *As mentioned in the introduction to this recipe, new potatoes and salad leaves can also be added to this dish.*

Very thinly sliced carrots cooked with the herrings or onions also work very well. A separate warm potato salad, dressed with soured cream, lemon juice and chives, eats well as an accompaniment.

Roast Pigeon 'Hearts' with a Spinach and Chicory Salad

Serves 4

100–175 g (4–6 oz) young spinach leaves

2 heads of Belgian endive/chicory

4 wood pigeons, breasts removed and skinned (legs and carcasses can be made into Game Stock, page 202)

25g (1 oz) butter

salt and pepper

For the Dressing

1 teaspoon Dijon mustard

1 teaspoon wholegrain mustard

½ teaspoon clear honey

1–2 tablespoons red-wine vinegar

6 tablespoons walnut or olive oil (the walnut works very well with pigeon)

2 tablespoons groundnut oil

salt and pepper

Introduction Salads were originally a combination of salted or pickled vegetables (the word 'salad' deriving from the Latin *sal*, salt). The word then described a simple mixture of green leaves and, in Britain, developed in the seventeenth and eighteenth centuries into a virtual banquet of items and flavours on one plate.

Salads today are basically whatever you want them to be, this one having a gamey flavour, which is combined with a few other ingredients.

The 'hearts' are, in fact, the pigeon breasts. These are pan-fried for 2–3 minutes on each side before being cut open to create a heart shape. For a very simple starter, one 'heart' may well be sufficient, but wood pigeons are quite small, so I suggest two per person. The legs and carcasses from the pigeons can be made into a Game Stock or *Jus* (see page 202). Either will freeze well for another day, but a little can also be kept back to drizzle around the salad just before serving, which will enhance the overall game flavour. (If using game stock, reduce it to an almost syrupy consistency.)

The rest of the salad consists of young spinach leaves and Belgian chicory, with a mustard and red-wine dressing sweetened with a touch of honey to counter the chicory bitterness. Many other ingredients could be added – fried bread croûtons, French beans, mangetout, pine kernels, olives, red onions, new potatoes, broad beans, walnuts and so on.

Method Start by making the dressing: either of the mustards can be used alone by simply doubling the quantity to 2 teaspoons. However, the combination of both does work very well with this salad. Whisk together the mustards, honey and 1 tablespoon of red-wine vinegar. Mix the two oils and whisk slowly into the mustards. Season with salt and pepper. For a sharper finished flavour, add the remaining tablespoon of red-wine vinegar.

Pick and wash the spinach leaves, draining in a colander. Cut the base from the endive, discarding any damaged or discoloured outer leaves. Separate the leaves and cut or tear any of the larger ones from 'corner to corner', creating a simpler shape for eating. Wash if necessary.

Season the pigeon breasts with salt and pepper. Melt the butter in a frying pan and, once bubbling, place the breasts in. Fry for 2–3 minutes before turning and continuing to fry for the same length of time. Remove from the pan and leave to rest for 6–8 minutes.

Meanwhile, mix the spinach and endive together (along with any other salad ingredients chosen), adding half of the dressing. Gently fold the dressing into the leaves; this will guarantee a full flavour with every bite. Divide the salad leaves between four bowls or plates.

Once rested, the breasts can be sliced. Cut along the rounded side towards the straight line of meat (base of breast when on the bone), but not quite through. The medium-rare breasts will now open like a book, creating the heart shape. Arrange one or two per portion on top of the salad and season with a twist of pepper.

The remaining dressing can now be spooned over the breasts and around the salad before serving or finishing with a few drops of game stock or *jus*, if using, as mentioned in the introduction.

Two-onion, Two-cheese Potato Tart

Serves 6 (8 if using a large flan tin)

knob of butter

1 quantity Shortcrust Pastry (page 211)

1–2 teaspoons chopped fresh thyme (optional)

2 tablespoons olive oil

2 onions, finely sliced

6–8 spring onions, finely sliced

225 g (8 oz) new potatoes, cooked until tender (preferably Jersey Royals when in season, page 147)

100 g (4 oz) cream cheese

1 egg and 1 egg yolk, beaten

200 ml (7 fl oz) whipping cream

6 slices Gruyère cheese

salt and pepper

For the Dressing

onion juices (see method)

5–6 tablespoons olive oil

2 teaspoons red-wine vinegar

salt and pepper

Introduction Quiche Lorraine must be the best known of savoury tarts, and it is today considered to be a combination of onions, bacon and cheese, but that's not exactly how it started. The French area of Lorraine became well known for its egg- and cream-filled tart, called a quiche, but the most popular version, *quiche au lard*, which had bacon in it (and sometimes onions and cheese) was soon to be generally referred to as *the* quiche Lorraine. In this recipe, I'm using two types of onions, the everyday variety and spring onions, working alongside a cream cheese filling and finished with a topping slice of melting Swiss Gruyère cheese. The potatoes are an added extra that can be omitted from the recipe, but do eat very well, giving a completely different texture to enjoy. Salad leaves can be used as an accompaniment to the tartlet, but a simple drizzle of olive oil, onion and red-wine dressing is a tasty little finish. Six individual tartlets or one large flan can be made. The choice is yours. Although a very good starter, this dish can be eaten at almost any time of day and occasion, and would be a lovely addition to a summer buffet.

Method You will need six 10 cm (4 in) diameter, 2.5 cm (1 in) deep invididual tartlet tins or a 23–25 cm (9–10 in) diameter, 2.5 cm (1 in) deep flan tin. Butter the tin(s).

Make the pastry, adding the thyme, if using, to the flour. Roll out the pastry thinly and line the tin(s) (see Notes). Once lined, refrigerate to set for 30 minutes before baking.

Pre-heat the oven to 200ºC/400ºF/Gas 6. Line the pastry case(s) with greaseproof paper and fill with baking beans or rice. Bake in the pre-heated oven for 15–20 minutes until the pastry has set with a golden edge. Remove the paper and beans, checking that the base of the pastry is cooked. If not, return to the oven for a further 4–5 minutes. Leave to cool.

Warm the olive oil in a saucepan and add the sliced onions. Cook on a medium heat for 6–7 minutes, until softening and taking on a golden colour. Add the spring onions and continue to cook for a few minutes more until also softened. A tablespoon or two of water can now be added, creating an onion juice to help flavour the dressing. Season with salt and pepper. Drain the onions in a colander or sieve, collecting any excess juices to use in the dressing.

Halve the cooked potatoes. These can be used as they are, or be pan-fried in butter to give a sautéd crispy edge.

To make the filling, soften the cream cheese, adding the egg and egg yolk and cream. Season with salt and pepper. Divide the onions between the tartlets or cover the base of the large tart and place the potatoes on top. Pour in the cream cheese mix, filling to the brim of the pastry, leaving the edges of the potatoes exposed. Reduce the oven temperature to 150ºC/300°F/Gas 2 and bake for 25–30 minutes, or 30–35 for the large tart, until the mix has just set. Remove from the oven and leave to rest for 5 minutes (10–15 minutes for large tart) before removing from the tin(s). Finish and serve immediately or leave to relax to room temperature. The tart(s) will eat at their best slightly warm. Just before serving, lay a slice of Gruyère on top of each tart (3 or 4 will be needed for the large one) and gratinate under a pre-heated grill, allowing the cheese to melt over the sides of the pastry for a real home-made finish.

To make the dressing, whisk the saved onion juices with the olive oil and red-wine vinegar, adding more vinegar if preferred, and seasoning with salt and pepper. Spoon the dressing over and around the tartlets just before serving.

Notes: *When lining the tin(s), leave any excess pastry hanging over while cooking. This will prevent the pastry from shrinking and, once cooked, can be cut away to leave a perfect all round finish*

The finely grated zest of one lemon can be added to the pastry recipe, working alongside the fresh thyme to enhance the total flavour.

appetizers

soups

fish

mains

vegetables

desserts

savouries

basic recipes

menus

soups

Mushroom and Butter Bean Soup

Serves 6

175 g (6 oz) dried butter beans, or 400 g (14 oz) tin of butter beans, drained

25 g (1 oz) butter, plus a knob for pan-frying the mushroom garnish

1 large onion, finely chopped

1 garlic clove, crushed

350 g (12 oz) cup or chestnut mushrooms (or buttons, if others unavailable), sliced

600 ml (1 pint) Vegetable or Chicken Stock (page 204 or 201) or alternative

300 ml (½ pint) milk

150 ml (5 fl oz) single cream (optional)

salt and pepper

1 tablespoon chopped fresh flatleaf parsley, to garnish

Introduction A combination of beans and mushrooms in soup has been popular for hundreds of years. So although this is certainly not a new idea, it's perhaps slightly more refined.

Dried beans have been a staple for centuries, and butter beans, or lima beans, are perfect for creamed and broth soups.

Mushrooms come in many varieties, shapes and sizes. Because of their high water content, many – particularly the cultivated varieties – do not have a lot of flavour; although they work well in some dishes, they often struggle in others. Cultivated cup, open and flat varieties of mushroom all hold a 'meatier' flavour, and the chestnut is even stronger. After that, it's the wild mushrooms, among them chanterelles, oysters, morels, ceps, shiitake and so on, each holding its own very distinctive flavour. For this recipe it's best to use either the cup or chestnut mushroom. The soup is going to be puréed and creamed, which will maximize the fungus flavour. Wild mushrooms can always be used to garnish the finished dish.

Method If using dried butter beans, they will need a minimum 12 hours' soaking in cold water. It's important, when buying any dried beans, to check the expiry date. The longer life the bean has, the more tender it will be. Once soaked, drain and rinse. Place the beans in the pan with the stock and bring to a gentle simmer. Cover with a lid kept slightly askew and cook for 1 hour until the beans are tender. Lift some of the beans and keep for garnishing (for this it's best to remove the shells). If using tinned butter beans, drain off the liquor and set aside a few beans for each portion's garnish.

Melt the butter in a saucepan and, once bubbling, add the chopped onion and garlic. Cook without colouring for 8–10 minutes until the onions are beginning to soften. Add two-thirds of the mushrooms, saving a third to garnish, and continue to cook for 10–15 minutes until also softening. Add the beans to the onion/mushroom mix and warm through. Add the stock and bring to the simmer. Cook on a medium heat for 15–20 minutes.

Add the milk and return to the simmer. Season with salt and pepper. Liquidize and strain through a sieve to a smooth consistency. Add the single cream, if using and check the seasoning.

When ready to serve, heat a frying pan and pan-fry the remaining mushroom slices in the knob of butter. This is best achieved on a high heat to colour the mushrooms golden brown. The reserved butter beans can be warmed in the soup or microwaved separately. Divide the soup between the bowls, and garnish with the beans, mushrooms and chopped parsley.

Note: *A spoonful of cooked spinach is also a very nice garnish for this soup, eating well with the butter beans and mushrooms.*

Fisherman's Soup – the British Bouillabaisse

Serves 6

For the Red-mullet Base

Makes approx. 3.4 litres (6 pints)

3 tablespoons olive oil

1 large fennel, roughly chopped

2 celery sticks, finely sliced

2 large onions or 8 shallots, finely sliced

4 carrots, peeled and finely sliced

3 garlic cloves, sliced

1 small dried red chilli

½ teaspoon coriander seeds, crushed

generous pinch of saffron

few sprigs of fresh basil

few sprigs of fresh tarragon

200 ml (7 fl oz) Pernod

½ bottle white wine

3–4 frozen red mullets, defrosted and chopped, including head, tail and all bones

400 g (14 oz) tin of tomatoes, or 2 tins for extra tomato flavour, or 12 fresh over-ripe tomatoes, chopped for fresher flavour

juice of 1 orange and 3 pieces of orange zest

3.4 litres (6 pints) Fish Stock (page 201) or alternative

salt and cayenne pepper

For the Fisherman's Soup

350 g (12 oz) cod fillet, cut into 50 g (2 oz) pieces

butter

450 g (1 lb) lemon sole, filleted and skinned

12–18 headless raw king prawns, defrosted if frozen, shelled, tail fan left on

350 g (12 oz) sea bass fillet or 3–4 red mullet fillets

seasoned flour (optional)

olive oil

3 celery sticks, finely shredded

1 medium fennel or 2–3 baby fennels, finely shredded

1 leek, finely shredded

1.2 litres (2 pints) Red-mullet Base

3 tomatoes, preferably plum, blanched (page 209) and cut into 5 mm (¼ in) strips

1 tablespoon chopped fresh flatleaf parsley

1 tablespoon 1 cm (½ in) fresh chive sticks

1 tablespoon chopped fresh tarragon

1 tablespoon chopped fresh chervil

Salt, pepper and a squeeze of lemon juice

For the Croûtons

12 thick slices of French bread

olive oil, for brushing

4 large fresh sage leaves, chopped

175–225 g (6–8 oz) Cheddar cheese, grated

Introduction Bouillabaisse is probably the king of all fish soup-stews, and it is a speciality of southern France, particularly the area around Marseilles. It's basically a collection of many fish and, traditionally, *rascasse*, the Mediterranean red scorpion fish (difficult to find in Britain), has to be part of its make-up. The pieces of fish are poached in a soup base with fennel, garlic, tomatoes, herbs and many more flavourings, and presented in a large bowl with all the cooked vegetables. Meanwhile, the liquor is reduced and emulsified with olive oil to increase its flavour, and it's from this boiling that the dish found its name – *bouillon abaissé*, which translates as 'lowered broth', what we would call 'reduced'.

There are many traditional fish soup-stews in the British culinary canon, but most of them are fairly simple in essence. Now into the twenty-first century, many flavours and tastes have long since been introduced to the soup and accepted into our eating habits, so this recipe is a combination of many influences.

For the poaching liquid, I'm making a soup base with red mullet. If the fish stock listed is replaced with water, the red mullet quantity will need to be doubled, or simply add 1 kg (2¼ lb) of chopped fish bones to the ingredients. The soup base can be used in many more dishes and freezes very well. Long-term thinking provides long-term pleasure.

Bouillabaisse accompaniments usually include garlic *croûtes* and *rouille* (a spicy mayonnaise). For a more British touch, this soup would be helped along with warm sage and Cheddar olive oil toasts.

Any type of fish can be used in this soup, and the quantity is not crucial either. Choose from a combination of cod, haddock, sole, sea bass, grey mullet, salmon, red mullet, mackerel, lobsters, scallops, mussels, clams or prawns.

This soup could be a starter, middle course, main course or supper dish. Whichever, it's an experience.

Method Make the soup base first. Heat the olive oil in a large saucepan. Add the fennel, celery, onions, carrots and garlic. Cook on a gentle heat for 15–20 minutes, with a lid on, until the vegetables have softened. Add the spices, saffron, herbs and Pernod and reduce by half. Add the white wine, also reducing by half. The red mullet pieces (and bones if using), tomatoes, orange juice, zest and stock or water can now all be added. Bring to the simmer and cook for 45 minutes.

Once cooked, remove from the heat and rest for 15 minutes before liquidizing and straining through a coarse sieve, extracting all the juices. For a smooth, non-grainy finish, also strain through a very fine sieve. The mullet soup base is now made, carrying quite a strong, sweet fish flavour. This can be served as it is or lightly creamed and offered with bread croûtons (page 210) flavoured with garlic and Parmesan cheese. Or freeze some or all of the soup for future use. Check for seasoning before serving.

To make the soup, first pre-heat the oven to 170°C/325°F/Gas 3. As discussed in the introduction, choose any fish you like. I've selected four that work very well. These can all be steamed or poached; however, I prefer to pan-fry or grill sea bass or red mullet. These add another texture to the dish. Put the cod pieces in a buttered and seasoned roasting pan or ovenproof dish. The sole will provide two small and two large flat fillets. Split the two large ones diagonally in half and then fold all six in half, creating looped fillets. Run a knife down the back of each prawn to remove the black vein. Place the cod, sole and prawns in the dish. Season with salt, add a knob of the butter and 100 ml (3½ fl oz) of water. Cover with a lid, bring to a soft simmer and cook in the pre-heated oven for 2–3 minutes, until just firm to the touch. Remove from the oven.

The sea bass or red mullet fillets, divided into six portions, can be lightly dusted, on the skin side, in flour seasoned with salt and cayenne pepper and brushed with butter before pan-frying skin-side down for a few minutes until crispy. Turn over and cook for a further minute.

To finish the soup, warm 2 tablespoons of olive oil, adding the celery and fennel. Cook for a few minutes without colouring until beginning to soften slightly. Add the shredded leek and continue to cook for 1 minute. While the vegetables are cooking, the red-mullet base can be re-heated, poured on to the vegetables and returned to the simmer. Add a knob of butter, check for seasoning, flavour with the lemon juice and stir in the tomatoes and herbs.

To make the croûtons, brush the French bread slices on each side with olive oil. Toast until crisp and golden brown. These can also be baked in a medium oven for a crisper finish. Mix the chopped sage leaves with the Cheddar and divide between the 12 toasts. Now simply gratinate under a hot grill, melting the Cheddar over the toasts.

The complete dish is now ready to be served, dividing the fish portions between bowls and spooning the soup over. This can be finished with a few drops of olive oil, offering the croûtons separately.

Notes: *Frozen red mullet fillets are best used for the soup base. These provide enough flavour and texture for the soup, and also cost a lot less than fresh.*

Classic fish soups are generally offered from one large pot on the table. It's up to you, the eater, to help yourself to the 'fruits of the sea' available. If you wish to serve in this manner, re-heat the mullet base and continue as per the recipe with the fennel and celery. Once softened, add the leeks and all the fish. Simmer very gently for 2 minutes before finishing with the butter, herbs and tomatoes. Trickle with olive oil and serve.

Potato, Onion and Garlic Parsley Soup with Parmesan Toasts

Serves 6

2 tablespoons olive oil

knob of butter

2 onions, peeled and sliced

1 bay leaf

4 large garlic cloves (2–4 more for garlic-lovers)

600 ml (1 pint) milk

1 lb (450 g) potatoes, peeled and cut into 1 cm (½ in) rough dice

600 ml (1 pint) Vegetable Stock (page 204) or alternative

salt and pepper

For the Parsley Coulis (optional)

small bunch of fresh flatleaf parsley

small bunch of fresh curly parsley

1 tablespoon groundnut oil

1 tablespoon water

salt and ground white pepper

For the Parmesan Toasts

4–6 slices of medium white processed bread

4–6 tablespoons freshly grated Parmesan cheese

For the Garnishes

1 large jacket potato, cut into 1 cm (½ in) dice, cooked until tender (optional)

1 dessertspoon chopped fresh flatleaf parsley (optional)

Introduction Garlic, with its powerful little cloves, holds a very strong history as one of the most ancient flavours known to man, becoming a staple ingredient to the majority of the world's population. Its reputation held many qualities and strengths. In particular, it was given to Egyptian labourers during the building of the Great Pyramids to keep them healthy. It was also used to relieve many ailments, such as toothache, headache and the pain of childbirth.

I'm continuing the history within this dish, using its qualities to bond well with the onion and calming its strengths with the addition of the potato.

This soup works very well as part of a two- or three-course lunch menu. Its quite creamy and thickish consistency is very 'mealy' on its own. Fish or pasta with salad will follow on just nicely, and, for a third course, if necessary, simple fresh fruits.

Method To make the parsley coulis, blanch both types of parsley in boiling, salted water for a few minutes until tender. Drain well and liquidize to a purée along with the groundnut oil and water. Season with salt and pepper and push through a sieve to leave a smooth 'sauce'.

Next make the Parmesan toasts: these are simply Melba toasts gratinated with Parmesan cheese, creating cheesy crisps to dunk in the soup.

Toast the bread on both sides. Then cut away the crusts and split the slice through the middle, each slice now doubling in volume. Scrape away the crumbs and cut each piece into two triangles. The quantity listed will give three or four triangles per portion. Place all the slices, untoasted-side up, on a baking tray, and cook in a warm oven (120°C/250°F/Gas ½) or under a warmed grill for a few minutes until dry, crispy and curled. These are best finished with the cheese just before serving the soup. Sprinkle with the Parmesan and melt in the oven or under the grill. Serve warm.

To make the soup, warm the olive oil and knob of butter in the pan and add the sliced onions, with the bay leaf. Stir and cover with a lid, cooking on a medium heat until tender. While the onions are sweating, peel the garlic cloves, split in half and place, with the milk, in a saucepan. Bring to the simmer and remove from the heat, leaving to infuse. Add the potatoes to the onions and continue to cook for a further 10 minutes until they are beginning to soften. Pour on the vegetable stock and garlic milk, garlics included, bringing to the simmer. Cook for 15–20 minutes until the potatoes have overcooked. Remove the bay leaf and blitz to a smooth finish. Check for seasoning with salt and pepper. The soup is now ready to serve.

If using the cooked diced potatoes for a garnish, either microwave or warm them in a drop of water. Divide the potatoes between bowls, sprinkle with the chopped parsley, if using, and pour the soup over.

To finish, drizzle, if using, with the parsley coulis. Offer the warm Parmesan toasts separately to be enjoyed with this quite delicious soup.

Notes: *The parsley coulis is not essential but does give the dish quite a new edge. As you eat the soup, the coulis begins to emulsify and sets off new sensations in the taste buds.*

The potato dice garnish is not essential but, again, gives a new taste.

Cream of Tomato Soup

Serves 4–6

2 tablespoons olive oil

25 g (1 oz) butter

2 onions, finely chopped

1 small carrot, finely chopped

2 celery sticks, finely chopped

2 garlic cloves, crushed

1 bay leaf

1 kg (2¼ lb) fresh over-ripe tomatoes, cut into eight

pinch of sugar

600–750 ml (1–1½ pints) Chicken or Vegetable Stock (page 201 or 204) or alternative

100 ml (3½ fl oz) single or whipping cream

salt and pepper

Introduction Tomatoes originated in South America, and didn't reach Europe until the sixteenth century. They were looked upon with suspicion at first, and had a bad reputation for being the cause of gout among other things. Cooking them was the only answer, and no one ever thought of eating them raw until at least the eighteenth century. It's really quite amazing to me that one of our most popular ingredients and flavours only really started to be accepted and taken seriously here in Britain during the last 50–60 years of the twentieth century.

Tomato soup is probably the most famous canned soup in the world. Fresh tomato soup, using simple basic ingredients, offers a completely different finish. Many believe the best way to make a tomato soup is simply to chop and stew the over-ripe fruits until tender and puréed. Once sieved, the soup is made.

Method Warm the oil and butter together. Once bubbling, add the chopped onions, carrots, celery, garlic and bay leaf. Cook with a lid on for 15–20 minutes, until softened.

Add the chopped tomatoes, sugar, salt and pepper. Return the lid and, on a low heat, cook for a further 25–30 minutes. The tomatoes will now have stewed and softened, ready for the addition of 600 ml (1 pint) of the stock. Bring to the simmer and cook for a few minutes before removing from the heat and liquidizing to a purée. For a good smooth finish, and to remove any seeds, it's best also to strain it through a sieve. Return to a pan and stir in the cream. If the soup is too thick for your liking, add more of the stock until the correct consistency is achieved. At this point, it's important the soup does not boil. Boiling of almost any finished vegetable soup impairs its natural flavour.

Notes: *Between a teaspoon and tablespoon of tomato purée can be added to the chopped tomatoes if they are not over-ripe and as flavoursome.*

Here are a few garnishes that will work very well with the dish.

- *Bread Croûtons or Home-made Crunchy Breadsticks (both page 210)*
- *Fresh tomato dice (page 209)*
- *Shavings of Parmesan cheese*
- *Trickles of extra virgin olive oil.*

tomatoes

Oxtail Soup

Serves 10–12

2 oxtails, divided between joints by your butcher

2 tablespoons flour

2 tablespoons cooking oil

knob of butter

2 onions, peeled and chopped

3 large carrots, peeled and chopped

4 celery sticks, chopped

4 flat mushrooms, chopped

2 bay leaves (optional)

fresh thyme sprig (optional)

pinch of ground allspice (optional)

250 ml (9 fl oz) Madeira or sherry

600 ml (1 pint) Veal or Beef Stock (page 203) or canned consommé

3 litres (5¼ pints) water

squeeze of lemon juice

salt and pepper

Introduction Oxtail has to be my favourite of all meats. (It's a pleasure to have it back again after being banned, as with all beef on the bone, for a period between 1997 and 1999.) You'll find the local butcher stocks oxtail mostly through the winter months. Personally, I would cook oxtail in any shape or form at any time of year. It is usually encountered in the form of stew, but this time I've turned to soup, which has a long history in Britain. Soup acknowledges the meat's strength of flavour and natural gelatinous qualities, and this particular version is more like a clear consommé (but without all the egg white needed to clarify it). It's best made 24 hours in advance; when refrigerated overnight, any excess fats will have formed a set crust which can be removed in one fell swoop (a lot easier than continual skimming with a ladle or 'lifting' with kitchen paper). And, of course, cooking in advance simplifies the day's preparation.

The ingredients list is for 10–12 portions, and although this can be easily halved, oxtail soup does freeze so well.

Method Cut away excess fat from the oxtails. Season with salt and pepper and dust with the flour. Heat a large braising pan with the cooking oil and butter. Once bubbling, add the tails, cooking on a medium heat until all are well coloured and sealed. Remove the tails from the pan, keeping to one side and pour away any excess oil. Add the chopped vegetables and mushrooms, plus the bay leaves, thyme and allspice, if using, and cook for 10–15 minutes until all have coloured. Return the tails to the pan, also adding the Madeira/sherry, stock and water. Bring to the simmer; at this point, skim all excess white scum from the stock. Cover with a lid.

There are now two options: to cook very slowly for 3–3½ hours either on top of the stove or in a pre-heated oven at 150°C/300°F/Gas 2. Once cooked and the oxtail meat is close to falling off the bone, remove from the oven, lifting the tails from the rich stock. Strain the 'soup' through a very fine sieve, preferably with a muslin cloth, allowing the juices to completely free themselves from the vegetables.

At this point, lightly skim and, once cool, place in the refrigerator for several hours, preferably overnight, to set. Any excess fats will form a 'plate' that can easily be removed. Separate the meat from the oxtail bones and shred or tear into strands. These are best kept immersed in a ladle or two of the stock to retain their moistness. Bring the soup to the boil and check its total oxtail strength; if it's tasting a little shallow, which I doubt, reduce until a good flavour is achieved, then add the squeeze of lemon juice. Warm the oxtail strands in their stock and divide a tablespoon or two between bowls (any extra can be frozen or used in a fried beef hash or fritters), pouring the rich oxtail soup over.

Notes: *Here are a few extra garnishes that will work very well in this dish.*

- *Chopped parsley can be sprinkled over*
- *Extra Madeira or sherry can be added at the last moment, for a richer finish*
- *A splash of Worcestershire sauce will fire up its finish*
- *Small, neat dice of onions, carrots and celery can be cooked separately and added with the oxtail strands to replace the vegetables strained away*
- *Tomato dice (page 209) add a nice sweetness to this soup.*

Lettuce Soup finished with French Dressing

Serves 4

knob of butter

1 large onion, chopped

600 ml (1 pint) hot Vegetable or Chicken Stock (page 204 or 201) or alternative (milk can be used to replace the stock, lending a creamier finish)

2 round lettuce picked, rinsed and roughly chopped

2 egg yolks

4 tablespoons double or whipping cream

salt, pepper and freshly grated nutmeg

For the French Dressing

1 teaspoon Dijon mustard

1 teaspoon white wine vinegar

1 teaspoon lemon juice

pinch of caster sugar

2 tablespoons olive oil and 2 tablespoons groundnut oil (or 4 tablespoons groundnut oil only)

salt and pepper

1 teaspoon chopped fresh chives

For the Garnish

½ small iceberg lettuce, finely shredded

coarse sea salt (optional)

twist of black pepper

Introduction As I've said in the past, salads are a perfect excuse to use your culinary licence. You must express your personality, but always remember not to *over*-flavour, which will overpower the freshness of the leaves themselves. Here I've extended my culinary licence quite considerably, turning a salad into a soup for spring or summer eating. It's not a new idea, as lettuce soups have been with us for almost as long as the vegetable itself. There are now hundreds of varieties of lettuce to choose from, and they are available all year round.

I've chosen the loose, round variety which doesn't take too long to wilt, consequently maintaining its colour and flavour. I've also added shredded iceberg as a crisp garnish, to help the French dressing.

There are many versions of French dressing or vinaigrette on record. The great Auguste Escoffier, executive chef at the Savoy Hotel in the early 1900s, coupled vinaigrette with ravigote sauce (translated as 'pick me up'), and included capers and herbs. Usually, though, a vinaigrette is at heart a combination of oil and vinegar. Many recipes add a little extra in the way of chopped herbs, mustard, sugar, garlic, lemon juice and more. My recipe here is quite basic, but adds a subtle piquancy to the finished soup.

Method Make the French dressing first. Mix together the mustard, vinegar, lemon juice and caster sugar. Whisk in the olive and/or groundnut oil(s) and season with salt and pepper. This will have a split/curdled consistency but all the flavours work together well. All the ingredients can be placed in a small screw-top jar and literally just shaken until mixed. The chopped chives should not be added until the last moment: this prevents a colour loss due to the rich acidity.

To make the soup, melt the butter in a large saucepan and, once bubbling, add the chopped onion. Cook on a low heat until translucent and tender. While cooking the onions, bring the stock (or milk) to the boil. Chop the lettuce leaves and add to the onions, allowing the broken leaves to wilt. Pour on 600 ml (1 pint) of the hot stock, season with salt, pepper and nutmeg and simmer, uncovered, for 10–12 minutes. Remove from the heat and stand for a few minutes before blitzing in a liquidizer or blender to a purée. Push through a sieve to remove any coarse fibres from the lettuce. Return to the stove.

Whisk the yolks with a few tablespoons of the soup. Once the soup is approaching simmering point, whisk in, not allowing it to boil or the yolks will begin to scramble as they warm. The soup will thicken. Pour in the cream, check for seasoning and the soup is ready. If too thick and a looser consistency is preferred, simply add any remaining stock or milk as required. Divide between bowls. Season the crispy iceberg with sea salt and black pepper and sit a little in the centre of each bowl. Add the chives to the French dressing and drizzle over.

Note: *A handful or two of spinach leaves can be added with the lettuce to leave a deeper green in the finished soup.*

Cock-a-leekie Soup

Serves 6–8

1.3 kg (3 lb) chicken (preferably free-range)

2–3 tablespoons cooking oil

900 g (2 lb) chicken wings, chopped

1½ carrots, peeled

2 celery sticks

1½ leeks (using the coarser greens for stock)

1½ large onions

225 g (8 oz) flat mushrooms, sliced

fresh thyme sprig

few black peppercorns

2 bay leaves

3 litres (5¼ pints) water (a chicken stock cube can be added for increased flavour)

2–3 glasses of white wine (optional)

For the Clarification

½ carrot, finely chopped

1 celery stick, finely chopped

½ leek, finely chopped

½ onion, finely chopped

½ teaspoon salt

2 large egg whites, slightly beaten

6 tomatoes, chopped

For the Garnish

1 leek, sliced, using white and green

8–10 ready-to-eat prunes, stoned and cut into thin strips

'I believe that I once considerably scandalised her by declaring that clear soup was a more important factor in life than a clear conscience.'

SAKI (H.H. Munro), 1870–1916
The Blind Spot

Introduction Cock-a-leekie, a classic and traditional Scottish soup which consists of a chicken – once an old cockerel past his crowing best – cooked in a stock flavoured with leeks and prunes, may have had a slight French influence too, in that originally the chicken and the broth were often served as two separate courses. In some recipes, onions were used instead of leeks, and raisins instead of prunes.

For me, the combination of shredded leeks (I like to include some of the tender greens as well as traditional whites), strips of chicken and prunes works perfectly. But I take the whole concept of the soup even further, turning it into a consommé, the most refined and clearest of soups. This takes more planning and time, but you're paid back by the great flavours and the soup's own display of great pride. The recipe can be made without following the clarifying process, resulting in a very tasty cock-a-leekie broth.

Method Remove the chicken legs. Skin and bone the legs, then mince, finely chop or process the meat. Heat the cooking oil in a large saucepan. Add the chopped chicken wings and fry until a deep golden brown. Chop and add all the soup base vegetables, along with the flat mushrooms. Continue to fry until also well coloured. All of the remaining ingredients can now be added – chicken, leg bones, herbs, water plus stock cube and white wine, if using (but reserve the minced chicken). Bring to the simmer, skimming off any impurities rising to the top. This stock/broth can now be simmered very gently on a low heat for 2–2½ hours. Once cooked, turn off the heat and rest for 15–20 minutes. Remove the chicken and take off the breasts, cutting into strips for the garnish. Put aside. Strain the broth through a sieve/colander, allowing every last drop to fall naturally from the ingredients. This can now be poured through a double layer of muslin, collecting any impurities. Once passed, the soup base is best left to cool and then refrigerated for 24 hours.

When taken from the fridge, the fat will have formed a crust, easily removable in one swoop. If you wish to use the consommé on the same day, dab kitchen paper from the surface to remove any fat easily. Leave to cool to room temperature. When the chicken is cool enough to handle, remove the breast meat and shred it.

To make the clarification, mix the finely chopped vegetables with the minced chicken, adding the salt and slightly beaten egg whites. This can be quickly achieved in a food processor, adding the tomato pieces and blitzing to a pulp. The soup base is now best brought to a liquid consistency before whisking in the clarification.

Now bring this consommé mix to a rapid simmer, stirring or whisking from time to time, making sure it does not stick to the base of the pan. Once close to boiling, reduce the temperature to a very gentle soft simmer, whisk for the last time and leave to cook slowly for a minimum of 1 hour. During this cooking time, a thick crust will have formed; this collects all the impurities, leaving a rich amber consommé, flavoured from the chicken and its fellow ingredients. Usually, a crack will have formed in the edge of the crust. For the last 15 minutes of cooking time, spoon a little of the crust

Cod *Brandade* Soup with Leeks and Potatoes

away, leaving a gap to ladle from once cooked. The consommé can now be gently ladled out, passing it through fresh muslin into a suitable bowl or saucepan. Once almost all is strained, if any excess is becoming slightly cloudy, spoon into a small separate pan. This can be used to warm the chicken strips.

Taste the soup; if it appears to be slightly weak, boil and reduce by a quarter or third if necessary.

When ready to serve this shiny, glossy bowl of magic, simply warm the reserved chicken strips in the excess stock mentioned, or use a little water.

Heat 1 ladle of consommé separately and, once boiling, add the shredded leeks; cook for 30 seconds until tender. Add the prunes and, once warmed, spoon some of the leeks, chicken strips and prunes, without the heating liquor, as this will have become cloudy, over the hot consommé. The cock-a-leekie is ready to serve.

This recipe may seem a little intense and full of headaches, but the hardest part is just the chopping of the vegetables. The rest is down to slow simmering, releasing lots of exciting smells in your kitchen. As I mentioned in the introduction, you can simply make the stock, pass it through the double muslin and the broth is ready. If you only ever make this once, you'll be very glad you did.

Notes: *The clarification process is achieved by the albumen of the egg white coagulating with the meat, rising to the top of the liquid, carrying other solid ingredients. The gentle simmer of the liquid below will keep the crust afloat.*

Beef consommé can also be made, replacing the whole chicken and wings by volume with oxtails. These, pan-fried and boiled, will give a deep beef flavour. For the crust, add 175 g (6 oz) of finely minced beef, replacing the chicken leg meat.

Serves 6

For the *Brandade*

450 g (1 lb) cod fillet

2 tablespoons coarse sea salt

For the Soup

600 ml (1 pint) milk, plus extra for poaching (optional)

4–6 garlic cloves, sliced

2 tablespoons olive oil

knob of butter

2 onions, finely chopped

2 leeks, white only, cut into 5 mm (¼ in) rough dice (reserve greens for garnish)

2 potatoes, cut into 5 mm (¼ in) rough dice

600 ml (1 pint) Fish Stock (page 201) or alternative, or water

pepper

For the Garnish

1 large or 2 medium potatoes, cut into 5 mm (¼ in) dice

knob of butter

leek greens, finely sliced

olive oil, to serve

Introduction *Brandade* has been a classic of the Languedoc and Provence for hundreds of years, although it wasn't until about 1830 that the recipe first appeared in a cookery book. Salted dried cod is popular all over southern Europe, particularly in Spain and Portugal, and *brandade* is the French way of making an unpromising ingredient palatable. The cod is soaked in cold water, to remove excess salt and to rehydrate it, for at least 48 hours, and is then cooked and 'pummelled' to a paste with the addition of milk and oil, forming a salt cod cream-pâté.

Many other features have since been added to the dish. Garlic is thought to be essential to *brandade* now, but in fact was used more as a seasoning than flavouring originally. Another addition, thought of today as a standard requirement, is potato. Apparently this was introduced in northern France, where olive oil was less prevalent, to help calm the strong salted flavour.

This *brandade*, served as a soup, will please everybody. You can buy ready-salted cod, but here it's going to be made fresh. To enjoy this dish, therefore, you must start 48 hours in advance.

Method To make the *brandade*, leave the skin on the cod fillet and remove any bones. Lay skin-side down on a tray and sprinkle salt over the flesh. Cover with cling film and refrigerate for 24 hours.

Wash away any excess salt before soaking the cod in cold water, refrigerated, for a minimum of 12 hours, changing the water two or three times.

Once soaked, cut a central piece (350 g/ 12 oz) of the fish, keeping it to poach later for the garnish. All the trimmings can now be put to one side for the soup.

To make the soup, warm the milk with the garlic slices and leave to one side to infuse. Warm the olive oil in a saucepan

Cod *Brandade* Soup with Leeks and Potatoes

with the knob of butter and, once bubbling, add the onions and top with a lid. Cook, without colouring, for a few minutes until softening. Add the white chopped leeks and potatoes and continue to cook for 10–12 minutes until beginning to soften. Add the fish stock or water, bring to the simmer and cook for 15–20 minutes until the vegetables are tender. Pour in the milk and garlic and add the salt-cod trimmings, discarding the skin. Return to the simmer and cook for a further 2–3 minutes. Liquidize the soup and strain through a sieve, squeezing any excess juices from the grainy cod pulp. This does not need to be pushed through: its flavour is already in the soup, and the potatoes and vegetables are its thickening agents.

Check the soup for seasoning with pepper (salt will probably not be needed due to the *brandade*).

Now make the garnishes. Place the reserved salt cod fillet in a dish, bring enough extra milk to cover it to the boil in a separate saucepan and pour over the fillet. Cover with a lid. After a few minutes, the cod will have cooked. The milk can be used to loosen the soup or discarded. The fish flesh can now be broken into flakes and divided between bowls. Another alternative is to simply steam the fish over simmering water for a few minutes until cooked; then flake it.

Cook the diced potato in water until tender. Drain and keep warm to one side. Melt a small knob of butter in a saucepan. Wash the shredded leek greens, drain well and add them to the pan. The natural water from the leeks will create steam while cooking on a medium heat, the leeks becoming tender within minutes.

To finish, divide the warm diced potatoes and leeks between the bowls, topping with the rich salt-cod soup. Drizzle with olive oil and serve.

Notes: *Thick toasts eat very well with this dish, just as they used to be served with the original* brandade, *almost like pâté with toast.*

Some of the leek greens can be kept for placing on top of the soup before trickling with oil.

The parsley coulis in the recipe for Potato, Onion and Garlic Parsley Soup (page 44) can also be used to trickle over this soup.

'Meat and Two Veg' Soup

Serves 4 as a main course or 8 as a starter

900 g (2 lb) piece of gammon

bouquet garni of thyme, sage and bay leaf and a few black peppercorns, tied in leek, or bought ready-made bouquet garni

4 medium potatoes, peeled and quartered

16 baby onions, peeled

knob of butter plus 50 g (2 oz)

4 medium carrots, peeled and split and cut into 3 cm (1¼ in) pieces

2 tablespoons chopped mixed fresh herbs e.g. parsley, sage and chervil

salt and pepper

Introduction Eating soups at the family table is a memory I love to re-live. It's a 'tradition' that I feel every family should keep. This soup can also be served as a starter at dinner parties. It has the great ability of bringing people together and relaxing situations.

This recipe is one that really must be served from a large casserole dish or bowl in the centre of the table, with each person happily helping themselves. Small portions can then be had without that feeling of obligation of having to eat everything put in front of you.

The meat I'm using is gammon, which feeds the water its rich flavour, creating the stock-soup itself. Other meats can be used in its place, such as chicken or rabbit.

The gammon will need to be ordered in advance, giving time for it to be soaked and refrigerated for 24 hours, changing the water several times.

Method Rinse the soaked gammon and place in a saucepan with cold water to cover. Bring to the boil and refresh under cold water. Now the gammon, along with the bouquet garni, can be topped once more with cold water just to cover, covered with a lid and brought to the simmer. Cook with the lid ajar for 2½ hours. The meat will be so tender and succulent to eat. The vegetables and potatoes will need to be added during the cooking process. Here's the method.

Forty-five minutes before the meat has finished, the potato quarters can be added. This gives them plenty of time to cook and begin to break, slightly thickening the liquor. Place the button onions in a saucepan of cold water and bring to the simmer. Drain. Melt a knob of butter in a frying pan and sauté the onions until well coloured. These can now be added to the soup, giving a slightly 'roasted' flavour. The carrots can also be added.

After the gammon's cooking time, cover with the lid and leave to rest for 10–15 minutes. Return to a gentle simmer, remove the bouquet garni and add the 50 g (2 oz) of butter and chopped herbs, check for seasoning and the 'meal' is ready to offer to the family. The gammon will 'carve' with a spoon, and you can help yourself to potatoes, the two vegetables and herby stock to go with it.

Notes: *If using chicken or rabbit, the cooking time can be reduced to 1–1½ hours.*

Many other vegetables can be added – cauliflower, swedes, turnips, mushrooms cabbage, sprouts, broccoli, peas and cabbage. If using green vegetables, cook separately to maintain their colour and add just before serving.

Smoky Lentil Soup

Serves 4–6

1 tablespoon cooking oil

175 g (6 oz) piece of smoked streaky bacon, cut into 5 mm (¼ in) dice

2 onions, finely chopped, or 75 g (3 oz) button onions, peeled and halved

2 carrots, cut into 5 mm (¼ in) dice

2 celery sticks, cut into 5 mm (¼ in) dice

1 garlic clove, crushed (optional)

175 g (6 oz) *lentilles de Puy* (small greeny-blue lentils)

900 ml (1½ pints) Chicken Stock (page 201)

150–300 ml (5–10 fl oz) whipping cream

knob of butter

salt and pepper

1 tablespoon chopped fresh flatleaf parsley (optional), to garnish

Introduction Lentils come in many colours, shapes and flavours, and have been enjoyed for thousands of years around the world – European prehistoric sites have revealed lentil remains. The most common varieties are green or brown, which hold their colours through cooking; for soups they will need a good hour of stewing. Whole red lentils have a distinctive salmon colour, and cook very quickly; that rich redness turns to a yellow tone. The split red lentil, which also fades to yellow, is probably the spiciest-flavoured of them all. And then there are the small Puy lentils, which are French, the most expensive, but also the best, having a slight peppery flavour. I'm using these for this soup. The green or brown varieties would also work, but for a few extra pence, the results will be money well spent. Smoky bacon infuses its flavours into the soup, bringing a coarser consistency as well. This dish can be enjoyed in two forms – loose or creamed – and the details for both are offered below.

Method Warm the oil in a saucepan. Add the diced bacon pieces and fry on a medium heat for a few minutes until well coloured. The bacon will now have released its own fats in the pan. It's important not to drain this away, instead, add the vegetables and garlic (if using) and cook on a medium heat for 8–10 minutes until beginning to soften. The bacon fat will now have infused the vegetables with its smoky flavour. Rinse the lentils and add to the pan. Stir and add the chicken stock. Bring to the simmer and cook gently for 45 minutes, until the lentils are completely tender and have 'thickened' the stock. If you prefer the lentils to have a slight bite, cook for only 30 minutes.

To finish, add enough cream to suit your taste. Add a knob of butter, season with salt and pepper and finish with the chopped parsley, if using. The smoky soup is ready to serve. This eats well as an almost complete meal, offering the Home-made Crunchy Breadsticks (page 210) to accompany the soup.

Notes: *The cream and butter can both be omitted from this recipe for a less rich finish.*

To make the creamed soup, place the bacon, keeping it as one piece, in a saucepan with the stock, along with the vegetables. The vegetables can simply be roughly chopped. Top with the stock and bring to the simmer, cooking for 40 minutes. Remove the piece of bacon. Add the rinsed lentils and return to the simmer, cook for 45 minutes, remove from the heat and purée in a liquidizer or food processor, pushing through a sieve (not essential) for the smoothest finish. Add the cream to taste, dice the cooked bacon and re-heat in the soup. Finish with chopped parsley and serve. The breadsticks or Bread Croûtons (page 210) will both work well with this version.

Fresh Spinach Soup with Goat's Cheese and Sweet Pepper Pancakes

Serves 4–6

675 g ($1\frac{1}{2}$ lb) spinach leaves

1.2 litres (2 pints) Vegetable Stock (page 204)

50 g (2 oz) butter

1 small onion, chopped finely

1 medium potato, cut into rough 1 cm ($\frac{1}{2}$ in) dice

1 garlic clove, crushed (optional)

salt, pepper and freshly grated nutmeg

2–3 tablespoons crème fraîche or whipping cream (optional)

1 quantity Goat's Cheese and Sweet Pepper Pancakes (page 209)

Introduction The word 'spinach' suggests natural strength, and among professional and, I hope, home cooks it is highly respected. Probably made famous by our old favourite cartoon character Popeye, the wonderful green-leaved vegetable has become accepted as a rich component of our daily diets. The beautiful leaves have an astonishing ability to absorb melting butter, and once tender give back that faintly bitter-sweet taste. Spinach deserves the honourable title of prince of vegetables.

Spinach does have one disadvantage, and that, of course, is its immense volume reduction during the cooking process. To serve as a vegetable (page 142), you will need at least 900 g (2 lb) for four good portions. A very natural soup can be made with just the leaves and stock cooked and blitzed together, but as you will see, I've included one or two more ingredients for a smoother and fuller consistency and flavour.

The pancakes are a wonderful optional extra, with that cheese flavour working so well with the soup itself.

Method Discard any bruised spinach leaves and remove the central stalks. The spinach must now be washed carefully 2–3 times, removing any grit deposited by rain.

Bring the vegetable stock to the boil. Drop the leaves into the bubbling liquor and allow to cook for a few minutes, until tender. Drain in a colander allowing the stock to fall into a suitable bowl or saucepan. Squeeze any excess stock out of the spinach and set aside.

Melt 25 g (1 oz) of the butter in a saucepan. Once bubbling, add the chopped onion, potato and garlic, if using. Place a lid on top and bubble gently for 8–10 minutes until the potatoes are beginning to soften. Pour the saved stock over and bring to the simmer. Cook on a medium heat until the potatoes are cooked through. This will generally take 12–15 minutes. Season with salt, pepper and nutmeg and leave to cool.

Once cold, mix with the cooked spinach and liquidize to a smooth finish. For a cleaner finish, the soup is best pushed through a sieve, too.

When it's time to eat, warm the soup, whisking in the crème fraîche (if using) and remaining 25 g (1 oz) of butter. An electric hand blender will help emulsify all the ingredients, also leaving the soup with a cappuccino-style froth. A little sprinkling of extra nutmeg can be sprinkled over before serving.

Notes: *If making the vegetable stock recipe, the lemon is best omitted. This prevents its acidity discolouring the bright green spinach.*

An alternative accompaniment to goat's cheese pancakes is fried bread croûtons rolled in Parmesan cheese (page 210).

It is like the few handfuls of good soil cast on the surface to receive the sown seed. To soup you owe your first impression of being well looked after at table.

Marquis de Cussy

Fresh Herb Broth

Serves 4

1 dessertspoon chopped fresh flatleaf parsley

1 dessertspoon chopped fresh curly parsley, plus stalks and a few leaves for the stock

1 dessertspoon chopped fresh chervil, plus stalks and a few leaves for the stock

1 dessertspoon chopped fresh chives, plus stalks and a few leaves for the stock

1 dessertspoon chopped fresh tarragon, plus stalks and a few leaves for the stock

1 dessertspoon picked fresh marjoram leaves, plus a few leaves for the stock

750 ml (1½ pints) Vegetable or Chicken Stock (page 204 or 201) or alternative

50 g (2 oz) butter

1 large potato, cut into 1 cm (½ in) dice

1 large leek, cut into 5 mm (¼ in) thick rings

salt, pepper and a squeeze of lime juice (optional)

'Excellent herbs had our fathers of old –
Excellent herbs to ease their pain –
Alexanders and Marigold,
Eyebright, Orris and Elecampane –
Basil, Rocket, Valerian, Rue,
(Almost singing themselves they run)
Vervain, Dittany, Call-me-to-you –
Cowslip, melilot, rose of the sun.
Anything green that grew out of the mould
Was an excellent herb to our fathers of old.'

RUDYARD KIPLING (1865–1936)
Our Fathers of Old

Introduction 'Broth' is a word normally used to describe the liquid within which meat and other flavourings have been cooked, similar to the French *bouillon*. It is, in a sense, the stage between stock and soup, in that a good broth can be eaten (or drunk) when combined with other ingredients, whereas a plain stock cannot, being an ingredient rather than a finished product.

Kipling noted the excellence of herbs and here I've included many that all work together, standing out from the other ingredients. The addition of potato and leek help with texture and blending of flavours. They can be replaced with some rice (25 g /1 oz) simply cooked in the stock. I prefer this dish as a stock garnished with the potatoes, leeks and chopped herbs. For a thicker, creamier herb soup, rather than a broth, liquidize to a smooth purée before adding the chopped herbs.

When chopping herbs, unless this is carefully executed with a sharp knife and at the last moment, the beautiful flavoured leaves become bruised and weep, losing a lot of their natural taste. Although I am listing them as chopped, tearing them will give you a cleaner and more flavoursome finish, with no loss of colour.

Obviously, the majority of the herbs will need to be picked before chopping; it's important that all the stalks are kept as these will then infuse the stock, helping the overall finish.

Method Place all the herb stalks, plus any surplus leaves, in a saucepan, and cover with the stock. Bring to the simmer and gently cook for 5 minutes. Remove from the heat and leave to infuse for a further 15 minutes.

Melt the butter in a saucepan; once bubbling, add the diced potato. Cook on a gentle heat with a lid on for 6–8 minutes. If they begin to stick at any point of this cooking time, lightly moisten with a ladle of the 'herb' stock. Add the leek rings and continue to cook, without a lid, for a few minutes. Boil the stock and strain into the vegetables. Bring to the simmer and cook on a medium heat until both vegetables are tender.

Season with salt and pepper and a squeeze of lime juice, if using. This is now a loose broth that can also be liquidized to a creamy consistency. Add the mixed herbs to finish and serve.

It's important that the herbs are added just before serving because this guarantees their lively, fresh and very individual flavours. Quite a superb dish to serve as a starter or soup course with plenty going on in the bowl, but without becoming too much. It's best to offer a soft-centred, crusty bread with this, which will lift and absorb every last drop.

Smoked Haddock Soup with Welsh Rarebit Gnocchi

Serves 4–6

For the Soup

300 ml (10 fl oz) milk

600 ml (1 pint) Fish Stock (page 201) or alternative, or water

350 g (12 oz) natural smoked haddock fillet

knob of butter

1 leek, white only, roughly chopped

1 onion, roughly chopped

1 large potato, peeled and roughly chopped

100 ml (3½ fl oz) single cream (optional)

salt and pepper

For the Gnocchi (makes 30–35)

450 g (1 lb) potatoes, skin left on

75–100 g (3–4 oz) Cheddar cheese, grated

1–2 teaspoons English mustard

few dashes of Worcestershire sauce

100 g (4 oz) plain flour

1 egg, plus 1 yolk for extra-rich flavour

salt and pepper

butter or olive oil, for cooking

To Serve

2 tomatoes, blanched (page 209) and diced

1–2 tablespoons chopped fresh chives

olive oil, for drizzling

Introduction Smoked haddock is a great Scottish speciality. Naturally cold-smoked Finnan haddock, originally from Findon in Aberdeenshire, is the fish required for this soup. Many fish sold as smoked haddock have been dyed yellow and quite often have not even been smoked, but instead chemically treated to create that smoky flavour. Choosing your haddock is actually quite simple: always opt for the natural, slightly off-white fillets, which will give you the flavour we're after.

There are several traditional soups made with smoked haddock, but my version is garnished with chopped tomatoes, chives and Welsh rarebit gnocchi. Gnocchi of course are a form of Italian dumpling, and they can be made from semolina or potato. I'm using potato and Cheddar cheese, with the addition of Worcestershire sauce to give the 'dumplings' that Welsh rarebit finish.

Method The gnocchi can be made and cooked well in advance, ready to pan-fry 'to order'. Cook the unpeeled potatoes whole in salted, boiling water until tender (generally approximately 20 minutes, depending on size). Peel the warm potatoes and mash to a smooth texture. At this point, 75 g (3 oz) of the cheese can be added; while the potato is still warm, the cheese will melt into them. For a more cheesy flavour, add the remaining 25 g (1 oz). Add the mustard and Worcestershire sauce, tasting for strength. More can always be added. Add the flour, egg and yolk, if using, season with salt and pepper and the dumpling dough is ready to be rolled into 1–2 cm (½–¾ in) balls. Simply take a good teaspoon of the mix and roll with floured hands or on a floured surface. Once all are rolled, the dumplings are ready to poach in simmering water for 3–4 minutes: 5 minutes is the maximum they will need. It's best to cook a handful at a time. Drop carefully into the water; you'll notice as cooking time passes that they will rise to the top of the pan. It's at this point that they are ready.
If not using immediately, refresh in iced water. They can be made to this stage well in advance.

Once cooled, refrigerate the dumplings on trays and cover with cling film. They can be re-heated by pan-frying whenever needed.

To pan-fry, melt a knob of butter along with a drop of olive oil in a frying-pan. Once the butter is beginning to bubble, add the dumplings. Fry on a medium heat until golden brown. This will have created another texture in the dumplings and completely warmed them through. They are now ready to serve.

To make the soup, boil together the milk and stock or water. Place the smoked haddock fillet in a dish and pour the hot liquor over. Cover and leave to stand for

Creamy Roast Chicken Soup

15–20 minutes. This will cook the smoked haddock without boiling its lovely soft, succulent flakes.

While the haddock is resting, melt the butter in a saucepan and, once bubbling, add the chopped leek, onion and potato. Cook on a medium heat, covering with a lid to create a steam. Allow the vegetables to simmer in the butter until softening. Drain the milk liquor from the haddock fillet, pouring it over the vegetables. To ensure the moist texture of the haddock is maintained, cover with cling film. Return the soup to the simmer and cook until completely tender; this will take a further 15–20 minutes.

The soup can now be liquidized to a purée and strained for a smooth finish. Season with salt and pepper, adding single cream if using. The smoked haddock fillet can now be flaked and warmed in the soup when ready to serve.

To finish the dish, warm the soup with the flakes of poached smoked haddock. Just before ladling into bowls, add the tomato dice and chopped chives. Now garnish with the pan-fried Welsh rarebit gnocchi and drizzle with olive oil. This soup has so much happening in the bowl. The soup itself is full of smoky flavour with the translucent flakes to bite into. The tomatoes bring a slight sweetness, working with the oniony chives while the nuggets of Welsh rarebit lend a cheesy edge with a mustard and spicy Worcestershire bite.

Serves 6-8

1.1 kg (2½ lb) chicken, preferably free-range

1 tablespoon cooking oil

25 g (1 oz) butter

900 ml (1½ pints) Chicken Stock (page 201) or alternative

150 ml (5 fl oz) single cream

salt and pepper

25–50 ml (1–2 fl oz) dry sherry (optional)

Optional Vegetables and Flavourings

1 onion, roughly chopped

½ leek, roughly chopped

1–2 celery sticks, roughly chopped

2 garlic cloves, peeled

1 bay leaf

fresh thyme sprig

For the Roux Sauce

knob of butter

50 g (2 oz) plain flour

450 ml (15 fl oz) milk

Introduction Chicken soup was always one of my favourite 'convenience' meals as a child – the thick, creamy variety from the tin, eaten with lots of crusty bread. Even just coming from the tin, I felt it was a culinary treat. It was probably being able to mop up every last drop from the bowl with the bread that excited me.

This version involves a little extra work and cooking time, but does give quite a basic soup a very different finish. If you don't fancy the wait, then simply make the soup with the stock, poaching one or two breasts in it for garnish. You will still have a very tasty chicken soup, but without the roasted flavour.

Method Pre-heat the oven, to 200°C/400°F/ Gas 6. Season the chicken with salt and pepper and heat a frying pan with the cooking oil. Place the chicken on its side in the pan and fry until golden brown, turning to repeat the same roasted flavour and effect. If using the optional vegetables and flavourings, melt a knob of butter in a suitable pot or roasting pan, sprinkle the vegetables, garlic cloves and herbs around, and cook for a few minutes until softened. Add the chicken to the pan before adding the chicken stock and bringing to the simmer. The chicken can now be pot-roasted (this makes a wonderful main course) in the pre-heated oven for 50–60 minutes, basting from time to time with the stock.

While the chicken is roasting, make the roux. Melt the butter in a saucepan. Once bubbling, add the flour, cooking over a medium heat and stirring from time to time until it reaches a pale hazelnut colour. This is a 'roux' base used for the making of many white, blond sauces. Bring the milk to the boil and pour on to the roux, whisking to a smooth consistency. Remove from the stove, covering with cling film to prevent a skin from forming.

Creamy Roast
Chicken Soup

Remove the chicken from the oven, lift out of the stock and keep warm on one side. Strain the cooking liquor through a fine sieve, discarding the vegetables. Once the chicken stock has been strained, re-heat the roux sauce and continue to add stock to it until a creamy soup consistency is achieved. This can now be gently simmered, stirring occasionally, for 20–30 minutes, cooking the flour base into the milk and stock. The soup may need loosening with more stock before adding the single cream. Strain through a sieve. Once a perfect soft, loose, spoon-coating finish has been achieved, any remaining chicken stock can be boiled and reduced by two-thirds, increasing its depth of flavour, before also adding to the finished pot of roast chicken soup. Season with salt and pepper. The sherry can now be added as an optional taste, giving quite a different finish to the dish.

To serve, the chicken breasts and bones can now be cut from the bird, removing the thigh and drumstick meat. Carve both cuts and divide between individual bowls, pouring the soup around. For a 'cappuccino' finish to the soup, loosen a ladle or two with warm semi-skimmed milk before blitzing with an electric hand blender or whisk and spooning over the chicken. The surprise to the dish is finding the succulent pieces of roast chicken sitting underneath the light fluffy soup almost souffléing on top.

Notes: *The pot-roast chicken can be served as a complete main course, with potatoes and vegetable dishes featured in the book. The soup can then be made as above, using the stock. This will give you two dishes from one pot. Alternatively, one breast and leg can be used as the garnish, still leaving half a bird to be enjoyed in sandwiches or with salad.*

A little olive oil (or Tarragon Oil, page 207) can be drizzled around the finished soup.

Vichyssoise

Serves 6, generously

675 g (1½ lb) leeks, white parts only

50 g (2 oz) butter

1 large onion, finely chopped

2 medium potatoes, cut into rough 1 cm (½ in) dice

900 ml (1½ pints) Chicken or Vegetable Stock (page 201 or 204) or alternative

300 ml (10 fl oz) milk

150–300 ml (5–10 fl oz) whipping or double cream

salt and pepper

For the garnish

3 tablespoons snipped fresh chives

freshly grated nutmeg (optional)

Leeks

Introduction You'd expect this soup to have come from the town of Vichy in France. The inspiration does, but the dish doesn't. This internationally known soup was the invention of a Frenchman, Louis Diat, while he was head chef at the Ritz-Carlton Hotel, New York, in 1917. He was from the Vichy area of France and remembered a soup his mother would often serve, made with leeks and potatoes. Diat discovered how well the soup would eat cold during the hot New York summer months. And, as with all chefs, he added his own little touch, that familiar sprinkling of chopped chives. Here's my version of that French-American classic.

Method Remove any tough outer leaves from the leeks, then wash and roughly chop. It's important the finished weight is 675 g (1½ lb) of whites only. If the green is used, the vegetable becomes very discoloured, giving an almost 'depressing' finish to the dish. Melt the butter in a large saucepan and, once bubbling, add the chopped leeks, onion and potatoes. Stir and allow to bubble gently, covering with a lid and cooking for 10–15 minutes until beginning to soften. Pour over the stock and bring to the simmer. Cook for 20–25 minutes.

Add the milk, return to the simmer and remove from the heat. Season with salt and pepper and leave to cool slightly before liquidizing to a smooth purée. It's now best to push it through a fine sieve into a bowl sitting on ice. Refrigerate and, once chilled, stir in 150 ml (5 fl oz) of the cream. If you prefer a creamier finish, add the remaining cream. Check for seasoning and the vichyssoise is made.

To serve, sprinkle each portion liberally with snipped chives and a quick grating of fresh nutmeg (if using). Eating this soup on a hot summer's day becomes a meal on its own, especially if offered with Home-made Crunchy Breadsticks (page 210) and a green salad. A simple cream of leek and potato soup, over 80 years old and it's never lost a year; thank you, Monsieur Diat.

Note: *A shellfish alternative to this soup can be achieved by substituting crab or lobster stock for the chicken or vegetable stock. Follow the recipe method, garnishing with cooked flaked white crab meat or soft dice of lobster.*

Onion Soup with Steak and Kidney 'Sausage' Dumplings

Serves 4

For the Dumplings (makes 12)

75 g (3 oz) lamb or beef kidneys (lamb kidneys give a more subtle flavour)

50 g (2 oz) beef suet, chopped finely or dried alternative

225 g (8 oz) beef skirt, coarsely minced

salt and pepper

1 egg

1 small onion, finely chopped and cooked in butter without colour

25–50 g (1–2 oz) fresh white breadcrumbs

dash of Worcestershire sauce

flour, for rolling

cooking oil and butter, for frying

For the Soup

25 g (1 oz) butter or beef dripping

900 g (2 lb) onions, finely sliced

1 bay leaf

pinch of brown sugar

675–900 ml (1–1½ pints) Beef or dark Chicken Stock (page 203 or 201)

salt and pepper

100 g (4 oz) Gruyère cheese, grated, to serve (optional)

Introduction The best-known onion soup is probably French onion soup, once the passport to a Continental menu, and now quite out of fashion. In France, it's known for its pick-me-up qualities, particularly useful when wines have been flowing too rapidly and too well. I've introduced a traditional British feeling to the French classic, moulding a steak and kidney sausage mix into small dumplings, ready to help soak up the onion flavour. This gives the soup a 'sausage and onion gravy' touch and, when finished with the melting Gruyère cheese (as per the classic French soup recipe), brings the dish back to the heights of fashion.

Method First prepare the dumpling ingredients because they should be well chilled. Clean and trim the kidneys of any sinews before chopping/cutting into small dice. Mix with the suet, quickly blitzing in a food processor, or chopping by hand to combine but not purée the two ingredients together. Keep refrigerated.

Now make the soup. Melt the butter or beef dripping in a saucepan and, once melted, add the sliced onions and bay leaf. Stir-fry, allowing them to become golden brown and form an amalgamated mass. Add the sugar and cook for a few minutes more, until slightly caramelizing. Pour 600 ml

Winter Vegetable Soup (*Crème Garbure*)

(1 pint) of the stock on top, season with salt and pepper and cook for 10–15 minutes. The soup is now ready, with its familiar 'thickness' of onions bound within the stock.

For a looser finish, add the remaining 225 ml (8 fl oz) of stock.

To make the dumplings, place the minced beef in a bowl over ice and season well with salt and pepper. Add the egg, stirring and working it into the beef. Add the cooked, chopped onion along with the suet mix. Finally add 25 g (1 oz) of the breadcrumbs and dash of Worcestershire sauce, re-checking the seasoning. To check the sausage texture and taste, pan-fry a small 'burger' for a few minutes on each side. If the mixture is too moist, add the remaining 25 g (1 oz) of breadcrumbs, re-seasoning if necessary.

The dumpling mix can be made several hours beforehand, refrigerating and setting. To finish, simply roll in floured hands into 12 nuggets (3 per portion). Heat the cooking oil and butter together and pan-fry the dumplings until golden brown – about 6–8 minutes. Transfer to the soup during its last few minutes of cooking, allowing the kidney flavour to enhance the soup. Either serve in one large tureen or divide between four large soup bowls. Sprinkle with the Gruyère cheese, if using, and gratinate under a pre-heated grill. The English onion soup is ready to serve.

Note: *The dumplings can be omitted, replacing with a thick slice of French bread per portion, toasted, placed on top of the soup, sprinkled with cheese and also melted under the grill. That's classic French onion soup.*

Serves 6

1 onion or 2 shallots

2 medium carrots

1 celery stick

1 small swede or medium turnip

1 medium potato

1 small leek

25 g (1 oz) butter

1.2 litres (2 pints) Vegetable Stock (page 204) or alternative

150 ml (5 fl oz) single cream or milk or half of each (optional)

salt and pepper

Introduction The French name for this soup – *crème garbure* – literally translates as 'garbage cream'! The basic idea was to use up any vegetable trimmings, creating a thick, tasty and very cheap soup. This is ideal in winter, with all the winter root vegetables available, but the soup can also be made in spring. If making a spring version, I'd prefer to use baby vegetable varieties, and enjoy them lightly cooked in the stock as a broth.

Method Each of the vegetables can first be peeled, also removing the outside layer from the leek, before cutting all into rough 1 cm (½ in) pieces. Gently melt the butter, not allowing it to brown. Add all the vegetables, leaving the potatoes to one side, allowing them to cook for 5–6 minutes until beginning to soften. Add the potatoes and continue to cook in the butter for a further 2 minutes before pouring the vegetable stock over. Season with a good pinch of salt and twist of pepper before bringing to the simmer and skimming off any impurities. Cover with a lid, allowing steam to release, and cook for 20–25 minutes until all the vegetables and potatoes are tender. Liquidize in stages to a smooth purée, returning to a saucepan. If using the cream or milk for a richer finish, simply add and return to the simmer, season again with salt and pepper and the soup is ready to serve.

Notes: *The Home-made Crunchy Breadsticks (page 210) or Croûtons for Soup (page 210) will both work as accompaniments to this dish.*

Extra butter can be whisked in to the soup to enrich it a stage further.

Two or three tomatoes, chopped and added with the potatoes, will add a slightly sweet and fruity finish to the soup.

fish

Roast Sea Bass with Glazed Crab Mashed Potatoes

Serves 4

flour, for dusting

4 × 175 g (6 oz) sea bass fillet portions, scaled and pin-boned (page 13)

large knob of butter, melted

2 tablespoons cooking oil

100 g (4 oz) white crab meat

450g–675 g (1–1½ lb) Mashed Potatoes (page 142)

2 heaped tablespoons chopped fresh chives

salt and pepper

For the Crab Sauce

½ × 400 g (14 oz) tin of crab bisque soup (or lobster/seafood bisque soup)

50 g (2 oz) Cheddar cheese, grated

1 teaspoon ready-made English mustard

1 tablespoon brandy (optional)

squeeze of lemon juice

1 egg yolk

50 ml (2 fl oz) double or whipping cream

salt and pepper

For the Quick Lemon Sauce (optional)

juice of ½ lemon

50 g (2 oz) cold butter, cubed

salt and pepper

olive oil, for drizzling

Introduction The sea bass fillet here is not actually roasted at all, but pan-fried in butter. This leaves a crisp, nutty-flavoured skin which looks as though it has been roasted. As for the crab mashed potatoes, these are very special, the warmed white crab meat worked through the potatoes with chives and glazed with a crab bisque sauce. The sauce is poured over the crab mashed potatoes and glazed under the grill to a golden brown. When you cut through the glaze, it mixes with the potatoes, spreading its flavour throughout. (In fact, this potato dish will work with almost any pan-fried, roasted or grilled fish, whether it be salmon, cod, halibut or even smoked haddock.)

The white crab meat can be purchased completely clean and flaked. I recommend this way of buying, unless you intend to make your own bisque using the shell and brown meat. Although already clean, the flakes are best checked for any pieces of shell that have got through at this stage.

Method Start by making the crab sauce. This is best made, up to the egg stage, no more than 20–30 minutes before serving. Bring the soup to a rapid simmer and reduce by a quarter. This will slightly thicken and increase the seafood flavour. While hot, add the Cheddar cheese and stir in over a low heat, not allowing the soup to boil as this will begin to separate the oils from the cheese. Once melted, add the mustard, brandy, if using, lemon juice and egg yolk. Continue to cook, not even allowing a simmer, or this will scramble the egg. After a minute or two the sauce will have thickened. Remove from the stove and continue to stir. If the pan is too hot, then transfer to a cold bowl. This will prevent the egg from continuing to cook. Season with salt and pepper and keep to one side.

Lightly flour the skin of the sea bass fillets before brushing with melted butter and seasoning with salt and pepper. Heat the cooking oil in a large frying pan (two pans may be needed) and, once hot, lay the fillets in, skin-side down. Cook on a medium heat for 6–7 minutes. This will crisp the skin, creating a roasted flavour. While the sea bass is roasting, gently warm the crab meat in the remaining melted butter before adding to the mashed potatoes with the chopped chives. Turn the bass fillets and continue to fry for a further minute or two.

To finish the sauce, lightly whip the cream to soft peaks before folding it into the sauce mixture.

Now spoon the crab and chive mashed potatoes into an ovenproof dish about 5–6 cm (2–2½ in) deep, before pouring the sauce over to cover and glazing under a pre-heated grill. (Any remaining sauce can be offered separately.) Once golden brown, the potatoes are ready.

Present the sea bass on plates and serve. The fish can be finished with a drizzle of lemon sauce. A very quick version can be made by warming the lemon juice with 2 tablespoons of water before whisking in the cold chopped butter. The butter will emulsify into the liquor, creating a sauce consistency. Season with salt and pepper before spooning over. A trickle of olive oil also works very well across the fish, along with just a few drops on top of the glazed potatoes for an even shinier finish.

Notes: *The sea bass fillets can also be grilled, crisping the skin side following the same cooking time. If grilling, the fillets will not need to be turned over.*

Strain the whipped cream through a sieve before adding to the sauce to remove any grainy texture often found in tinned fish soups.

The English Spinach on page 142, or a simple green salad, will eat very well with this dish.

Roast Monkfish with Crispy Bacon or Parma Ham

Serves 6

6 × 275–350 g (10–12 oz) monkfish tails, skinned and thin grey membranes removed

flour, for dusting

knob of butter, melted

2–3 tablespoons cooking oil

12 rashers of streaky bacon or 6 slices of Parma ham

salt and pepper

For the Aïoli (6 generous portions)

1 large jacket potato, steamed or boiled in its skin

2 large garlic cloves, crushed

2–3 eggs, boiled for 7 minutes

150 ml (5 fl oz) Mayonnaise (page 207) or bought ready-made mayonnaise

pinch of saffron, warmed in 2 tablespoons warm water (optional)

100 ml (3½ fl oz) olive oil

2–3 teaspoons lemon juice

salt and cayenne pepper

For the Garnishes (optional)

10–12 tablespoons Red-wine Fish Gravy (page 204)

2–3 tablespoons Lemon Oil (page 84)

watercress

1 lime or lemon, cut into 6

Introduction Monkfish, or angler fish, has only really become familiar to us in the last 20–30 years. During the 1960s and early 1970s, monkfish was generally considered to be second-rate, and it sold very cheaply. However, it is now one of the more expensive fish, because its true merits have been recognized.

The beauty of this quite ugly fish – very rarely seen whole, its head being quite huge and certainly not carrying the looks of many others – is the texture and flavour of the tail meat. The fillets are joined by one thick central bone that does not include the many small pin bones that almost every round fish carries. Consequently, the skin and fillets are very easy to remove, recreating a very white and firm flesh, which is often associated with and compared to that of succulent lobster.

Bacon is a superb accompaniment for monkfish, but I must confess that a crisp slice of Parma ham is even better. *Aïoli* also eats very well with monkfish. This is a sauce made in a mayonnaise style, flavoured with garlic, and given texture and flavour by potatoes that have been baked, boiled or steamed in their skins. It's best to serve this sauce at room temperature, and immediately.

Method To make the aïoli, peel and break up the cooked potato and, while still warm, place in a food processor. Add the crushed garlic, cooked egg yolks (discard the cooked whites), mayonnaise and saffron (with its water, if using). Blitz briefly to mix and slowly pour in the olive oil, along with 2 teaspoons of the lemon juice. Season with salt and cayenne pepper and blitz again quickly before tasting for seasoning and for the acidity provided by the lemon juice. The aïoli is now ready and has a thick consistency, almost like a dip rather than a sauce. This is best served at room temperature.

Pre-heat the oven to 200ºC/400º/Gas 6. Season the monkfish tails with salt and pepper before dusting with flour. Brush each presentation side with butter. Heat a roasting tray or frying pan with 2 tablespoons of cooking oil and, once hot, place the tails in, buttered-side down. Fry to a rich golden brown before turning and continuing to fry for a further 2–3 minutes. Place in the pre-heated oven and roast for 8–10 minutes.

While the monkfish is roasting, the bacon can be cooked. Warm a frying pan to a medium heat and place the bacon rashers in the dry pan. These will now begin to release their own fat content. Fry for 3–4 minutes before turning the rashers over and continuing for a further few minutes; the rashers will now have released excess water and fat, resulting in a crispy finish. You might find they need longer to cook – this will be determined by the thickness of the rashers. These can now be kept warm in the oven, becoming even crispier. If serving Parma ham, cook as above but add a tablespoon of oil to the pan before frying. The Parma ham becomes totally crispy, giving it a completely new flavour.

Remove the monkfish from the oven and leave to rest for at least 2 minutes.

The garnish ingredients are all optional because we have aïoli to accompany the finished dish. However, the flavours of the gravy work well with the roasted fish, and the lemon oil lends another bite.

To present the dish, place the roasted monkfish tails on plates and trickle with the gravy, if using. This can be artistically applied using a squeezy bottle. Drizzle lemon oil around, if using, and garnish each plate with a sprig of watercress and a wedge of lime or lemon. Sit two bacon rashers or a slice of crispy Parma ham on top of the fish and serve. The aïoli can now be offered in small dishes or one large bowl.

Steamed Monkfish 'Scampi' with a Minestrone Sauce

Serves 6

1 kg (2½ lb) monkfish tail fillet, skinned, or 6 × 175 g (6 oz) portions

knob of butter

salt

For the Minestrone Sauce

2 tablespoons olive oil

knob of butter

2 carrots, cut into 5 mm (¼ in) dice

2 onions, cut into 5 mm (¼ in) dice

3 celery sticks, cut into 5 mm (¼ in) dice

1.2–1.5 litres (2–2½ pints) Red Mullet Base (page 42)

1 large courgette, cut into 5 mm (¼ in) dice

1 × 200 g (7 oz) tin of borlotti beans (an Italian bean used in many regional soups and stews)

75 g (3 oz) macaroni, cooked as per packet instructions

3 tomatoes, blanched (page 209) and cut into 5 mm (¼ in) dice

6 fresh basil leaves, torn

1–3 teaspoons grated Parmesan cheese

25 g (1 oz) of butter, for finishing

salt and pepper

olive oil, to serve

Introduction Monkfish, despite its ugliness, has a firm white flesh with a succulent finish more commonly associated with lobster. The actual taste of the fish is similar, rather like langoustines, which is obviously where the 'scampi' of the recipe title comes from. The story goes that scampi – which are Dublin Bay prawns or langoustines – were so expensive that this 'cheap' fish, monkfish or angler fish, was used in their place. Fingers were cut from the monkfish, and once breadcrumbed or battered, who'd know the difference? Whether the story is true or false, monkfish can give lobsters and langoustines a run for their money, especially in the following recipe. Biting through the meaty succulence into a rich minestrone with all its flavours is quite something. This recipe is for six main-course portions, but if you're looking to serve it as a starter or fish course, reduce the quantities by a third to half minimum.

Method Cut the monkfish into thumb-size strips. Seven or eight per portion will be plenty. These can now be placed on buttered and seasoned baking parchment ready to be steamed. If a suitable steamer is unavailable, an ovenproof dish will be needed to re-create the steaming process in an oven pre-heated to 180°C/350°F/Gas 4.

For the minestrone, heat the olive oil in a large saucepan with the butter, and, once bubbling, add the neatly diced carrots, onions and celery. Cook on a medium heat, without colouring, for 8–10 minutes until the vegetables are softening. At this point, add the red mullet base. Bring to the simmer and cook on a gentle heat for 15–20 minutes.

While the 'soup' is simmering, boil a small saucepan of salted water. Add the diced courgette, checking the tenderness of the vegetable after 45 seconds to 1 minute; they should still have a slight bite. If ready, drain and keep to one side. Rinse the borlotti beans under a cold tap and leave to drain.

Shortly before you're ready to eat, add the courgettes, beans and macaroni to the soup. Bring to the simmer and cook for a minute before adding the chopped tomatoes, basil leaves, Parmesan cheese to taste (without becoming too overpowering) and butter. Check for seasoning. The minestrone is ready to serve.

About 8–10 minutes before the soup is quite finished, the 'scampi' can be steamed. If steaming, sit over simmering water (with the paper), not boiling, as this over-tightens the fish, and cook for 5–6 minutes until firming but also succulent to the touch.

If cooking in the oven, season the fingers in the dish and barely cover the base with water. Bring to the simmer and cook in the oven for the same time as steaming. Spoon the minestrone into large bowls, placing each portion of naturally steamed monkfish on top. Trickle with olive oil, if desired, and serve.

As a main course, this is very much a complete dish. A good, and probably its best, accompaniment is crusty bread to help soak up all that rich soup.

Steamed Baby Turbot on English Spinach with a 'Moules Marinière' Sauce

Serves 4

knob of butter

2 × 675–900 g (1½–2 lb) baby (chicken) turbots, filleted, with skin and skirt left on

150 ml (5 fl oz) water

cooking oil, for frying

flour, for dusting

salt and pepper

For the Moules Marinière

1 kg (2¼ lb) mussels, washed and 'beards' removed

50 g (2 oz) butter

2 shallots, roughly chopped

200 ml (7 fl oz) white wine

300 ml (10 fl oz) Fish Stock (page 201) or water

2 baby fennel, cut into rings

2–3 shallots (preferably large or banana shallots), cut into rings

150 ml (5 fl oz) double cream

salt, pepper and a squeeze of lemon juice

2 tablespoons picked fresh flatleaf parsley

buttered English Spinach (page 142), to serve

Introduction Baby turbot are also known in England as chicken turbot, and in France as *turbotin*. Very small 450-550 g (16–18 oz) fish can be found, and eat well just grilled and served with a parsley lemon butter or hollandaise sauce.

In this recipe, the fish are to be filleted, offering two fillets per portion, so two 675–900 g (1½–2 lb) fish will be needed. If you're asking the fishmonger to fillet them, please ask for the skirt (the flesh attached to the surrounding fin) to be left attached to the skin. These we can then remove carefully from the skin and pan- or deep-fry as a tasty garnish. The skin on the fillets will be left in place, which protects the fish during the cooking, keeping the flesh moist to eat.

Moules marinière is a great French classic – mussels cooked in their shells with shallots, white wine and butter. For this sauce they are cooked in a similar fashion, but well in advance, then shelled and creamed. The quantities listed here are for four main courses. For a fish course or starter, simply halve them.

Method The mussels can be cooked in advance and re-warmed when needed. It's important to wash and scrub them, removing the 'beard' that's found along the straight edge of the shell.

Once cleaned, melt 25 g (1 oz) of the butter in a large saucepan and add the chopped shallots. Cook for a few minutes without colouring before adding the white wine and fish stock (or water). Bring to a rapid simmer before adding the mussels. Place a lid on top and cook on a medium heat, shaking the pan to help create an even cooking. After a minute or two, remove the lid and stir until all have opened and cooked. You may find a few that haven't opened: these should be discarded. Strain in a colander, saving all the juices, which will now have taken on a rich mussel flavour.

Once cooled slightly, the mussels can be picked from their shells, checking all beards have been removed. For extra security, these can be rinsed in a bowl of their own stock two or three times; this will guarantee the mussels are totally clean without losing their rich flavour. Now strain the mussel liquor through a very fine sieve or muslin cloth. Pour a third of the liquor on to the mussels to keep them moist until needed.

Pre-heat the oven to 190°C/350°F/Gas 5.

To finish the 'sauce', melt the remaining knob of butter in a saucepan and, once bubbling, add the fennel and shallot rings. Gently cook, without colouring, for 5–6 minutes until softened. Add the mussels, including the liquor they are in, and bring to a soft simmer. While the fennel rings are cooking, boil the remaining two-thirds of stock and reduce by half. Add the double cream and simmer for a few minutes before checking the seasoning with salt and pepper and finishing with a squeeze of lemon juice. Once the fish is cooked, this sauce can be blitzed with an electric hand blender for a lighter frothy finish. Add the flatleaf parsley to the mussels and they are ready to serve.

To cook the turbot, butter a suitable ovenproof dish or baking tray before seasoning with salt and pepper. Split the fillets lengthways, leaving eight individual pieces. With a sharp knife, gently cut away the skirts (fins) attached to each and remove the skin from them.

Lay the turbot fillets, flesh-side down, in the dish or tray and pour over the water. White wine can also be used but, though water will give nothing in flavour, it takes nothing away from the moist, natural flavour of the fish. Cover with foil before bringing gently to the simmer. Place in the pre-heated oven and cook for 6–8 minutes, until just firm to the touch.

While poaching/steaming the turbot, heat 2 cm (¾ in) of oil in a frying pan. Season the turbot skirts with salt and pepper before gently dusting in flour. These can now be fried for a few minutes until golden brown. Remove and drain on kitchen paper, sprinkling with a pinch of salt.

To serve the dish, divide the spinach between four plates. Remove the skin from the cooked fillets and place one large and one small fillet per portion on top of the spinach.

Divide the *moules marinière* between four small bowls (or one large) with their own liquor. Spoon the frothy cream sauce around the turbot and also on top of the mussels, creating a cappuccino-style finish.

The last component of the dish, the skirts, can now be placed on top of the turbot before serving.

Notes: *Large turbot fillets can be used: simply purchase 175–225 g (6–8 oz) portions. Any bones from the baby turbots will make superb fish stock (page 201) or can be frozen to make the stock another day.*

The 'skirts' used in this recipe are really not essential at all, but it is nice using every ingredient and wasting none.

The flatleaf parsley can be pre-blanched in boiling water to soften and tenderize it. Some parsley leaves can be quite coarse and tough.

A lot of other fish will also work in this dish, such as brill, lemon sole, sea bass and salmon.

Roast Fish on the Bone with a Chicken, Lemon and Thyme Liquor

Serve 4–6

1.3 kg (3 lb) turbot or brill, trimmed and washed

6 rashers of streaky bacon (or more, if preferred)

flour, for dusting

3 tablespoons groundnut or cooking oil

225–350 g (8–12 oz) fresh or frozen peas, cooked, to serve

large knob of butter

salt and pepper

For the Sauce

2 tablespoons very finely chopped shallots

juice of 1 lemon (more can be added for a sharper flavour)

300 ml (10 fl oz) Chicken Stock (page 201) or alternative

100 ml (3½ fl oz) crème fraîche or double cream (optional)

2 teaspoons picked and lightly chopped fresh thyme

75 g (3 oz) unsalted butter, chilled and cubed

salt and pepper

Introduction Almost any fish can be roasted or baked whole on the bone (depending on size, of course). For this recipe turbot is first choice, although a good, and cheaper, substitute would be brill. Brill doesn't carry quite the sweetness associated with turbot, but is still an extremely good fish to eat. They look quite similar, especially as brill get bigger, but to be sure of what you're buying, simply run your fingers across the dark skin of the fish: turbot will feel 'bumpy' while the brill is a lot smoother.

Bacon rashers provide the fat in which to fry the fish before roasting, the bacony flavour permeating the fillets without overpowering their very definite fresh taste. Fresh (or frozen) peas add a sweetness that always works well with a roasted flavour, whether fish or meat. And the chicken sauce? Its meaty but not too strong flavour, with the addition of lemon juice and thyme, provides a lighter way of finishing the dish. The fish will eat and look its absolute best if presented whole at table. Use a fish slice and fork to carve away the moist, rich flesh. The Mousseline Mashed Potatoes or Jersey Royals (if in season) on pages 142 and 147 would both suit this quite magnificent dish.

Roast Fish on the Bone with a Chicken, Lemon and Thyme Liquor

Method To roast the fish, pre-heat the oven to 190°C/350°F/Gas 5. The head can be left on the fish, to maintain the shape for presentation. This is not essential, so if you'd prefer to have it removed, I'm sure your fishmonger will oblige. Both skins should be left on as these will protect the actual fish, helping keep the moistness within the fillets. It's best to wash the fish well and have the fins and tail trimmed.

The rashers of bacon are best cooked in advance. Place on a lightly oiled baking tray. To maintain the flat bacon-rasher shape, place another tray on top before cooking in a pre-heated oven 200°C/400°F/Gas 6 for 10–15 minutes. Once crispy, remove the rashers and keep to one side.

To roast the fish, heat a large roasting tray or frying pan on top of the stove. Season the fish on both sides, first making sure it is dry, before dusting on both sides with flour. Add the oil to the heated tray/pan. Once hot, place the fish, white-skin-side down and pan-fry to create a golden-brown presentation side. Turn the fish over – a roasting fork will help to do this, piercing towards the head – and continue to fry on the dark-skin-side for a few minutes to seal, before adding the butter. Once melted, begin to baste before placing in the oven and roasting for 15–20 minutes until cooked through. Remove from the oven.

While the fish is roasting, the sauce can be made. Place the very finely chopped shallots and lemon juice in a small saucepan and bring to the simmer. Cook and reduce by half. Add the chicken stock and bring to the boil, also reducing by half to two-thirds. If using the cream, add it now, as this will help to emulsify the flavours and give the sauce a silkier finish; return to the simmer.

Add the chopped thyme and slowly whisk in the butter, to emulsify. Season with salt and pepper, adding an extra squeeze of lemon if needed.

To present the dish, lift the whole fish, using two large fish slices, on to a suitable large plate or dish.

The peas can simply be re-heated with a knob of butter in the microwave or returned to a pan of hot water for a minute. To create another texture, heat 2–3 tablespoons of peas in the sauce. Spoon the sauce over the fish and garnish with the crispy bacon. Any excess peas can be offered separately. The roast is ready to serve.

Notes: *Lemon and watercress can also be used to garnish this dish.*

The bacon rashers can also be pan-fried or grilled to your liking.

Tunafish Steaks on Bitter Red-wine Onions

Serves 4

675–900 g (1½–2 lb) piece of tuna

3 glasses of red wine, boiled to reduce by half (optional)

400 ml (14 fl oz) Veal/Beef Stock (page 203) or alternative (optional)

2 tablespoons groundnut or vegetable oil

4 onions, halved and sliced

1 tablespoon red-wine vinegar, preferably Cabernet Sauvignon

2 glasses of red wine

150 ml (5 fl oz) Red-wine Fish Gravy (page 204)

knob of butter

salt and pepper

Introduction A good thick tuna steak simply grilled would work with the bitter-sweet red-wine onions featured here, but as the fish holds a very firm and close texture, it will stand up to many alternative methods of cooking. For me, the ultimate is to cook and eat this particular fish the same way I do a beef fillet steak – rare–medium rare. In this recipe the fish is poached in a veal or beef stock, just as you might meat. A gentle warmth surrounds the fish, cooking it so evenly that, once cut, the usual grey outer border hardly exists. Instead its pure, soft succulence with oozing juices just demands to be eaten. However, if you prefer, the tunafish steaks can be roasted instead.

Method To prepare the tunafish steaks, it's best to buy a 675–900 g (1½–2 lb) piece of tuna, which isn't too large in diameter. Cut the fillet in half lengthways and trim each piece to give two cylindrical ones. Roll the cylinders in 2–3 layers of cling film, twisting tightly to give a round shape. Refrigerate for several hours to set. Any trimmings can be kept for a tunafish salad.

While still wrapped in the cling film, which will be kept on during the cooking process to maintain the shape, cut the tuna: you should end up with four 150–175 g (5–6 oz) steaks.

To prepare the poaching liquor, mix the reduced 3 glasses of red wine with the veal or beef stock. This is entirely optional: the tuna can just be pan-fried and roasted but this changes the texture. Bring the stock to a warm temperature, below simmering.

Meanwhile, heat a frying pan or wok with a tablespoon of the oil. Add the sliced onions and pan-fry, allowing lots of colour with tinges of burn. Once softened and coloured well, add the red-wine vinegar and reduce until almost dry. Add the 2 glasses of red wine and also reduce until almost dry. Season with salt and pepper. Loosen with 50 ml (2 fl oz) of the fish gravy, saving the remainder to drizzle around each plate. The onions can be made well in advance, simply re-heating them when the fish gravy is added.

Heat another frying pan with the other tablespoon of oil and the knob of butter. Season the tunafish top and bottom with salt and pepper. Once the butter is bubbling, place the fillets in the pan and fry on a high heat until sealed and golden brown. Turn the tunas over and repeat. The cling film will shrivel slightly when placed in the pan. Place the fillets in the poaching liquor, if using, and cook for 4–6 minutes (4 minutes will keep the steaks at a good medium-rare stage; 6 will be more of a good medium). Bring the liquor to a soft simmer, remove from the heat, add the steaks and cover with a lid. Do not return the pan to the stove: this guarantees the steaks' temperature cannot be increased. Once cooked, remove from the pan and leave to rest for 3–4 minutes. If not poaching, cook the steaks in a pre-heated oven (180ºC/350ºF/Gas 4) for the same cooking times.

Re-heat the onions and spoon between four bowls/plates, pouring a little of the red-wine gravy around each. Remove the cling film from the fish and cut each through the middle to reveal the pink medallions.

Present two pieces per portion on top of the onions, keeping the pink open side of both pieces as total presentation. The dish can be served as it is or with a béarnaise sauce *au poivre vert* (with green peppercorns).

Note: *To make the béarnaise* au poivre vert, *follow the recipe for Sauce Béarnaise (page 205), adding 1 dessertspoon of crushed tinned or bottled green peppercorns to the crushed black peppercorns. Once the sauce is made, add a further teaspoon of chopped green peppercorns along with the chopped tarragon to finish.*

Steamed and Roasted Salt Cod with Baby Fennel and Lemon-garlic Potatoes

Serves 4

675–900 g (1½–2 lb) cod fillet with skin left on (not tail end, as this becomes over-salty)

3 tablespoons coarse sea salt

6 spring onions, trimmed and split lengthways

large knob of butter, melted

8–12 baby fennel

juice of ½–1 lemon

2–3 small potatoes, peeled and cut into 2 cm (¾ in) rough chunks

flour, for dusting

1 tablespoon olive oil or cooking oil, for frying

salt and pepper

For the Sauce

1 dessertspoon olive oil

1 large shallot, roughly chopped

2 garlic cloves, sliced

2 star anise

150 ml (5 fl oz) dry white wine

200 ml (7 fl oz) Fish or Chicken Stock (page 201) or alternative

50 ml (2 fl oz) Pernod (optional)

100–150 ml (3½–5 fl oz) double cream or crème fraîche (optional)

25–50 g (1–2 oz) butter (optional)

salt and pepper

1–2 teaspoons chopped fennel herb (picked fennel tops can be used)

For the Lemon-garlic Butter (optional)

1 teaspoon lemon juice

1 small garlic clove (or half clove), finely crushed

25 g (1 oz) butter

pinch of cayenne pepper

Introduction It's not essential to salt the cod in this recipe; fresh cod fillet will work equally well. The two cooking methods – steaming and roasting – apply to two separate components of the fish: the fillet will be steamed while the skin is pan-fried to a 'roasted' and crispy stage.

The herb fennel has been revered for centuries, and was used in cooking and for medicinal purposes. It's actually known as *the* herb to accompany fish, and it works very well with salted fish such as cod.

The bulb fennel we use as a vegetable was developed in the seventeenth century in Italy. It can be eaten boiled, grilled and pan-fried, all of which help bring out its distinctive aniseed flavour. (If ever thinking of serving a raw fennel salad, always make sure it is sliced very thinly, preferably on a mandolin. Season with salt and pepper and dress with olive oil and lemon juice.) Fennel bulbs come in many sizes, from young, thin 'babies' to some as large as fists. For this particular dish, I'm using small individual heads. Cut away the core at the base of each bulb with the point of a small sharp knife, which will help an even cooking. Salt cod is more often turned into the French classic *brandade*, puréed with garlic and potatoes. With this recipe the flavour of the garlic lends itself to the sauce, and the potatoes and the fennel become part of the garnish.

Method Lay the cod fillet(s), skin-side down, on a tray and sprinkle the coarse sea salt over the flesh. Cover with cling film and refrigerate for 24 hours (48 hours for a stronger salt-cured flavour).

After salting time is complete, remove from the fridge and rinse away any excess salt grains. Now it's best to soak in cold water, refreshing the water 2–3 times, while the fish is refrigerated for 12 hours.

If baking the cod, pre-heat the oven to 180°C/350°F/Gas 4. Once soaked, remove the cod from the water and pat dry. Cut the fillet(s) into four portions, carefully cutting away the skin from each. The skin can be kept to one side, ready to be pan-fried when needed.

Blanch the spring onions in boiling water for 30 seconds before removing and allowing to cool and dry on kitchen paper. Butter and pepper four pieces of greaseproof paper. Lay three spring onions, folding each in half, on the paper. Each portion of fish can now be laid on top, brushing each with butter. These can now be refrigerated until needed.

To cook the baby fennel, trim the top and the core base of each, saving all the trimmings for the sauce. Place the bulbs in a saucepan and squeeze over the juice of half a lemon. Add a pinch of salt and enough water barely to cover. Bring to the simmer, covering the fennels with a butter paper. Poach for 8–10 minutes until the bulbs have become tender. Once tender, increase the heat, remove the paper and allow the liquor to reduce, with the bulbs still in it. This will increase in flavour and, once boiled to just 3–4 tablespoons, will have taken on a good fennel flavour. Keep warm to one side.

While the fennel is cooking, the potato chunks can be cooked, by either boiling in salted water or steaming for 5–6 minutes, until they have become tender.

Meanwhile, make the sauce. Warm the olive oil in a large saucepan. Add any fennel bulb trimmings, roughly chopped, along with the shallot, garlic and star anise. Cook, without colouring, on a medium heat for a few minutes. Once softened, add the white wine and bring to the boil before reducing by three-quarters. Add the fish or chicken stock, bring to the simmer and cook until reduced by half. The Pernod, if using can now be added. If using the cream, add 100 ml (3½ fl oz) and return to the simmer. Season with salt, pepper and a squeeze of lemon juice to enhance the sauce flavour. The remaining 50 ml (2 fl oz) of cream can be added for a richer finish. Strain through a fine sieve, squeezing all the juices from the fennel trimmings. If not using cream, the liquor can be left as it is with natural flavours and consistency, or add 25–50 g (1–2 oz) of butter, to enrich.

The lemon-garlic butter for the potatoes, if using, can be made well in advance. Mix the lemon juice with the garlic and add to the butter along with the cayenne pepper. Refrigerate until needed.

The cod can now be steamed for 8–10 minutes over simmering water, covered with a lid, or place in a baking tray with 2–3 tablespoons of water, bring to the simmer, cover and cook in the pre-heated oven also for 8–10 minutes. This cooking time for either method will work well with an average-sized cod fillet. If the fillets are thick, increase the cooking time by at least 2–3 minutes.

While cooking the fillets, roast the skin. Lightly flour the skin on the dark side only and brush with butter. Heat a tablespoon of olive or cooking oil in a frying pan and, once hot, insert the skins, buttered-side down. Pan-fry, pressing the skins with a fish slice, for 6–7 minutes. The skin will become crispy and rich in colour. Turn the skins and continue to cook until completely crispy.

To serve the dish, place the fennels and spring onions around the plates. Roll the steamed potatoes in the lemon-garlic butter, if you have made it, before also sprinkling around the plate. Place the salt cod fillets in the centre, straining any liquor left on the papers through a tea strainer into the sauce. Add the chopped fennel herb to the sauce and spoon over the fish and around the plate. The 'roasted' cod skin can now be presented on top of the fish fillet. The dish is now ready to serve.

Notes: *Although this dish contains quite a few components, it really is very easy to make. The fennel can be cooked in advance and re-warmed in its cooking liquor, or microwaved (as can the potatoes). The sauce and flavoured butter can also both be made well in advance.*

For a slightly different finish and texture, the steamed potato chunks can be pan-fried once cooked, giving them a sautéd edge and flavour, before rolling in the butter.

Once poached, the fennels can be finished on a hot grill plate to give a barbecued look and slightly bitter flavour.

In the hands of a clever cook fish can become an inexhaustible source of endless enjoyment.

Brillat-Savarin

Rich Fish Stew

Serves 4

butter, for brushing and frying

4 × 100 g (4 oz) red mullet fillets, pin-boned (page 13)

450 g (1 lb) sea bass fillet, cut into 4

350 g (12 oz) smoked haddock fillet

150 ml (5 fl oz) milk

salt and cracked white peppercorns

For the Broth

2 tablespoons olive oil

3 baby fennels, sliced into rings

2 banana shallots, sliced into rings

2 large garlic cloves

2 strips of orange zest

300 ml (10 fl oz) white wine

pinch of saffron

600 ml (1 pint) Fish Stock (page 201), or alternative

1 medium leek, sliced into rings, or 4–6 spring onions

2 tomatoes, preferably plum, blanched (page 209) and cut into 1 cm (½ in) dice

8 orange segments, halved

25 g (1 oz) butter

1 tablespoon chopped fresh flatleaf parsley

1 teaspoon chopped fresh tarragon

salt and pepper

Introduction The richness of this dish comes from both the sauce and the fish included in it. The sauce-liquor borrows its flavours from the famous classic fish soup-stew bouillabaisse, and they include saffron, garlic, tomatoes, onions and parsley. The fish featured here are red mullet and sea bass, with the unusual addition of natural smoked haddock. Mullet and sea bass are expensive (another reason for the 'rich' of the recipe title), but also hold very distinctive flavours that will cope with the highly flavoured broth. Salmon and cod fillet could both be used to replace them. As for the smoked haddock, I've found biting into the large flaky pieces with a smoky flavour really enjoyable, giving this stew a different edge. Shellfish such as scallops, crab, lobster and mussels can also be included, as they are often found in one or other of the many bouillabaisse variations. The quantities here will be enough for four main courses or at least six fish or starter portions. For a fish course or starter, halve each red-mullet fillet and cut the sea bass fillet into six (or even eight).

Method Start by making the broth. Heat the olive oil in a large saucepan. Add the fennel and shallot rings, along with the garlic and orange zest. Cook on a medium heat for 5–6 minutes, without colouring, until softening. Add the white wine, bring to the boil and reduce by three-quarters. Add the saffron and cook for a few minutes before pouring in the fish stock and returning to the boil. Reduce by a quarter before seasoning with salt and pepper. The broth can now be removed from the heat and left to infuse while the fish is cooked.

To cook the fish, place the mullet fillets on a buttered and seasoned baking tray, brushing the skins with butter and seasoning with a sprinkling of salt. Place under a pre-heated grill for 3–4 minutes, until golden brown and crispy.

While cooking the red mullet, heat a frying pan with a knob of butter. Once bubbling, place the sea bass portions in, skin-side down, and pan-fry on a medium heat for 3–4 minutes before turning and continuing to cook for a further 2–3 minutes.

While the bass are frying the smoked haddock fillet can also be cooked. Place the fillet in a dish and boil the milk, then pour it over the fillet. Cover with a lid and, after a few minutes, the fillet will be cooked. This can now be broken into portions and kept warm to one side.

To finish the fish stew, return the broth to the simmer. Remove the orange zest before adding the leek rings and cooking for a few minutes until tender. Add the tomato dice, orange segments, butter and herbs, and check the seasoning.

Place the fish in a large serving dish and spoon the broth over. The rich fish stew is now ready to present on the table.

Notes: *Cooked new potatoes can also be added to the liquor to complete the main course.*

Garlic bruschetta toasts can be offered separately to soak up the cooking liquor. To make these, follow the method for the toasts used in the recipe for Mushroom Toasts with Melting Swiss Cheese, page 196, calculating on two or three, 1–2 cm (½–¾ in) thick slices of French bread per portion.

Pan-fried Sea Bass with Blackberry Shallots and Creamy Hollandaise Sauce

Serves 4 as a fish course

30 g (1½ oz) butter

450 g (1 lb) large shallots, cut into rings

2 glasses of red wine

2 teaspoons demerara sugar

2–3 tablespoons *crème de mûre* (*crème de cassis*, the blackcurrant variety, can also be used)

4 × 100–175 g (4–6 oz) sea bass fillet portions, skin scaled and left on

flour, for dusting

1 tablespoon cooking oil

salt and pepper

For the Hollandaise Sauce (optional)

1 quantity Simple Hollandaise Sauce (page 206)

100 ml (3½ fl oz) double cream (150 ml/ 5 fl oz can be used for a creamier finish)

Introduction Sea bass is a fish of many varieties, among them the North American striped and black bass and, moving east across the Atlantic, the silvery fish native to Europe. It has the advantage of being available all year round, and an extra bonus is that it has few bones. Sea bass, over the years, has become highly prized – the 'caviar' of round fish. For this recipe I'm using fillets, which you can get the fishmonger to prepare. Before filleting, please ask for the fish to be scaled; this prevents the flesh from becoming damaged and leaves a neater finish

The blackberry flavour to the shallots – which are a perfect accompaniment to the fine flavour of sea bass – is not due to the actual fruit itself, but to the French blackberry liqueur *crème de mûre*. (Similar liqueurs can actually be home-made, and these are often called ratafias. You simply steep the fruit in up to 70 per cent proof alcohol, along with ground cloves, cinnamon and sugar, for up to a month, before straining through muslin.) The *crème de mûre* gives the red-wine-braised shallots a new finish that works well with the flavour a sea bass has to offer.

This particular fish recipe is best suited as a starter or fish course. If it were to be served as a main course, Jersey Royals (page 147) and English Spinach (page 142) would eat well as accompaniments.

Method To make the shallots, melt half the butter in a saucepan and, once bubbling, add the shallot rings. Cook for 2–3 minutes and, once beginning to soften, add the red wine and 1 teaspoon of the sugar. The heat can now be increased to create a gentle bubble. This braises the shallots. Once the wine has reduced by three-quarters, the *crème de mûre* can be added, also allowing it to reduce slightly. If the flavour is over-sharp, the remaining teaspoon of sugar can be added. The shallots are best left now to cool and marinate in the cooking syrup for a few hours. (If left overnight, the flavour becomes even more intense.)

Season the sea bass fillets with salt and pepper and lightly flour the skin side of the fish. Using the remaining half of the butter, brush each floured side.

Heat a tablespoon of cooking oil in a frying pan. Place the fillets, skin-side down, in the pan. Cook on a medium heat without shaking the pan, allowing the butter to melt and bubble along with the flour, creating a crisp finish. Cook for 4–5 minutes before turning and frying for a further 2 minutes. While pan-frying the fish, re-heat the shallots.

To serve, spoon the shallots into the centre of four plates, trickling the rich syrup around. The crisp sea bass fillets can now be placed on top.

If serving the hollandaise, lightly whip the double cream and gently fold in. The sauce is now ready to offer, providing a soft, creamy balance to the richness of the complete dish.

Warm Salmon 'Quiche Lorraine'

Serves 6

butter, for greasing and frying

1 quantity Shortcrust Pastry (page 212), or 225 g (8 oz) Puff Pastry (page 212) or bought ready-made puff pastry

flour, for rolling pastry

2 shallots or ½ onion, finely chopped

75 ml (3 fl oz) white wine

225g–275 g (8–10 oz) salmon fillet, cut into 1 cm (½ in) squares

1 medium leek, finely shredded and washed

4 spring onions, finely shredded

3 eggs

300 ml (10 fl oz) double cream

1–2 tablespoons chopped fresh chives

salt and pepper

For the Sauce

1 quantity Lemon Butter Sauce (page 87), made with 100 g (4 oz) butter and omitting the single cream

1–2 tablespoons soured cream or crème fraîche

4–5 sorrel leaves, finely shredded

salt and pepper

Introduction Fish tarts work well at so many different eating times, whether as a starter, fish course, main course, supper or lunch dish, or as part of a buffet. I'm using fresh salmon, because it's so easily obtainable and will hold its moistness while baking. I suggest you add some smoked salmon trimmings, which are often found at fishmongers and supermarket fish counters. The smoky flavour works wonders with the fresh fish.

As for the sauce, I'm suggesting the lemon butter sauce offered with the Whole Round Fish Cake with Melting Swiss Cheese (page 87), but with the addition of soured cream or crème fraîche and finely shredded sorrel. (A mayonnaise could also be flavoured in the same way: use roughly 1–2 tablespoons of either cream per 150 ml/5 fl oz of mayonnaise.)

For this recipe, a 25 cm (10 in) flan tin, 4 cm (1½ in) deep and preferably loose-bottomed, is being used. If using home-made shortcrust pastry to line the ring, the finely grated zest of a lemon can be added to sharpen its finished flavour. This recipe will give enough for at least six main-course portions, and 8–10 (perhaps even 12) starters or fish courses.

Method Butter the flan tin, then flour a work surface and roll out the pastry. Use it to line the tin or ring, leaving any excess pastry overhanging the edge; once cooked, this can be carefully cut away to give an even finish. Refrigerate for 20 minutes.

Pre-heat the oven to 200°F/400°F/Gas 6. Line the pastry with greaseproof paper and fill with baking beans or rice. Bake in the pre-heated oven for 20–25 minutes, then remove and allow to cool. Reduce the oven temperature to 180°F/350°F/Gas 4.

Remove the paper and beans/rice from the pastry case, trimming away the excess pastry to finish with a smooth edge.

Place the chopped shallots or onion in a baking tray and season with salt and pepper, adding the white wine. Place the salmon on top of the shallots, season again and cover with foil. Bake for 5–6 minutes. The fish should be starting to set, still keeping a medium-rare, pink texture. If still too soft and rare, continue to bake, checking every 1–2 minutes. Once at its medium-rare stage, remove from the oven, taking the salmon from the baking tray.

Any shallots and juices can now be transferred to a small saucepan, boiled and reduced until almost dry. Leave to cool.

Melt a knob of butter in a large saucepan and, once bubbling, add the leeks and spring onions; these, along with the chives – all members of the onion family – will lend their own individual flavours and at the same time complement one another. Cook for 2–3 minutes until beginning to soften. Season and leave to cool.

Mix together the leeks, spring onions and salmon and scatter in the cooked pastry case. Whisk the eggs into the cream, adding the chopped chives and white wine and shallot reduction. Season well with salt and pepper before pouring into the flan case. Bake in the pre-heated oven for 20–25 minutes, until just set.

Remove from the oven and leave to rest for at least 15–20 minutes. Eaten hot, the texture of quiche is never quite right, but, like roast meats, once relaxed, all the flavours become fuller.

While the quiche is resting, the lemon butter sauce can be made. Whisk in the sour cream or crème fraîche, seasoning with salt and pepper, before adding the shredded sorrel leaves.

The 'quiche' and sauce are now ready to serve. Just a good glass of white wine will make the best accompaniment for this dish.

Creamy Smoked Haddock 'Shepherd's Pie'

Serves 6

900 g (2 lb) natural smoked haddock fillet, skinned and pin-boned (page 13); (the yellow-dyed variety can also be used)

1 small onion

1 bay leaf

1 clove

450 ml (15 fl oz) milk

20 g (½ oz) butter

20 g (½ oz) flour

150 ml (5 fl oz) single cream

lemon juice or white wine

2–3 eggs, hard-boiled for 7½ minutes and refreshed in cold water

75 g (3 oz) frozen peas, defrosted

1 tablespoon fresh chopped chives

1 tablespoon fresh chopped parsley

salt and pepper

For the Topping

2 tablespoons very finely chopped shallots or onions (optional)

knob of butter, melted

900 g (2 lb) Mashed Potatoes (page 142)

50–100 g (2–4 oz) Cheddar cheese, grated

Introduction Shepherd's pie is, of course, chopped (or minced) lamb cooked with vegetables, spices and gravy before being topped with soft mashed potato and baked. It's the potato topping used here that transforms this smoked haddock dish into a 'shepherd's'. The haddock is warmed in milk, which is then used to make the sauce, spreading its slight smokiness throughout the dish. Frozen peas are also included and, although these are not essential, they add a sweetness to all the other savoury flavours involved. You'll notice the peas are not cooked: once defrosted and softened, they are tender enough, and will warm through in the pie. Dishes like this can be adapted to suit any personal taste. You can add other flavours, whatever you prefer. For instance, a small dice of quickly fried bacon and/or Italian Fontina cheese, which softens so well, can be sprinkled over the fish before topping with the potato.

Method Lay the smoked haddock fillet in a dish. Pierce the small onion with the bay leaf and clove before placing in a saucepan with the milk. Bring to the boil, then pour the milk over the fish (keeping the onion in the saucepan). Cover with a lid and leave to stand for 10 minutes. The heat of the boiled milk will have cooked the fish, while maintaining maximum moistness and translucent flakes.

Pour the milk back on top of the onion and return to the simmer. Melt the butter in a saucepan and add the flour. Cook on a medium heat for 3–4 minutes, not allowing the roux (the culinary term for this combination of fat and flour) to colour. Add a ladleful of the milk at a time, stirring into the roux. This will create a white sauce (béchamel). Once all the milk has been stirred in, add the onion to the sauce. Reduce the temperature to the gentlest of simmers and cook, stirring from time to time to prevent the sauce from sticking, for 15–20 minutes.

Add the single cream and season with salt and pepper, being careful not to over-salt as the smoky flavour of the milk will have already influenced the total flavour. Add a squeeze or two of lemon juice to liven the sauce or, if available, a few splashes of white wine.

While the sauce is cooking, the smoked haddock can be broken into generous flakes and sprinkled into a buttered ovenproof dish. Shell and roughly chop the hard-boiled eggs and sprinkle into the dish, along with the defrosted peas and the chives and parsley.

The sauce can now be strained over the fish mixture. Leave to set and allow to cool completely.

Pre-heat the oven to 200°C/400°F/Gas 6 while making the topping. Cook the shallots (or onions) in the knob of butter for a few minutes, without colouring, until tender. These can now be added to the hot mash along with 50 g (2 oz) of Cheddar cheese. Taste and, if not cheesy enough, add more, melting it into the potatoes, to suit your taste; 100 g (4 oz) will be plenty. Spoon and spread the potatoes over the haddock mix. The pie topping can be slightly 'dented' with a palette knife to create a 'fishscale' effect. Brush with butter, then bake in the pre-heated oven for 25–35 minutes, until golden brown.

Notes: *If the pie has been refrigerated, it will take 35–40 minutes to bake through.*

A teaspoon or two of English or French Dijon mustard can be added to the mashed potatoes for a warmer finish.

Two Salmons with Sorrel-flavoured Leeks and Crème Fraîche Mashed Potatoes

Serves 4

1–1½ quantity Basic Butter Sauce (page 206), replacing the star anise and cardamom pods with 4–6 leaves of sorrel

50 g (2 oz) butter

3–4 medium leeks, cut into 1 cm (½ in) thick slices, washed

450 g (1 lb) Mashed Potatoes (page 142), made without cream

50–75 g (2–3 oz) crème fraîche

4 × 75–100 g (3–4 oz) slices of smoked salmon

4 × 75–100 g (3–4 oz) slices of fresh salmon

4 leaves of sorrel, finely shredded (for leeks)

salt, pepper and a squeeze of lemon juice (optional)

Introduction The flavours in this recipe were just made for one another. The slightly soured creamy potatoes work well with the steamed smoked salmon and, on the other side, the leeks and lemony sorrel lift the pan-fried flavour from the fresh salmon, sharpening the rest of the flavours on the plate.

Sorrel's name is derived from the word 'sour' – which it is – and it has been used in cooking and medicine in England for centuries. The leaves have a smooth, spinach-like texture and shrink quite dramatically when cooked, like spinach, due to the high water content. One disadvantage is that they lose their colour, becoming almost brown with a slimy texture when cooked; as a result, sorrel is used primarily to flavour other foods, rather than as a vegetable. In this dish it works perfectly, the sorrel butter sauce eating very well with the leeks.

Method First make the butter sauce as described on page 206, but replace the star anise and cardamom pods with the sorrel leaves. Once the sauce is seasoned and sieved, a squeeze or two of lemon juice can be added to lift the sorrel flavour.

Melt 25 g (1 oz) of the butter in a large saucepan. Once bubbling, add the leeks, with 2–3 tablespoons of water. Season with salt and pepper and stir before placing a lid on top. Stir from time to time until the leeks have become tender. This generally takes 6–7 minutes. The mashed potatoes can be finished with the crème fraîche while the leeks are cooking.

Warm a frying pan with the remaining butter, along with a steamer for the smoked salmon. Place the slices of smoked salmon on buttered and seasoned rectangles of greaseproof paper and place in the steamer. Place the slices of fresh salmon, presentation-side down, in the frying pan of bubbling butter. Season the fresh salmon while frying and cook until golden and cooked halfway through. The steamed fish should also just be warmed enough to cook halfway, keeping a rich, translucent pink bite through. Both take only a few minutes.

While the salmon is cooking, add the fresh shredded sorrel to the leeks and spoon on to the right-hand side of the plate, also spooning the mashed potatoes on the left. Spoon the butter sauce over the leeks before placing the pan-fried salmon on top of the leeks and the steamed salmon on the crème fraîche potatoes. The dish is now ready to eat as a complete course.

Note: *The Mousseline Mashed Potatoes (page 142) can be made to the full quantity for real mash lovers.*

Fillets of John Dory Poached in Shiraz Wine on Creamed Celeriac and Cabbage

Serves 4

bottle of Shiraz red wine, preferably spicy flavoured

900 g–1.2 kg (2–2½ lb) John Dory, filleted, skinned and portioned as mentioned in the introduction

3 white sugar cubes (brown can also be used)

75 g (3 oz) butter, cubed

salt

For the Creamed Celeriac and Cabbage

½ savoy cabbage, finely shredded

2–3 small carrots, thinly sliced

225 g (8 oz) celeriac, peeled and cut into 5 mm (¼ in) dice

50 g (2 oz) butter

squeeze of lemon juice

100 g (4 oz) streaky bacon rashers, cut into thin strips

100–150 ml (3½–5 fl oz) double cream

salt and pepper

Introduction John Dory is known as St Pierre in France. The fish has two black spots, one on either side, and these marks are where St Peter himself was supposed to have held the fish before throwing it back into the water. Although John Dory is quite thin-looking, its fillets are usually thick, with a slightly meaty but tender finish.

Shiraz is the Australian name for the Syrah, a grape used to make the classic wines of the Rhône. The flavour of an Australian Shiraz can vary from a rich, full ripeness to a spicy, peppery finish. In this dish, the fish is actually going to be poached in the wine itself. I prefer to use a spicy variety, which lifts and does not mask the richness of the fish. The quantity of fish suggested will give you approximately 175 g (6 oz) portions for main courses, and at least six healthy cuts for a fish course or starter. Two fillets will be taken from the fish, which can each be divided into three fingers; the two largest can then be cut in half diagonally, providing in total eight fingers of fish, two per portion.

Method The vegetables can all be cooked individually and mixed together just before serving. If so, blanch the cabbage in boiling, salted water for 1–2 minutes until tender, before draining in a colander and leaving to cool naturally (this will release excess water, rather than soaking up water as happens when cooled in iced water). The carrots and celeriac can both be cooked in a similar fashion. Melt a knob of the butter in two separate pans. Squeeze lemon on to the celeriac dice to protect their colour before adding to the butter. Cook the carrots gently in the other pan. A tablespoon or two of water can be added to each to create steam; this will cook the vegetables a lot more quickly. Once tender, remove and allow to cool.

Fry the bacon in a hot, dry pan until crispy. When needed, melt the remaining butter and re-fry the bacon, adding the carrots and celeriac. As soon as they are warmed, add the cabbage, seasoning everything with salt and pepper. Add 100 ml (3½ fl oz) of the cream and bring to the simmer. Enough cream must be added to coat and moisten the vegetables, bringing them all together. If needed, add the remaining cream.

Alternatively, cook everything in the same pan, frying the bacon before adding the carrots and celeriac. Cook reasonably gently before adding the cabbage. After 2–3 minutes the vegetables will be ready for the cream and seasoning with salt and pepper.

To cook the fish, warm the Shiraz in a roasting pan/poaching dish, bringing to the boil, and then reduce the heat to a gentle simmer. Salt the fish before poaching directly in the wine for 4–5 minutes. The fillets should now be tender. Remove from the wine; the fillets will now have a very distinctive burgundy colour and full Shiraz flavour. Keep warm, preferably cling-filmed. Meanwhile reduce the red wine/liquor by three-quarters before adding the sugar cubes and whisking in the butter. (All the spices from the sea-trout version of red-wine sauce (page 86) can be added to give another edge to the finished sauce, but are not essential with this particular wine.)

To present the dish, divide the creamed cabbage and celeriac mix between four plates, sitting them in a circular fashion in the centre. Place the John Dory fillets, two per portion, on top before drizzling with the rich Shiraz red-wine sauce.

Fresh Salmon on Slowly Caramelized Lemon Chicory

Serves 6

knob of butter

6 × 175–225 g (6–8 oz) salmon fillet portions, skinned and pin-boned (page 13)

12 pieces (2 halves per portion) Slowly Caramelized Lemon Chicory (page 152)

salt and pepper

For the Herb Butter Sauce

175 g (6 oz) unsalted butter, diced and chilled

2 shallots or ½ onion finely chopped

1 bay leaf

fresh parsley stalks

generous fresh tarragon sprig

generous fresh marjoram sprig

generous fresh chervil sprig

2–3 fresh mint leaves

2 tablespoons white-wine vinegar or sherry vinegar

4 tablespoons white wine

100 ml (3½ fl oz) water or Fish, Vegetable or Chicken Stock (pages 201, 204 or 201) or alternative

3 tablespoons single cream or crème fraîche

salt and pepper

For the Sauce Garnish

1 teaspoon torn or chopped fresh tarragon

1 teaspoon torn or chopped fresh marjoram

1 teaspoon torn or chopped fresh flatleaf parsley

1 teaspoon torn or chopped fresh chervil

Introduction Chicory does not excite everyone's palate as it can sometimes be bitter. However, here the slow caramelizing counters that bitterness, and the reduced sweetness of the juices impregnates the cooked vegetable. To complement and balance this flavour, the fresh salmon is best steamed rather than pan-fried or grilled. The butter sauce to go with the dish is flavoured with lots of fresh herbs, and can also be sharpened with the addition of a sherry-vinegar reduction to complement the chicory.

If you want to serve this recipe as a starter or fish course, serve half a chicory head with a 100 g (4 oz) salmon portion.

Method First, make the sauce. Melt a small knob of the butter in a saucepan and, once bubbling, add the chopped shallot or onion, bay leaf, parsley stalks and other herbs. Cook for 5–6 minutes without allowing the shallots to colour. Add the vinegar and reduce by three-quarters. Add the white wine and also reduce by three-quarters. Pour in the water or stock of your choice, reducing this time by half. Add the single cream (or crème fraîche). Bring to the simmer and whisk in the remaining diced butter. Season with salt and pepper before straining through a sieve. If the sauce is too thick, loosen with water or lemon juice. The butter sauce is ready and, for a smoother and lighter finish, blitz with an electric hand blender. Just before serving, the fresh herb garnishes can be added.

To cook the salmon, butter greaseproof paper squares and season with salt and pepper. Brush the salmon with butter and place, skinned-side up, on the papers.

These can now be steamed over simmering water – not boiling too rapidly, as this over-tightens the fish – covered with a lid, for 7–8 minutes. Thickly sliced salmon may well take up to 10 minutes. Check by pressing the fillets; texturally, they should be firm but just giving. This will tell you they are medium-rare to medium, with a rich pink centre.

Place two pieces of chicory (1 whole chicory) on each plate. Spoon the finished herb butter sauce over and around before sitting the salmon on top. Any juices left in the paper should be poured over each fish before serving.

Notes: *The herb sauce can also be spooned over the fish.*

For an extra flavour, make a quick lemon oil: mix 2–3 tablespoons of olive oil with 1 tablespoon of lemon juice, seasoned with salt and pepper, and drizzle around the dish.

The salmon skins can be kept and pan-fried as for the cod skin on page 73, sitting it on top of the steamed fillets before serving.

Seared Red Mullet with Leeks, Butter Fondant Potatoes and Red-wine Sauce

Serves 4

2 × 500–675 g (1¼–1½ lb) red mullets, scaled, filleted and pin-boned (page 13)

flour, for dusting

25 g (1 oz) unsalted butter

2 tablespoons olive oil

4 medium leeks, washed and cut into 1 cm (½ in) thick rounds

salt and freshly ground white pepper

Butter Fondant Potatoes (page 151)

For the Red-wine Sauce

300 ml (10 fl oz) red wine

150 ml (5 fl oz) Veal or Beef Stock/*Jus* (page 203) or alternative

Optional Extra Sauce Flavourings

1 large shallot, chopped

1 garlic clove, split

fresh thyme sprig

1 bay leaf

150 ml (5 fl oz) Fish Stock, (page 201)

Introduction Red mullet is one of the most prized of fish, with its own very individual colour, texture and flavour. This dish will work very well as a fish or main course; the ingredients here are enough for four main-course portions. Butter fondant potatoes feature on restaurant menus on a fairly regular basis; they are a 'naughty' accompaniment, the potatoes cooking in and absorbing lots of butter. My excuse for this is that the leeks are almost steamed, so they keep a very natural flavour, balancing the potatoes. Three or four new potatoes will probably be enough per person, but it's always a good idea to cook five portions, offering the 'extras' separately.

Method Pre-heat the oven to 180°C/350°F/Gas 4.

First, make the sauce. The red wine and veal or beef stock/*jus* are the basic ingredients for a quick red-wine sauce. Simply reduce the wine by three-quarters before adding the stock/*jus* and cooking for 10–15 minutes to a coating consistency. There are a few more flavours that can be added to increase its flavour. If doing this, add the shallot, garlic, thyme and bay leaf to the red wine. Reduce as for the quick version before adding the fish stock, returning to the boil and reducing again by three-quarters. The stock/*jus* can now be added, simmering to a sauce consistency. Strain through a sieve and the sauce is ready.

To make the potatoes, follow the recipe on page 151. These can be cooked several hours in advance. To re-heat, warm through in a pre-heated oven for 15–20 minutes.

Now season the flesh side of the fish with salt and pepper. The red skin should just be sprinkled with salt before dusting lightly with the flour. Brush the fillets with two-thirds of the butter. Heat a frying pan and a saucepan. Heat the olive oil in the frying pan and the remaining knob of butter in the saucepan. Once the butter is bubbling, add the leeks. These will be moist from washing; this will help create steam. Cook on a medium heat, stirring from time to time, and covering with a lid to help form the steam. The leeks will take 6–7 minutes to cook until tender. Once at this stage, season with salt and pepper.

When the frying pan is hot, place the fillets in, buttered skin-side down. Cook on a medium-high heat for 3–4 minutes. During this time, the skin will begin to crisp, giving the fish a better eating texture. Turn the fillets over and continue to cook for a further 2–3 minutes.

Divide the leeks between four plates, placing them on the right-hand side. If there is too much to place on the plates, offer any excess separately in a bowl.

Drizzle the warmed red-wine sauce on the left-hand side, sitting three or four buttered fondant potatoes on top. Finish the dish by presenting the red mullet on top of the leeks.

Note: *Excess butter may be left over once the potatoes are cooked. This can be used for finishing other vegetable dishes or basting roast meats.*

Seared Sea Trout with Fennel-flavoured Tender Sauerkraut and a Red-wine Sauce

Serves 4

4 × 175 g (6 oz) sea trout fillet portions, skinned and pin-boned (page 13)

flour for dusting

knob of butter

salt and pepper

2 tablespoons olive oil

For the Sauerkraut

½ small white cabbage, quartered and cored

100 ml (3½ fl oz) white wine

75 ml (3 fl oz) white-wine vinegar

bouquet garni of 1 teaspoon pickling spice, 3 lightly crushed juniper berries and 1 fresh thyme sprig, tied in a muslin cloth

50 g (2 oz) butter

2 medium onions, sliced

2 small fennel, finely sliced, saving any feathery tops

1 heaped teaspoon dill (optional)

squeeze of lemon juice

salt and pepper

For the Red-wine Sauce

2 cloves

3 juniper berries

2–3 strips of orange peel

4 black peppercorns, crushed

¼ cinnamon stick

bottle of red wine, preferably claret

3 white sugar cubes (brown can also be used)

75 g (3 oz) butter, cubed

salt and pepper

Introduction The sea trout, also known as the salmon trout, is caught mostly in rivers although, like salmon, it is a migrating fish and lives most of its life at sea. The flesh is also similar to that of salmon, if not quite the same rich and deep pink (which is determined by the proportion of crustaceans in its diet).

Sauerkraut has been eaten for over 2,000 years, and the basic pickling method has changed many times. At its simplest, shredded white cabbage is layered with salt before pressing and maturing over a two- to three-month period, which creates a most natural 'pickled' flavour. Instead of salting, I prefer to marinate shredded white cabbage, and do so for 24–48 hours with one or two spices, white wine and vinegar, along with some fennel to lend a mild aniseed flavour.

Method Make the sauerkraut first. As mentioned in the introduction, the cabbage is best marinated with the other ingredients (bar the fennel and onions) for 24–48 hours. This will guarantee the pickled flavour working into the cabbage. To do so, shred the cabbage very finely and place in a bowl with the white wine, white-wine vinegar, muslin bag of spices and a pinch of salt. Turn the cabbage to mix all of the flavours, cover with cling film and refrigerate, stirring every few hours. Once the marinating period is complete, drain in a sieve, collecting all the juice.

Melt a third of the butter in a large saucepan and, once bubbling, add the sliced onions. Allow to cook on a moderate heat, without colouring, until softened. Add the white cabbage, muslin bag of spices and a few tablespoons of the drained juices. Once simmering, cover with a lid and cook, stirring from time to time, to ensure an even cooking. The juices will quickly evaporate, so add a little more water to maintain the moist steaming. Continue cooking for 20–25 minutes until the cabbage has become tender with just the slightest of bite. Season with salt and pepper.

While the cabbage is cooking, melt a third of the butter in a separate saucepan and, once bubbling, add the sliced fennel. Cook, without colouring, until softened, and take care to maintain the slightest of bite. Season with salt and pepper and set the fennel aside.

Now make the sauce. Tie the cloves, juniper berries, orange peel, peppercorns and cinnamon stick in a piece of muslin. Place in a saucepan and pour over the red wine. Boil and reduce to 100 ml (3½ fl oz). Remove the muslin, squeezing any juices into the reduction, and discard.

Add the sugar cubes to the reduction and warm through. The sugar will dissolve, sweetening the sharp-flavoured wine sauce. To finish the sauce (best done just before serving), whisk in the cubes of cold butter, a few at a time. This will thicken the sauce and balance the wine and the sugar's sweet taste.

If it begins to split (curdle) when adding, an electric hand blender will help re-emulsify to a finished consistency. Season with salt and pepper; if still too sweet, add more butter until the correct flavour is achieved.

To cook the sea trout, season with salt and pepper and dust with flour on the skinned side. Brush this side with butter before placing in a frying pan heated with the olive oil. It's always important to start cooking the fish presentation-side down first. Cook on a medium heat for 6–7 minutes until golden brown before turning over and continuing to fry for a further 2 minutes. The fish will now still be pink in the centre.

Whole Round Fish Cake with Melting Swiss Cheese

While pan-frying the sea trout, add the fennel to the sauerkraut along with the remaining third of the butter. Heat and re-check for seasoning.

Any fennel tops can now be picked and lightly chopped (approximately 1 heaped teaspoon of dill can also be used) before adding to the sauerkraut with a squeeze of lemon juice.

Spoon the sauerkraut on to four plates, placing the trout fillets on top. Drizzle around the plate with the sweet, spicy red-wine butter sauce just before serving.

Notes: *The quantity of sauerkraut produced may be too much for one meal. This can be kept and served cold with salads or re-heated for another fish dish.*

All the spices and orange can be omitted from the red-wine sauce, simply using the wine itself, sugar and butter.

Buttered Jersey Royals or the Mousseline Mashed Potatoes (pages 147 and 142) eat very well with the sea trout.

Serves 4–6

50 g (2 oz) butter

2 shallots, finely chopped

350 g (12 oz) salmon fillet, skinned and pin-boned (page 13)

350 g (12 oz) cod or haddock fillet, skinned and pin-boned (page 13)

300 ml (10 fl oz) white wine

bunch of spring onions, finely shredded

675 g (1½ lb) Mashed Potatoes (page 142)

1 tablespoon chopped fresh parsley (optional)

1 tablespoon chopped fresh tarragon (optional)

1 tablespoon olive oil

50–100 g (2–4 oz) Gruyère or Cheddar cheese, grated

salt and pepper

Lemon Oil (page 84) to serve (optional)

For the Lemon Butter Sauce (optional)

100–175 g (4–6 oz) cold unsalted butter, cubed

juice of 1 small lemon

50 ml (2 fl oz) Chicken or Vegetable Stock (pages 201 or 204) or alternative, or water

50 ml (2 fl oz) single cream (optional)

salt and pepper

Introduction My salmon fish cake recipe has proved very popular over the years, and this is a new variant. Fish cakes are normally rolled in egg and breadcrumbs before deep-frying, to create a crispy outside encasing tender poached fish (salmon, cod, haddock and so on) bound with soft mashed potatoes. In this recipe, the breadcrumbs are omitted and the fish-potato mixture is pan-fried until golden brown before being topped with grated Swiss cheese and grilled. This makes the dish a lot easier to finish, and it becomes quite a feature when presented whole at the family dinner table, like a fresh gâteau, still sitting in the pan in which it has been baked. A lemon butter sauce (see overleaf) or lemon-flavoured mayonnaise make lovely accompaniments, along with a simple green salad.

Method Pre-heat the oven to 200°C/400°F/Gas 6.

Lightly butter an ovenproof dish in which to poach the fish. Once buttered, season with salt and pepper, sprinkling over the chopped shallots.

Place the salmon and cod in the dish and season with salt before pouring in the white wine. Cover with foil before placing in the pre-heated oven and baking for 8–10 minutes. The fish should be only just cooked, with the flesh taking on a firm touch and retaining most of its juices. Turn down the oven to 180°C/350°F/Gas 4. Remove the fish from the dish before pouring the wine, shallots and fish residue into a small saucepan and reducing by half to three-quarters, to an almost syrupy consistency.

Melt a knob of the butter in a large saucepan and, once bubbling, add the shredded spring onions. Cook for a few minutes, until softened. Remove and leave to cool.

Whole Round
Fish Cake with
Melting Swiss Cheese

The salmon and cod can now be gently broken down into chunks, saving half to sprinkle on top of the cake. Mix the remaining half with the potato. Add the spring onions, reduced cooking liquor and chopped herbs, if using, before seasoning with salt and pepper.

Melt the remaining butter with a tablespoon of olive oil in a non-stick ovenproof frying pan, until bubbling. Remove from the stove, spooning in the fish-cake mix. Spread to cover the pan but leave it fairly rustic, for a good home-made look. Return to a medium heat and pan-fry for 8–10 minutes, until the base is becoming golden brown. Cover with buttered foil before placing in the oven and cooking for 15 minutes, until warmed through.

Remove from the oven and take off the foil. Cover with the remaining chunks of cod and salmon. Sprinkle liberally with the grated cheese before melting under a pre-heated grill.

The family fish cake is now ready to serve. A little lemon oil (olive oil flavoured with lemon juice, to taste) can be trickled across the top to finish.

To make the sauce, place the chopped butter in a saucepan with the lemon juice, stock and cream, if using. Bring to the simmer, continuously whisking to emulsify the flavours. Do not allow the sauce to boil as this tends to separate the butter. If the sauce is too thick, a drop of water can be added, or more lemon juice to sharpen the taste. A very creamy consistency can be achieved by blitzing the sauce with an electric hand blender. Season with salt and pepper. The sauce is now ready to serve.

Notes: *Many other flavours can be added to the fish-cake mix; spinach works perfectly well, but here are a few others to think about: cooked, sliced button mushrooms; cooked, diced fennel; cooked, sliced leeks; cooked prawns or mussels, or lobster/ crab meat.*

Should the cod or salmon be larger than the other, I suggest cooking each in a separate dish. This will guarantee even cooking.

Blackened Cod Casserole

Serves 4

4 × 175–225 g (6–8 oz) cod fillet portions, pin-boned (page 13)

flour, for dusting

2–3 tablespoons cooking oil

knob of butter

salt and pepper

For the Vegetable Casserole

olive oil, for frying

1 large shallot, roughly chopped

juice from 1 large orange, plus 2 strips of peel

3–4 black peppercorns, lightly crushed

1 bay leaf

fresh lemon thyme sprig, plus ½ teaspoon picked lemon thyme leaves

bottle of red wine

150 ml (5 fl oz) Fish Stock (page 201) or alternative, or water

175 g (6 oz) baby onions, peeled

100–175 g (4–6 oz) small button mushrooms

2 carrots, peeled and cut into 1 cm (½ in) thick slices

2–3 celery sticks cut into 1 cm (½ in) thick slices

8–12 small new potatoes, cooked

knob of butter

1 leek, cut into 1 cm (½ in) thick slices

salt and pepper

To Finish the Sauce (optional)

2 tablespoons whipping cream

50 g (2 oz) cold butter, cubed

salt and pepper

Introduction Casserole cookery can be very convenient, with everything cooked in and served from the one pot. This dish is not quite a complete casserole, however; the vegetables are cooked and finished in the dish, but the fish is fried separately. It gives a very 'casseroley' impression, though, holding many different textures and flavours. The 'blackened' of the recipe title is created by over-cooking and almost burning the skin of the fish. It's not essential to do this, but it does provide a crisp bitterness, working beautifully with the moist texture of the flesh.

The vegetables included here are quite basic – carrots, celery, onions, and so on – but many others could be added, with asparagus, mangetout or snow peas all working very well. These vegetables are casseroled in a red-wine liquor. The red wine, helped by lemon thyme, gives the dish a very meaty edge, which is slightly sweetened by the flavour of fresh orange.

Method To prepare the vegetable casserole, warm a tablespoon of olive oil in a saucepan. Add the chopped shallot, orange peel, black peppercorns, bay leaf and sprig of lemon thyme. Cook on a medium heat for 4–5 minutes until the shallots are softening without colour. Add the red wine and bring to a rapid simmer. Continue to cook until reduced by two-thirds. The fish stock or water can now be added, returning to the simmer and cooking for 10 minutes. While the red-wine liquor is cooking, boil and reduce the orange juice to a syrupy consistency. This can now be added to the red wine before straining the liquor through a fine sieve. Season with a pinch of salt.

Place the baby onions in a saucepan and cover with cold water. Bring to the boil and, once boiling, strain and allow them to cool naturally. Heat a little cooking oil in a frying pan, adding the onions. Pan-fry on a medium heat until well coloured and beginning to soften. This process will take 7–10 minutes, depending on the size of the onions. The button mushrooms can now also be quickly pan-fried in an almost dry pan (adding just a drop of oil), allowing them to colour as they soften through.

Add the carrots and celery to the red-wine liquor and bring to the simmer. Cook for at least 10–15 minutes, until both vegetables have softened. For extra sauce (optional) pour off 150 ml (5 fl oz) of the liquor into a separate small saucepan. This can be finished by adding the whipping cream and returning to the simmer before whisking in the 50 g (2 oz) of butter. Season with salt and pepper. This extra sauce is best blitzed with an electric hand blender just before serving, to create a frothy, almost milkshake consistency.

Add the button onions and mushrooms to the carrots and celery in the remaining liquor. The potatoes are best served warm and added to the dish when presented, in case they discolour in the liquor.

To prepare and cook the fish, score the cod skin with several lines. Lightly flour and season with salt and pepper.

Heat a frying pan with the cooking oil and, once hot, place the fish in, skin-side down. Cook on a medium-high heat for 8–10 minutes, until the skin has become crispy and quite dark in colour. The heat can be increased during the last 2 minutes to guarantee the deep colouring. Add a knob of butter to the pan before turning the fish over and finishing the cooking for 2–3 minutes. While the cod is cooking, melt a small knob of butter in a saucepan and add 2–3 tablespoons of water. Once bubbling, add the leeks. Cook on a fast heat for a few minutes, until softened.

During these last few minutes of cooking, add a knob of butter to the

Roast Cod with Garlic Baked Beans and Chestnut Mushrooms

Blackened Cod Casserole

vegetables in the liquor, along with the lemon thyme leaves, and season with salt and pepper. The new potatoes and leeks can now be quickly added before dividing between serving plates or bowls. Place the cod fillets skin-side up in the centre and spoon, if using, the creamy, frothy red-wine sauce on top of the vegetables.

The blackened cod casserole is now ready to serve.

Note: *The carrots and celery, once cooked in the red-wine liquor, can be spooned into a separate pan with 2–3 tablespoons of the juices. Add a teaspoon of caster sugar and bring to the boil. As the liquor reduces, the sugar will slightly caramelize and become syrupy, sweetening the two vegetables. These can be spooned around the plates when serving.*

Serves 4

4 × 175–225 g (6–8 oz) cod fillet portions, skin left on, pin-boned (page 13)

flour

melted butter, for brushing

2–3 tablespoons olive oil or cooking oil

salt and pepper

For the Beans

knob of butter

1 shallot, finely chopped

1 carrot, peeled and halved

6 garlic cloves, halved

100 g (4 oz) dried white haricot beans

2–3 pieces of lemon peel

fresh tarragon sprig

For the Garnishes

25–50 g (1–2 oz) butter, chilled and cubed

2 large shallots, preferably banana shallots, cut into rings

2 teaspoons tarragon vinegar or sherry vinegar

225 g (8 oz) chestnut, cup or button mushrooms (an extra 25 g (1 oz) per portion can be added for mushroom lovers), sliced or quartered

2–3 tablespoons olive oil

12 picked fresh tarragon leaves, torn into small pieces

Introduction The beans used in this recipe are dried white haricot beans, which are smooth and oval rather than the more familiar kidney shape. It's best to rinse them before cooking.

Baked beans, bound in their tomato sauce, are a favourite in every British home (see Home-made Baked Beans on Toast, page 185), but I'm afraid that here there isn't a tomato in sight. The beans are baked with garlic and their cooking liquor forms the basis of an accompanying sauce. If you're not a tarragon fan, omit the herb and the tarragon vinegar from the recipe, using sherry vinegar instead.

Method Pre-heat the oven to 180°C/350°F/ Gas 4. For the beans, melt the knob of butter in a braising dish and, once bubbling, add the chopped shallot and the carrot (the carrot adds a sweet flavour), cooking for a few minutes without colouring. While the shallots are simmering, place the garlic cloves in a small saucepan and cover with cold water. Bring to the simmer, remove from the heat and rinse until cold. Repeat this process at least twice. This calms the flavour of the garlic, reducing its usually intense finish.

Once the shallots have softened, add the haricot beans along with the garlic pieces. Stir and cover with 600 ml (1 pint) of water. Bring to the simmer, covering with greaseproof paper before baking in the pre-heated oven for 1½–2 hours until tender. After the first 1½ hours, check the beans: if not quite tender, continue to bake, adding up to 300 ml/10 fl oz of water if necessary to loosen.

Once completely cooked, remove from the oven, adding the lemon peel and sprig of tarragon. Leave to stand for 30 minutes. The flavours will now have had time to infuse, increasing the bean liquor flavour.

Remove the carrot, lemon peel and tarragon before draining off the liquor. Cover and keep the beans and garlic pieces warm. Boil and reduce the liquor to increase its flavour, to 150–200 ml (5–7 fl oz). This will now become the sauce for the finished dish.

For the garnishes, melt a small knob of the butter in a saucepan and, once bubbling, add the shallot rings. Cook without colouring for a minute or two, until beginning to soften. Add the tarragon vinegar and cook on a medium heat until completely reduced and almost dry.

The chestnut mushrooms can now be either pan-fried in butter until slightly golden and just tender (2–3 minutes) or poached in a few tablespoons of the cooking liquor.

To create the bean sauce, whisk the butter into the stock to emulsify it. Add 2–3 tablespoons of olive oil to taste. The beans, mushrooms and shallot rings can now be either scattered around the plate or added to the sauce. Finish the sauce with the picked tarragon leaves before spooning around the cod.

The cod can be roasted while the sauce is being made and the garnishes are cooked. Season the fish with salt and pepper. Score the skin side with a sharp knife, creating 3–4 lines. Dust each skin with flour before brushing with melted butter.

Heat a frying pan (preferably ovenproof) with the olive oil or cooking oil. Once hot, place the fish in, skin-side down. Cook on a medium heat for 7–8 minutes until the skin has crisped, then turn over and bake in the pre-heated oven for a further 4–5 minutes.

The roasted cod will now be ready to serve. To create a shiny finish, brush the skins with olive oil before serving on the plates, surrounded by the baked beans.

Notes: *The juice of an orange can be boiled and reduced by two-thirds before adding it to the finished sauce. The sweet and sharp flavour of oranges works wonderfully with tarragon and garlic.*

A teaspoon or two of soured cream or crème fraîche can also be added for a creamy and piquant finish to the dish.

The beans need not be baked. They can simply be boiled and the recipe finished as in the method. It's important, however, when dried beans are being cooked, not to add salt or any acidic flavour as this will toughen rather than soften them. The cooking times for the beans are guidelines to their tenderness. Braising or boiling times depend on the quality and age of the beans; some will need up to 3 hours, in which case extra water should be added during this time.

Shellfish Pie Vol-au-vent

Serves 4

450 g (1 lb) Puff Pastry (page 212) or bought ready-made puff pastry

flour, for rolling pastry

butter, for greasing

1 egg, beaten

For the Filling

24–32 live mussels, depending on size, scrubbed and 'beards' removed

300 ml (10 fl oz) cider

1 shallot, roughly chopped

fresh parsley stalks

24 clams, well washed (cockles can also be used)

24 Atlantic prawns or 16 tiger prawns, shelled (keeping shells to flavour the sauce)

butter, for frying

175 g (6 oz) quartered chestnut, button or washed wild mushrooms (preferably girolles), sliced or quartered

1 tablespoon olive oil

8 large or 12 small/medium scallops, removed from shell and separated from roe

1 medium leek, outside 'skin' removed, cut into 1 cm (½ in) thick rings and washed, or 6–8 spring onions

150–300 ml (5–10 fl oz) whipping cream

1 tablespoon chopped fresh parsley

1 tablespoon chopped fresh chervil

salt, pepper and a squeeze of lemon juice, if necessary

Introduction The beauty of cooking fish with seafood shells is that a good stock is produced from their natural juices, so no extra fish stock is needed. The shellfish will all need to be cooked separately (the prawns, of course, are usually bought pre-cooked), but each will take only a few minutes to do so. Cider is included because it works particularly well with clams and mussels.

The mushrooms I'm using are chestnuts, but buttons are also possible. For a little extravagance, I suggest wild girolle mushrooms. These are often available in season (as are other wild fungi, such as pleurottes, oysters, shiitakes and morels), and they are not too expensive to buy.

The vol-au-vents are made from puff pastry, which you can buy ready-made if you like. This recipe will make four main-course vol-au-vents, or six smaller fish-course or starter portions.

Method Pre-heat the oven to 200°C/400°F/Gas 6. Roll out the puff pastry big enough to provide four 10 cm (4 in) discs. This will usually give you a 1 cm (½ in) thick pastry. Cut four discs and place on a baking tray, covered with a lightly buttered sheet of greaseproof paper. Refrigerate to set. Once cold, an 8.5 cm (3½ in) round cutter will be needed to mark an impression centrally on each pastry base. This, once baked, provides the lid when cut free. Carefully brush each pastry circle with the beaten egg, not allowing it to run down the edges, as this seals the pastry and prevents it from rising.

Bake in the pre-heated oven for 30–35 minutes. Check after 20 minutes. If already a rich, deep colour, gently cover with foil and reduce the oven temperature to 180°C/350°F/Gas 4. It's important to cook the cases through: undercooked puff pastry is very chewy.

Once baked, remove from the oven and leave to cool. Carefully cut out and save the lid, then remove all the central layers of pastry to leave a crisp case. These vol-au-vent cases can be baked well in advance and re-heated in the oven when needed.

To make the filling, heat a large saucepan and, once hot, put in the cleaned mussels. Add the cider, chopped shallot and parsley stalks. This will instantly create steam. Place a lid on top and cook on a high heat, shaking the pan from time to time, for 3–4 minutes, until the shells have opened (discard any that do not open). The mussels may take a couple of minutes longer if the pan was not hot enough. Strain through a sieve, returning the pan to the stove. Pour the stock (cider-mussel liquor) into the pan and, once bubbling, add the clams, repeating the same cooking process as for the mussels. Also strain, keeping the stock to one side.

Any prawn shells can now be added to the cooking liquor and brought to a gentle simmer. Cook for 15 minutes before straining through a fine sieve or muslin cloth. While the liquor is cooking, the mussels and clams can be removed from their shells, checking each for any grit, and also removing any remaining 'beards' from the mussels. Save all the juices and add to the liquor, before boiling and reducing by half. These molluscs can be cooked in advance and re-warmed in the sauce, but, for absolute perfection and to enjoy their maximum flavours, it's best to cook and eat them as soon as possible.

Heat a frying pan with a knob of butter. Once bubbling, add the mushrooms and pan-fry for a few minutes until tender; remove and set aside. Re-heat the frying pan and, once hot, add a tablespoon of olive oil. Once almost smoking, place the scallops in the pan. Cook for 2–3 minutes, creating a singed edge and golden colour before turning them over. Continue cooking

for a further 2 minutes. Remove from the pan and cut each one into a half-moon shape. The prawns can be gently warmed in 1–2 tablespoons of the liquor.

While cooking the scallops, warm a separate saucepan with a knob of butter. Once bubbling, add the leek, cooking and stirring for a few minutes before adding 2 tablespoons of water. The steam created will speed the cooking process: 2–3 minutes later the leek will be tender. Season with salt and pepper, straining off any excess water into the liquor. Mix together the mushrooms, mussels, clams, scallops and prawns.

The liquor simply needs to be re-heated and 150 ml (5 fl oz) of whipping cream added. Simmer for a minute or two, adding a squeeze of lemon juice (or white wine) and seasoning with salt and pepper to enhance its flavours. If it is too strong, or more sauce is preferred, add some or all of the remaining cream. Add the chopped herbs along with the shellfish filling. Place the warmed pastry cases on plates or in bowls before spooning the mix into and around each along with any sauce left in the pan. Top the 'pies' with the pastry lids before serving.

Notes: *The mushrooms and leeks can be cooked well before the shellfish. These will re-heat very quickly in a saucepan with a knob of butter. This will then prevent the use of too many pans on the stove at once.*

A pinch of saffron can be added to the juices before creaming to provide another flavour and colour to the dish.

One or two of the mussel and clam shells can be used to garnish the finished dish.

mains

Braised Creamy Rice and Poached Egg 'Pie'

Serves 4

2 tablespoons olive oil

1 onion, finely chopped

200 g (7 oz) arborio risotto rice

1 litre (1¾ pints) Vegetable Stock (page 204) or alternative

50 g (2 oz) butter

bunch of spring onions, thinly sliced

2 tablespoons grated Parmesan cheese

1 heaped tablespoon of mixed snipped fresh herbs e.g. parsley, chives, chervil and/or marjoram (optional)

salt and pepper

To Finish

4 Poached Eggs (page 209)

Parmesan shavings or 4 slices of Gruyère cheese soaked in milk for 1–2 hours, to soften

salt and pepper

Introduction Whenever the word 'pie' is used in a recipe title, one immediately expects pastry to be found in the ingredients list, whether to be used as a complete casing or simply as a lid. This recipe requires neither. The 'pie' – a creamy rice with a poached egg in the middle – is cooked in individual dishes, and topped with melting Swiss cheese: once the cheese is cut through, the 'pie' filling is found. In this vegetarian dish, the rice will be braised in the oven. Patna and basmati long-grain rices are normally used for braising, and both do so to perfection, but for this particular dish I prefer to use a risotto rice – arborio (Carnaroli and Viadone Navo are the best and the most expensive of this variety). The long-grain varieties braise just *too* well, staying loose and fluffy, but arborio releases its starch – as it does when used in a risotto – creating a creamy, thickened consistency. It is best to use individual dishes for this recipe, with the poached eggs set in the centre of each before melting the cheese on top.

Method Pre-heat the oven to 200°C/400°F/Gas 6. You will need four individual dishes, size 3 soufflé dishes are perfect.

Warm the olive oil in a braising pan, adding the chopped onion. Cook for a few minutes, without colouring, until softened. Add the rice and continue to cook for a further 2 minutes. Pour on three-quarters of the vegetable stock. Bring to the simmer, cover with greaseproof paper and a lid and braise in the oven for 20–25 minutes.

Meanwhile, prepare the poached eggs, as described on page 209. Set aside.

Remove the rice from the oven, checking it is cooked and still maintaining a slight bite. Most, if not all, of the stock will have been absorbed. More can now be added to loosen the consistency.

Melt the butter and quickly soften the sliced spring onions over a medium heat. These can now be added to the rice, checking for seasoning with salt and pepper. Add the grated Parmesan. This, along with the butter, will help to give a creamy consistency to the rice, at the same time slightly thickening it. More stock may need to be added to create a soft risotto texture. Add the mixed herbs, if using.

Re-heat the poached eggs for 1 minute in simmering water before drying on kitchen paper and seasoning with salt and pepper. Fill each pie dish a quarter deep with the rice. Place the poached eggs in the centre, then cover completely with the braised rice. Lay the Parmesan shavings or Gruyère cheese on top before melting under a pre-heated grill. Once bubbling, the 'pies' are ready to serve.

A large bowl of tossed green salad is probably the best accompaniment for this dish, along with thick olive oil and garlic French stick toasts.

Roast Salt and Peppered Duck Breast with Spicy Plums

Serves 4

4 duck breasts, preferably magrets (see introduction)

1 teaspoon coarse sea salt

1 teaspoon white peppercorns, coarsely cracked (see introduction)

1 tablespoon cooking oil

knob of butter

For the Plums

1 tablespoon cooking oil

6 plums, halved and stoned

knob of butter

1–2 teaspoons demerara or caster sugar

For the Spicy Sauce

150 ml (5 fl oz) red wine

2 tablespoons brandy

piece of cinnamon stick

3 cloves

1 star anise

juice of ½ orange

juice of ½ lemon

juice of ½ lime

pinch of five-spice powder

1 heaped teaspoon Dijon mustard

3–4 tablespoons redcurrant jelly

Introduction For this particular dish, I prefer to use *magret* duck breasts, very plump and usually sold vacuum-packed in pairs. They come from the French duck raised for producing *foie gras*. Any duck breast can be used for this dish, but be careful, as many are quite thin, and when roasted off the bone can shrink considerably. The coarse sea salt and cracked white peppercorns give a crunchier seasoned finish to the dish. (Simply lay the peppercorns between cling film sheets and crack with a rolling pin.)

Duck with plums is a wonderful combination of flavours (as for example, in Peking duck and its plum sauce). The plums here are first pan-fried before baking until tender, and then the dish is finished with a spicy and fruity sauce. For accompanying vegetables, I suggest serving Mousseline Mashed Potatoes and the English Spinach (page 142).

Method Make the sauce first. This can be made several days in advance but must be kept refrigerated in an airtight jar until needed. Place the red wine, brandy, cinnamon, cloves and star anise in a saucepan and bring to the simmer. Gently simmer for 10 minutes before adding the juice from all three fruits and bringing to the boil. The sauce can now be boiled to reduce by half before adding the five-spice powder, Dijon mustard and redcurrant jelly. Return to the simmer and cook for a further few minutes until the jelly has dissolved, before straining through a fine sieve. The sauce can now be left to cool, and refrigerated if not being used immediately. To appreciate the full flavour of this dressing, it's best served just warm rather than hot.

The plums can also be prepared a few hours in advance. Simply heat the oil in a frying pan, then sit the plums in it, flesh-side down, allowing to cook for a minute or two and colouring to a golden brown. Once at this stage, add a knob of butter along with a sprinkling (1–2 teaspoons) of the sugar. The sugar will now begin to caramelize with the butter. Add 2–3 tablespoons of water to create a syrup and turn the plums over in the pan.

The fruits can now be removed and placed on a baking tray, ready for re-heating when needed. Spoon the syrup in the frying pan over each plum half, giving them a glossy finish. The fruits will be re-heated while the duck breasts are roasting.

To cook the duck breasts, first pre-heat the oven to 200°C/400°F/Gas 6. Score the skin with a sharp knife in close lines from side to side. (This will help excess fat to be released, resulting in a crispy skin.) Once scored, sprinkle each skin with the coarse sea salt and cracked white peppercorns.

Warm an ovenproof frying pan or roasting pan with the cooking oil to a medium heat. This will prevent the skins from colouring too quickly. The breasts can now be laid in the pan, skin-side down. This slow-frying method will give you a much crispier finish. After 8–10 minutes of frying, a lot of excess fat will have melted from the skins and, at the same time, a good golden-brown finish achieved. It's now best, if possible, to pour away excess fat from the pan and, in its place, add a knob of butter. Once bubbling, turn the breasts over and place in the pre-heated oven, along with the plums, to re-heat, and cook for a further 5–6 minutes or maximum 8–10 minutes for particularly thick breasts. This will give you the duck cooked to a medium stage, guaranteeing a tender finish; very rare duck breasts can sometimes be chewy. Remove from the oven and baste with the butter in the pan before transferring to a separate dish to relax for 5–6 minutes. The plums can now be checked to see if completely heated through and tender. If not quite ready, continue cooking while the duck is resting.

Now it's time to present and serve the finished dish. I prefer not to slice the breasts and instead leave them whole. Slicing can lead to a lot of those flavoursome juices being left on a chopping board. Place the breasts on the right-hand side of the plates and a line of three plums to the left. To finish, drizzle the plums with the spicy-flavoured sauce and serve.

Notes: *If possible, I suggest sharp steak knives are offered when not pre-slicing the breasts. This will simply make life a lot easier when carving on the plate.*

The Spicy Sauce should be finished to a syrupy consistency. If it's too thin, simply continue to simmer until this stage is reached.

A plastic squeezy bottle can be used to drizzle the spicy sauce over the plums. This will help leave more even lines across the fruits. A few drops of olive oil can also be dotted around the breasts to finish the dish's presentation.

Steak and Kidney Sausages with Caramelized Onions

Serves 4

4 metres (4½ yards) sausage skins

450 g (1 lb) beef skirt, coarsely minced

225 g (8 oz) lamb or beef kidneys (lamb's kidneys give a more subtle flavour)

100 g (4 oz) beef suet, chopped finely, or dried alternative

knob of butter

1 onion, finely chopped

1 egg

50–75 g (2–3 oz) fresh white breadcrumbs

dash of Worcestershire sauce

lard, for frying

salt and pepper

For the Onions

4 medium–large onions, skin left on, split crossways through the middle

½ teaspoon demerara sugar (optional)

2 glasses of red wine (optional)

50 g (2 oz) butter (optional)

Introduction Sausages, which have been made in some form or another for thousands of years, fall into roughly three main categories: fresh (the most popular in Britain, and which need to be cooked); cured (e.g. salami); and pre-cooked or part-cooked (such as mortadella and frankfurters). In Britain, we have many famous varieties of fresh sausage, usually made with pork – Yorkshire, Oxford, Cumberland, Cambridge and Lincolnshire, to name but a few. All have different textures and seasonings, including nutmeg, mace, sage, garlic, ginger, cloves, thyme and more. These are all sausages that will never leave us, and I hope my steak and kidney sausages will sit proudly beside them.

The combination of steak and kidney is one we look upon as part of our British heritage, a strong British tradition. But, in fact it's a relatively new marriage of flavours, as most traditional recipes contain beef alone. Steak and kidney were first recorded as being introduced to each other in a recipe published in the mid-nineteenth century, and from that moment they became life-long friends. To find the two in a sausage is quite extraordinary: you can taste everything you'd find in a steak and kidney pudding, with the suet creating a slight dumpling texture.

The recipe makes eight large sausages, 12 medium, or 16 small. The caramelized onions give a very rich, bitter-sweet flavour, and, because of their moistness, can also act as a sauce. No separate sauce is needed as a result, but I have given one or two alternatives at the end of the recipe for a looser cooking liquor.

Method The caramalized onions need to be started at least 2 hours before eating. Pre-heat the oven to 160°C/325°F/Gas 3. Place the onions, flesh-side down, in a roasting tray. Put into the pre-heated oven. They will slowly begin to caramelize and will need up to 2 hours to be completely tender. During this cooking time, it's important to check they are not burning. If too dry, add up to 150 ml (5 fl oz) of water to the tray. This will moisten them and create steam for a softer cooking. Once totally tender, remove from the oven and leave to cool slightly. Each onion can now have the outside skin and inner layer removed, leaving just tender, caramelized onion 'discs'. Squeeze any juices from the skins into a pan and place on a medium heat. Once hot, add 300 ml (10 fl oz) of water and reduce by half. This will leave an onion-flavoured liquor.

For a richer sauce, sprinkle in ½ teaspoon of demerara sugar, following with the red wine and only 150 ml (5 fl oz) of water. Reduce by two-thirds, whisk in 50 g (2 oz) of butter and strain through a sieve. You now have a rich red-wine-onion 'gravy' to help moisten the onions.

The sausage skins (salted to keep them fresh) should be readily available from most butcher's. Before using, soak in cold, preferably running water. To be completely sure of cleaning and taking out the salt flavour, run the water through the actual skin. Now dry with a cloth before using.

I always cut the skins into 25 cm (10 in) lengths for the large sausages (shorter lengths for the smaller sausages), tying a knot in one end of each before filling. This will leave you with 5–8 cm (2–3 in) spare. During cooking, the skin shrinks around the filling, but, due to the excess, won't burst.

To make the sausages, ensure all the ingredients are chilled. The beef skirt should be totally fat-free and minced just once (ask your butcher) through a coarse blade. Clean and trim the kidneys of any sinews before chopping/cutting into small dice (maximum 5 mm/¼ in). Mix with the suet and quickly blitz in a food processor, or chop by hand, to combine but not purée the two together. Keep to one side.

Melt the butter in a small pan, add the chopped onion and cook until softened but not coloured. Place the minced beef in a bowl over ice and season well with salt and pepper. Add the egg, stirring and working it into the beef. Add the fried chopped onion, along with the kidney and suet mix. Finally, add 50 g (2 oz) of the breadcrumbs and a dash of Worcestershire sauce. To check the sausage texture and taste, pan-fry a small 'burger' of mix for a few minutes. Add more salt and pepper, if necessary, and if over-moist from the suet, simply add the remaining 25 g (1 oz) of crumbs.

Now, while the sausage mix is at this temperature and workable, it's time to fill the skins. Here's a tip for filling. Use a 1 cm (½ in) plain-tubed piping bag and only half fill it. This gives you more control. If it is overfilled, you can almost break your hand trying to squeeze the meat from it.

Take the skin and pull back to the knot; sit over the end of the piping tube and squeeze. Once the skin has been filled to the size of a standard sausage, remove the bag and make sure to push the sausage meat further in to give a good, plump shape. Push out any air left in the remaining sausages. It's best to rest the sausages in the fridge for at least 30 minutes before cooking.

The sausages can be grilled or pan-fried; I prefer to pan-fry. With this cooking method, you have total control of the heat. Melt the lard in a warm frying pan. Lay the sausages in the pan and fry gently, letting them take on a golden edge. The excess skin will quickly shrink around the sausage, stopping it from bursting unless you use extreme heat. I never prick sausage skin – I really can't see any point in it. The casing is there to hold in all those flavours and juices. If released, the meat will be very dry.

Beautiful, slowly cooked sausages will take 15-20 minutes. Well worth waiting every second for.

To serve the dish, place two pieces of onion on plates or in bowls and drizzle with the onion liquor before sitting two sausages on top of each.

The perfect accompaniment to this dish is Mousseline Mashed Potatoes (page 142).

Notes: *The steak and kidney mix can be enriched with a thick gravy, preferably flavoured with red wine, added to the sausage base: 70–80 ml (about 3 fl oz) will be plenty. If the gravy is available to use (perhaps left over from a roast-beef lunch), reduce to quite a thick pouring stage. Once cold, pour into the mix when adding the chopped onion.*

For an alternative onion garnish, simply pan-fry plenty of sliced onions until deep golden brown with a burnt edge to them. Add a sprinkling of demerara sugar and 2–3 glasses of red wine. Now reduce by three-quarters. Season with salt and pepper and the bittersweet red-wine onions are ready.

Red-wine Beef Lasagne

Serves 6

6 × 225 g (8 oz) individual chuck steak joints, trimmed and tied to retain shape

cooking oil, for frying

1 large onion, roughly chopped

1 large carrot, roughly chopped

3 tomatoes, cut into 8 wedges

1 garlic clove, chopped

fresh thyme sprig

1 bay leaf

bottle of red wine

600 ml (1 pint) Veal or Beef *Jus* (page 203)

6 pasta sheets 15 × 12 cm (6 × 5 in) (page 208), or ready-made fresh or dried lasagne

salt and pepper

For the Mushroom Sauce

200 ml (7 fl oz) white wine

300 ml (10 fl oz) Noilly Prat

25 g (1 oz) butter

4 shallots or 1 onion, finely sliced

175 g (6 oz) button mushrooms, sliced

juice of ½ lemon

50 g (2 oz) dried wild mushrooms, soaked in 150 ml (5 fl oz) cold water (optional)

150 ml (5 fl oz) Vegetable or Chicken Stock (page 204 or 201) if not using dried wild mushrooms

150 ml (5 fl oz) whipping cream

salt and pepper

For the Spinach and Mushroom Garnish

butter, for frying

1 kg (2¼ lb) picked and washed spinach

225 g (8 oz) fresh mixed wild mushrooms or sliced button or chestnut mushrooms

salt, pepper and freshly grated nutmeg

Introduction Beef lasagne doesn't sound like a British dish, but a lot of our eating habits today have been formed by influences from around the world. The 1980s and 1990s were very popular Italian years, with pizzas and pasta becoming very much part of our daily diet. This recipe isn't quite the lasagne we all know, the layered sheets of pasta with cooked mince between them and a cheese sauce on top. It's made of individual braised beef pieces, topped with a single pasta sheet and finished with a light, creamy mushroom sauce. There are one or two other flavours as well. The beef sits on top of spinach and mushrooms, both of which help turn this recipe into a complete meal. If you are not keen on pasta and mushroom sauce, you will still have the tasty red-wine beef to enjoy.

The beef I'm using is chuck steak. This cut has a very open texture which will absorb all the flavours and moistness of the cooking liquor. The meat will remain moist because it is braised in large pieces rather than the dice usually associated with chuck.

Method Begin by braising the beef. Pre-heat the oven to 180°C/350°F/Gas 4. Season the beef with salt and pepper. Heat an ovenproof braising dish on top of the stove with the cooking oil. (A frying pan can also be used for this stage.) Once hot, seal the beef pieces, colouring the meat completely. Remove the beef and add the onions and carrots to the pan. Cook for 10–15 minutes, until the vegetables have taken on colour, creating a caramelization. Add the tomato wedges, garlic, thyme and bay leaf, continuing to cook for a few minutes. Pour the wine over and bring to the simmer. Cook, reducing the wine by three-quarters. The *jus* and 300 ml (10 fl oz) of water can now be added. Return the meat to the pan and bring to the simmer. Cover with a lid and braise slowly in the oven for 2–2½ hours.

The meat will now be totally soft and tender. During the cooking time, it is important to check after each hour, skimming away any impurities collecting on the surface. Also, if the sauce is becoming too thick and strong, loosen with water as it's braising.

Once cooked, remove the beef pieces and keep to one side. Strain the sauce through a sieve. Pour half on top of the meat, reducing the remaining half to a good, rich, red-wine-sauce consistency. While reducing, check the flavour does not become too strong. Once at a good level, if too thin, loosen a teaspoon of cornflour with red wine and use to thicken the sauce to a coating consistency. The beef joints can now be kept warm in the liquor or refrigerated and re-heated when needed. If refrigerating (the beef set in the sauce keeps very well for up to 1 week in the fridge), the beef will need at least 45 minutes to 1 hour of gentle simmering before returning to its former glorious soft succulence.

An extra option when finishing the dish is to reduce 100 ml (3½ fl oz) of the re-heating liquor to a thick, sticky consistency. This can now be brushed over each beef joint once the string has been removed, to create a shiny glaze. This red-wine-braised beef recipe will stand as a dish completely on its own.

To make the mushroom sauce, boil and reduce the white wine by three-quarters. Pour off and keep to one side. In the same pan, boil and reduce the Noilly Prat by half. Add to the white wine. Now melt a knob of the butter in the pan and add the sliced shallots or onion. Cook on a medium heat for a few minutes, until beginning to soften and slightly colour. Add the button mushrooms, along with the lemon juice. Cook for 5–6 minutes before adding the soaked mushrooms (water included), if using. If unavailable, add the vegetable or chicken stock. Bring to the boil and reduce by half. Add the reduced white wine and Noilly Prat and simmer for 10–15 minutes.

Add the whipping cream and continue to simmer for a few more minutes. Season with salt and pepper before passing and pushing every last drop of sauce through the sieve. The mushrooms and shallots are added purely to create the flavour and can now be discarded (they can be added to the cooked spinach, if preferred).

The sauce is now ready and will be used to finish the dish, spooning it over the cooked pasta. A nice way to finish the sauce is blitzed with an electric hand blender: this creates a very light, frothy consistency, almost like a milkshake.

To finish the dish: melt a knob of butter in a large saucepan and, once bubbling, add the spinach. Stir as it cooks and becomes tender and wilted in the pan. This will take just a few minutes to achieve, with the water released by the spinach creating steam to help it cook. Season with salt and pepper (a pinch of nutmeg also works very well) before straining in a colander or sieve. Leave to stand for a few minutes, allowing excess water to drip away.

While the spinach is draining, heat a large frying pan with a large knob of butter. Once bubbling, add the wild or sliced mushrooms with salt and pepper and pan-fry to a tender golden brown. At this stage, add the cooked spinach, mixing everything together well.

Cook the pasta sheets in plenty of salted, boiling water for 2–3 minutes, or as instructed on the packet if using ready-made lasagne.

Divide the spinach and mushrooms between six plates or bowls. Place the beef joints (with string removed and brushed with glaze, if using) on top. Spoon 2–3 tablespoons of the separate red-wine sauce over each before placing the cooked pasta on top. This will cover the beef and spinach. Spoon the frothy mushroom sauce over the pasta. The beef lasagne is now ready to serve.

Notes: *Any red-wine sauce remaining will freeze very well for use at a later date.*

A trickle of truffle oil or olive oil can be spooned over the finished dish.

Boneless Potato Oxtail with Creamy Cabbage

Serves 8

2 whole oxtails, trimmed of excess fat, cut in half if too large for braising dish

flour, for dusting

cooking oil, for frying

knob of butter

2 large onions, roughly chopped

2 carrots, roughly chopped

3 celery sticks, roughly chopped

3 garlic cloves, roughly chopped (optional)

4 over-ripe large tomatoes, quartered

bottle of red wine

1.75–2.25 litres (3–4 pints) Veal or Beef Stock (not *Jus*), page 203

100 g (4 oz) pig's caul, soaked in water for 24 hours (see introduction)

6 potatoes, preferably Desiree, at least 8 cm (3½ in) long, peeled

salt and pepper

For the Stuffing

100 g (4 oz) frozen bone marrow (out of bone), soaked in water for at least 24 hours

100 g (4 oz) white breadcrumbs

1 egg

½ teaspoon chopped fresh thyme

salt and pepper

For the Creamy Cabbage

1 small savoy or green cabbage, quartered, stalk removed and layers cut into 5 cm (2 in) squares or pieces

knob of butter

100–150 ml (3–5 fl oz) whipping cream

salt, pepper and freshly grated nutmeg

Introduction Braised oxtail is one of my all-time favourites, a dish whose sticky succulence we have lacked recently because of the ban on beef on the bone. This recipe is taking the traditional braised oxtail a step further. Once braised, the meat is removed from the bone, arranged in a layer, and spread with a stuffing before cooked potato cylinders are placed along the centre to mimic the central bone. Once rolled, wrapped and set, these 'new' oxtails are cut and roasted like an individual joint of meat, the braising liquor becoming the tails' finished sauce. To guarantee that the oxtail is held together naturally, you will need pig's caul, the lacy lining of a pig's stomach. This virtually disintegrates during cooking, leaving little or no flavour. It can be obtained from your butcher if you give him enough notice, and has to be soaked in cold water for 24 hours before using. If unavailable, then roll the oxtail 'joints' in cling film several times. This can then only be removed by cutting away with scissors after the roasted tail has relaxed from the oven. Or you can place the tail meat on thinly sliced bacon or Parma ham before rolling in the cling film. The oxtail joints can be cooked and rolled at least 3–4 days in advance, and kept refrigerated until needing to be cut and finished.

Method To braise the oxtails, season and roll the tails in the flour. Heat a flameproof braising pan with 2–3 tablespoons of cooking oil, put in the tails and cook on a fairly high heat to colour all around.

While the tails are frying, heat a large saucepan or braising pan with a knob of butter. Add the chopped vegetables and garlic, if using, and cook on a medium heat for 15 minutes, allowing to soften and colour well. Add the tomatoes and continue to cook for a further 6–7 minutes. Pour in the red wine and bring to the boil. Boil and reduce by three-quarters before adding the veal or beef stock. Bring to the simmer and add the coloured oxtails. Once returned to the simmer, skim away any impurities and reduce the heat to a gentle simmering, covering with a lid ajar. These can now slowly cook for 2½–3 hours until completely tender. It's important to skim every 30 minutes to ensure the fats do not cook into the sauce. An alternative cooking method is to braise in a pre-heated oven (180°C/350°F/Gas 4) for the same cooking time (3 hours will probably be needed).

Once cooked, allow to relax and cool slightly (20 minutes) before removing the tails. Strain the oxtail stock through a fine sieve into a clean saucepan and return to the boil, allowing it to reduce to a rich sauce consistency. It's important to taste as it reduces. If the sauce reaches a strong, flavoursome stage but is too thin, simply thicken it with a touch of arrowroot or cornflour mixed with water (or red wine). For the cleanest of sauces, it's best, if possible, to strain again through muslin.

While the sauce is boiling, the tail meat can be removed from the bone. Lay two large squares of cling film on a clean work surface. Squeeze any excess water from the caul, if using, before opening and laying across the cling film. The tail meat can now be divided between the two, laying the meat closely to provide two rectangular shapes.

Cut six cylinders 7–8 cm (2¾–3¼ in) long and 1.5–2 cm (⅝–¾ in) wide from the potatoes, discarding the remainder. For this you need a cylinder cutter (like an apple corer and available from most kitchenware shops). Steam or boil the potatoes for 8–10 minutes until just tender. Once cooked, remove from the water and leave to cool.

To make the stuffing, blitz the bone

marrow in a food processor or liquidizer. Add the breadcrumbs, egg, thyme and seasonings and blitz again to a paste. This can now be spread into the central line of the oxtail rectangles, widely enough to be rolled around the potato cylinders.

Lay the cylinders, three per rectangle, top to tail along the stuffing. Now roll, keeping the caul on the outside and potato central, into a cylindrical shape. Wrap the caul around, along with the cling film. Re-roll each in another layer of cling film, twisting at either end to firm the oxtail cylinder. Foil can also be used as an extra layer. This will hold the shape very tightly. Refrigerate until needed.

The cabbage can also be pre-cooked. Place the cabbage pieces into a large saucepan of boiling, salted water, cooking without a lid for 3–4 minutes until tender. Drain in a large colander and leave to cool, or quickly refresh in iced water. This can be carried out several hours in advance, refrigerating until needed. To cook from raw, boil a knob of butter with 100 ml (3½ fl oz) of water, adding the cabbage. Cook and stir in the steam until tender. During this time, the liquor will have almost evaporated, ready for the cream to be added.

To cook the tails, pre-heat the oven to 200°C/400°F/Gas 6. Cut the oxtail parcels into eight fillet-steak-like portions, leaving the cling film on. Heat a roasting tray with 2 tablespoons of cooking oil. Place the tails in the pan and cook for a few minutes until golden brown before turning. Place in the pre-heated oven and roast for 15–18 minutes. This will heat them through thoroughly. Remove from the oven (the cling film does not melt but instead shrinks a little) and leave to rest for a few minutes. Cut away the cling film. The outsides of the tails can now be gently fried until well coloured. Meanwhile, re-heat the reduced sauce. The boned oxtails can now be presented in bowls, with the rich sauce spooned over and around.

To finish the cabbage, while the tails are resting, heat a knob of butter and tablespoon of water and add the blanched cabbage pieces. Season with salt, pepper and nutmeg and, once hot, pour in 100 ml (3 fl oz) of whipping cream. Stir and allow to reduce slightly, gently coating the cabbage leaves. The remaining 50 ml (2 fl oz) of cream can be added if needed.

The complete dish is now ready to serve.

Note: *Once the tails, rolled, wrapped and refrigerated, have completely set, they can be unwrapped and pan-fried in a hot roasting pan as complete cylinders. This will colour and begin to cook the caul fat surrounding them. Once well coloured, remove from the heat and leave to cool before re-wrapping in a double layer of cling film. This will save the job of having to fry the outsides of individual portions once cooked and rested. Instead, once cooked, the tail pieces will be ready to serve.*

To achieve a sticky glaze, 150 ml (5 fl oz) of the finished sauce can be reduced a little. Once reduced, this can be 'painted' over the tails for a stickier, glossier finish.

Aubergine Charlottes with Ratatouille Dressing

Serves 4

2 large or 3 medium aubergines

4 tablespoons olive oil

salt

For the Filling

olive oil, for frying

knob of butter

2 onions, finely chopped

2 garlic cloves, crushed

½ teaspoon ground cumin

½ teaspoon ground allspice

generous pinch of cayenne pepper

6 tomatoes, blanched and cut into 1 cm (½ in) dice (page 209)

1 heaped tablespoon currants

1 heaped tablespoon chopped fresh mint

1 heaped tablespoon chopped fresh coriander

salt and pepper

For the Ratatouille

1 tablespoon olive oil

knob of butter

1 small red pepper, seeded and cut into 1 cm (½ in) squares

1 small green pepper, seeded and cut into 1 cm (½ in) squares

1 small yellow pepper, seeded and cut into 1 cm (½ in) squares

1 large courgette, seeded and cut into 1 cm (½ in) dice

salt and pepper

For the Tomato Dressing

4 tablespoons passata (sieved tomatoes)

1 dessertspoon bottled tomato ketchup

1 tablespoon red-wine vinegar

2 teaspoons Worcestershire sauce

2–3 drops of Tabasco sauce

100–150 ml (3½–5 fl oz) olive oil

salt and pepper

For the Vegetarian Butter Sauce

75 g (3 oz) butter, chilled and cubed

1 shallot or ½ small onion, finely chopped

1 bay leaf

½ star anise (optional)

2 cardamom pods (optional)

2 tablespoons white-wine vinegar

4 tablespoons white wine

6 tablespoons Vegetable Stock (page 204) or water

2 tablespoons single cream

salt and pepper

Introduction A charlotte is a classic French dessert, and charlotte russe is said to have been invented by the great chef Antoine Carême. A mould is lined with either sponge fingers or bread, and then filled. The sponge-finger charlotte usually holds a flavoured sweet mousse and a jelly topping, and is served cold. The bread charlotte is baked, the most classic filling being apple, and although the origins may be French, the pudding seems very English because of its use of bread.

This savoury charlotte – a great vegetarian main course – uses the concept alone. Aubergine slices line individual moulds, and the remainder is cooked into a spicy filling. To finish the dish, sweet peppers are served with a tomato-based dressing, and spooned around the charlottes, along with a basic vegetable butter sauce. The 'charlottes' can be made up to 48 hours in advance, and placing them in plastic dishes means you can simply microwave them when needed.

Method First, make the charlottes: from each aubergine, cut two 1 cm (½ in) round slices from the middle. These will become the lids to sit on top of the moulds. Now quarter the aubergine pieces lengthways and cut away most of the flesh, leaving 3 mm (⅛ in) thick pieces of skin. The aubergine flesh can now be cut into 1 cm (½ in) dice. Lightly salt and stand in a colander for 20–30 minutes. This will draw the bitterness from the vegetable. The skin strips can now be cut in half lengthways, providing eight strips to line each mould.

Heat a frying pan with 2 tablespoons of the olive oil. The strips can now be pan-fried with little colour, turning after 2–3 minutes and adding more olive oil if necessary. Continue to fry for a further 2–3 minutes until tender. Remove from the pan on to kitchen paper to absorb any excess oil. Repeat the same process for the discs.

Now make the filling: fry the diced aubergine flesh in olive oil for a few minutes, until tender with golden edges. Once cooked, transfer to a bowl and set aside. Re-heat the pan with a knob of butter. Add the chopped onions, garlic, spices (including cayenne pepper) and tomatoes. Cook for 5 minutes before adding to the diced aubergines. The currants can now be added and, once cooled, the herbs. Check for seasoning with salt and pepper.

Butter four 150 ml (5 fl oz) plastic pudding basins. Line the moulds with the fried aubergine slices, slightly overlapping the strips. The filling can now be packed into the charlottes, topped with the cooked discs and any excess strips folded over. Cover each with cling film and lightly press. These can now be refrigerated until needed.

They should take no longer than 1 minute to re-heat, using a 750-watt microwave. For every 100 watts less, add 30 seconds – 1 minute. To check the filling is piping hot, pierce with a small knife, testing the heat of the blade against your lip.

To make the ratatouille, heat the olive oil and butter together in a saucepan. Once bubbling, add the sweet peppers and courgette. Cook for a few minutes, without colouring, until tender. Season to taste.

To make the dressing, mix together the passata, ketchup, red-wine vinegar, Worcestershire sauce and Tabasco sauce. Now gradually whisk in 100 ml (3½ fl oz) of the olive oil by hand or in a food processor/liquidizer, until completely emulsified. Season with salt and pepper. For a milder finish, add the remaining 50 ml (2 fl oz) of olive oil. This can now be kept in a squeezy bottle until needed. Any excess dressing can be kept refrigerated.

To make the vegetarian butter sauce, melt a small knob of butter and add the shallot or onion and bay leaf, and, if using, star anise and cardamom pods, and a twist of black pepper. Cook for a few minutes, without letting the vegetables colour, until softened. Add the vinegar and reduce by three-quarters. Add the wine and reduce by three-quarters. Pour in the stock or water and reduce again by half. Add the single cream to help emulsify the butter.

Bring the reduction to a simmer and whisk in the remaining butter, a few pieces at a time. Season with salt and pepper and strain through a sieve. If the sauce is too thick, loosen it with a few drops of water or lemon juice. The vegetarian butter sauce is now ready to use.

For a soft, creamy, frothy finish, simply blitz with an electric hand blender.

To finish the dish, turn the microwaved charlottes on to the centre of main-course plates. Scatter the sweet peppers and courgettes around, drizzling with the spicy tomato dressing. The vegetarian butter sauce is best offered separately, keeping the plates simple and very neat.

Notes: *As an alternative to aubergine strips, you can use one medium aubergine per portion. Cut each aubergine in half widthways to give you a thin and a round half. Scoop out the flesh from the rounder half, leaving a ½ cm (¼ in) border inside the skin. Brush the skins with olive oil and bake for 20–30 minutes at 180°C/350°F/Gas 4 until tender. While still warm, place the skins in the buttered moulds and they will take on the shape of the dish. Leave to cool. From the thinner halves, cut a round slice from the cut end (these will form the lids of the moulds) and put aside. Dice the scooped-out flesh and the rest of the thinner halves, and mix together. Cook and finish them as described in the main method. While this method doubles the number of aubergines required, it more than doubles the success of the dish.*

If plastic moulds are unavailable, four 7.5 cm (3 in) diameter metal rings (approximately 5–6 cm/2–2½ in deep) can be used. When lining with aubergine strips, place the rings on a buttered baking tray ready to be baked when needed. Place in a pre-heated oven, 200°C/400°F/Gas 6, for 20–25 minutes. Dress as described previously.

Instead of passata, 8 tablespoons of tomato juice, boiled to reduce by half, can be used.

Pigeon and Red Onion 'Pasty'

Serves 4

4 wood pigeons, breasts removed and skinned, legs and carcasses chopped for sauce

1 carrot, chopped

1 onion, chopped

few juniper berries and black peppercorns

1 bay leaf

2 garlic cloves, split

generous fresh marjoram sprig

½ bottle of red wine, preferably claret

600 ml (1 pint) Chicken Stock (page 201) or water

150 ml (5 fl oz) double cream

625–675 g (1 lb 6 oz–1 lb 8 oz) Quick Puff Pastry (page 212) or bought ready-made puff pastry

flour, for rolling pastry

2 small jacket potatoes

25 g (1 oz) butter

2 medium red onions, sliced

4 rashers of back bacon, lean 'eye' (round end of the rasher) removed and remainder thinly sliced (optional)

1 egg, beaten

salt and pepper

Introduction We all know the famous Cornish pasty, which is one of my favourite foods to eat – its thin strips of beef skirt with potato, onion and swede, all layered with spicy seasonings. However, this classic has had many different fillings since the Middle Ages, with every kind of meat, fish, vegetable and fruit working within that pastry case. They say that, originally, the pastry was purely a case to carry the food in, with such a tough texture that it was inedible. Quite often the meaty main course was found at one end of a pasty (the pastry initialled so you knew which was yours), with the sweet dessert at the other.

This pigeon-flavoured 'pasty' borrows the concept of layering with potato and red onion, but its shape is more in line with the French *pithiviers* (a dessert torte made with pastry and almond paste, circular in shape, usually decorated with spiral markings). Only the pigeon breasts are being used in the pasty, while the legs and carcasses are perfect for the sauce base. I've suggested the pigeon breasts are marinated in red wine for 24 hours. This is not essential, but does add more depth to the finished flavour.

Method Place the pigeon breasts in a bowl, with the carrot, onion, juniper berries, black peppercorns, bay leaf, garlic and half of the marjoram sprig. Pour in the red wine, then cover and refrigerate overnight or for at least 6–8 hours.

To make the sauce, fry the chopped pigeon legs and carcasses in a saucepan for 10 minutes until beginning to take on colour. Remove the breasts from the marinade and refrigerate until needed. Strain off the wine into a bowl, adding the chopped vegetables, spices and herbs to the carcasses. Continue to cook for a further 10–15 minutes before adding the red wine. Bring to the simmer and reduce by three-quarters. The chicken stock or water can now be added, also bringing to the simmer. Allow to cook gently for 30 minutes.

Increase the heat and reduce again by three-quarters. This stock can now be strained through a very fine sieve or muslin cloth. Return the reduced stock to the simmer and add the cream, cooking to a sauce consistency without becoming too thick. Season with salt and pepper. This sauce can become even lighter if blitzed with an electric hand blender to a frothy consistency just before serving. An extra glass or two of red wine can be boiled and reduced to increase the wine flavour.

To make the 'pasties', roll the puff pastry 2 mm (⅛ in) thick and cut four 10 cm (4 in) discs and four 14 cm (5½ in) discs. The pasties, as mentioned in the introduction, will be left round rather than folded. Lay the smaller base discs on large, buttered baking trays (or line the trays with baking parchment) and refrigerate, along with the larger discs, kept separate.

Boil or steam the potatoes in their skins until completely cooked and tender. Remove from the pan and leave to cool.

Meanwhile melt a knob of butter in a frying pan and fry the sliced red onions and sliced bacon, if using, to soften and slightly colour. It is important that the pan is hot: this will prevent the onions from bleeding too much of their tasty juices. Season with salt and pepper and leave to cool. Peel the cooled potatoes and cut into 5 mm (¼ in) slices. The remaining butter can now be melted and poured over the slices, before seasoning with salt and pepper. The remaining sprig of marjoram can now be picked, adding the small leaves to the cooked onions.

To build the pasties, place the potato slices on the four base discs, leaving a

1–1.5 cm (½–⅝ in) border around. Divide and spoon the marjoram red onions on top. Season the pigeon breasts and sit two on top of each pasty, laying an eye of bacon across the top, if using. The pasties are now ready to be topped with the larger pastry discs. First, brush around the border of the base discs with the beaten egg and cover, pressing the pastry around and sealing the two discs together. Refrigerate for 15 minutes to help set, then trim with a large round cutter (such as a flan ring) or shape/scallop using the back of a sharp knife.

Either leave the dome-shaped pasty totally plain, or score curved lines from the top central point to the border. Brush with the beaten egg to glaze, and chill again for 30 minutes.

Pre-heat the oven to 220°C/425°F/Gas 7. The pasties can now be baked for 18–20 minutes. The pastry will rise and become golden brown, with the breasts at a pink stage. Place the pasties in the centre of large plates or bowls, spooning the frothy pigeon sauce around.

Note: *A dressing can also be made to trickle around the dish. Boil and reduce 2 tablespoons of red-wine vinegar, preferably Cabernet Sauvignon, and mix with 2 tablespoons of walnut or hazelnut oil. The Game Jus (page 202) can be used to replace the cream sauce for a 'meatier' finish. 'Braised' Blue Cheese Leeks (page 146) or English Spinach (page 142) will both eat well with this dish.*

Côte de Boeuf with Caramelized Chicory Béarnaise Sauce

Serves 2

1 double rib (1 rib bone) of mature beef, French-trimmed, trimmings chopped

salt and pepper or cracked black peppercorns and sea salt

3 tablespoons cooking oil

25 g (1 oz) butter

300 ml (10 fl oz) water

watercress, to garnish (optional)

For the Sauce (optional)

⅔ quantity Sauce Béarnaise (page 205)

½ quantity Slowly Caramelized Lemon Chicory (page 152), see Note for Sauce Béarnaise addition

Introduction *Côte de boeuf* is a beef steak cutlet cut from the forerib. This recipe uses one double rib steak approximately 1.2 kg (2½ lb) with just one French-trimmed bone attached. (French trimming cuts the fat from the bones towards the 'eye' of the meat, leaving each bone scraped clean.) When ordering your 'steak', obviously British beef is the best, preferably from a two-year-old animal that has been hung for a minimum of 18–21 days. At this age, the meat will have a good marbling of fat which, through hanging, will work its way into the meat, ensuring moist and tender results. Once French-trimmed, ask your butcher to give you the trimmings. These can be roasted in the pan with the beef, helping to provide flavours for gravy.

As for cooking the steak, there are several options – grilling, pan-frying, barbecuing, roasting... Slow-roasting beef can often give you the most succulent of results, as cooking at a low heat prevents the meat from drying too quickly on the outside, instead allowing the marbled fats to melt and tenderize the whole piece. However, in this recipe I'm using a more intense heat.

The chicory béarnaise sauce is made from Slowly Caramelized Lemon Chicory (page 152), liquidized before being added to the béarnaise sauce. A straight béarnaise can be offered, perhaps serving the chicory as a vegetable accompaniment. Lyonnaise Potatoes (page 118) also eat very well with the roasted beef.

Method The chicory béarnaise sauce, if using, is best made before roasting the beef – refer to the Note on page 152 for the method. Keep aside at room temperature until ready to serve.

Pre-heat the oven to 200°C/400°F/Gas 6. Season the rib steak with salt and pepper or cracked peppercorns. Heat a roasting pan with the cooking oil. Once hot, place the rib in the pan along with the trimmings and cook for 5–6 minutes, colouring well. Turn the steak over and continue to cook until the rib is totally sealed. The bone is best wrapped in foil to prevent it from over-colouring. Add the butter, basting over the meat as it bubbles. Place in the pre-heated oven and roast for 5 minutes, then baste the meat with the butter and turn the meat over. Continue this process, turning every 5 minutes, until 20 minutes has passed. If the rib is particularly thick, cook for a further 5 minutes; this will give you medium-rare results. If you prefer the beef to be a little more cooked, add another 5–6 minutes for each stage, medium, medium-well done, and well done.

Remove the rib from the pan, cover and allow to relax for at least 10–15 minutes. Spoon away excess fat from the pan before re-heating on top of the stove. Pour in the water; once hot, the juices and sediment in the pan will be lifted, creating a loose roast gravy. Cook and reduce by a third before straining through a tea strainer. A knob of butter can be added to leave a silkier consistency.

The rib can now be presented on a suitable plate or carving board, garnished with the watercress (if using), ready to be sliced at the table. The chicory béarnaise sauce is best offered apart, along with any vegetable accompaniments, such as Lyonnaise Potatoes (page 118).

Note: *Grilled or fried mushrooms work very well with the rib, along with Red-wine Baby Carrots (page 150), Baked Mashed Potatoes (*Pommes Macaire, *page 141), Sautéd Butternut Squash (page 143), 'Braised' Blue Cheese Leeks (page 146), Roast (or Braised) Onions (page 144) and many more.*

Côte de Boeuf with Caramelized Chicory Béarnaise Sauce

Glazed Honey and Lemon Roasted Chicken with Buttered Forked Potatoes

Serves 4

2–3 tablespoons olive oil

1.6–1.8 kg (3½–4 lb) chicken, preferably free-range

butter, for spreading

2–3 tablespoons lemon honey (see Note)

salt and pepper

For the Potatoes

6 large baking potatoes

50 g (2 oz) butter, for forking

olive oil (optional)

2 tablespoons chopped fresh chives

coarse sea salt and pepper

For the Sauce

225 g (8 oz) chicken wings, chopped

1 tablespoon cooking oil

1 large carrot, roughly chopped

2 onions, roughly chopped

2 celery sticks, roughly chopped

fresh thyme sprig

1 bay leaf

1 dessertspoon honey

1 teaspoon golden syrup

juice of 1 lemon

750 ml (1½ pints) Chicken Stock (page 201)

150 ml (5 fl oz) Veal or Beef *Jus* (page 203), optional

potato flour or cornflour, for thickening (optional)

salt and pepper

Introduction This recipe will give a simple roast a new face and taste, with that wonderful nectar-of-flowers ingredient, honey, lending the chicken a slightly caramelized, sticky and sweet edge (helped along in the sauce by a little golden syrup). The buttered forked potatoes are baked before being peeled and forked to a soft but still textured mix. Seasoning with coarse sea salt helps give the potatoes an extra 'crunchy' texture.

Method Pre-heat the oven to 200°C/400°F/Gas 6. To make the sauce, pan-fry the chopped chicken wings in cooking oil until well coloured. Add the vegetables, allowing to colour slightly. Transfer all to a saucepan, adding the thyme, bay leaf, honey and golden syrup. Cook for 8–10 minutes, to a light caramel. Add the juice of the lemon, lifting all the flavours from the base of the pan. The chicken stock can now be added, brought to the simmer and cooked until reduced by three-quarters, before straining through a sieve. The stock will now have taken on a rich, deep caramel colour and chicken flavour. This can be served as it is – a loose cooking liquor – or thickened with potato flour or cornflour to a sauce consistency. Alternatively, the *jus* can be added to thicken the sauce to a gravy consistency. Season with salt and pepper.

To bake the potatoes, place on a baking tray previously sprinkled with coarse sea salt. Place in the pre-heated oven and cook for 50 minutes to 1 hour, until tender.

The chicken can also be roasted during this time; if so, the potatoes may need an extra 10–15 minutes.

Heat the olive oil in a roasting tray on top of the stove. Brush the chicken with butter before seasoning with salt and pepper. The bird can now be fried until golden brown on each side and breast and on the breast before sitting upright in the pan and roasting for 55 minutes to 1 hour. While roasting, baste the bird every 10–15 minutes. For the last 20 minutes, spoon 2–3 tablespoons of lemon honey over the chicken. During this time, baste frequently, lifting the honey from the pan and sharing it with the bird. As the honey cooks, it will reduce, becoming thicker and stickier developing a coating over the chicken.

Once cooked, remove from the oven, spooning any excess cooking liquor/honey over. If the lemon honey is still too thin, boil in the roasting tray on top of the stove until at a sticky stage, spooning the results over the bird. Leave to rest for 10 minutes.

Peel the baked potatoes and fork to a crumbly consistency before adding the butter and seasoning with coarse sea salt (if using) and pepper. It's important to maintain the crumble effect with a touch of creaminess rather than making the potatoes completely smooth. Olive oil can also be added for an extra flavour. Add the chopped chives just before serving.

The glazed honey and lemon chicken can now be carved, offering a leg or thigh with half a breast per portion. Finish with the gravy and forked potatoes and the dish is ready to be served. A lovely vegetable accompaniment is Red-wine Baby Carrots (page 150), the wine flavour working very well with the sweetness and sharpness offered by the chicken.

Note: *The lemon honey can be made in advance. Add the finely grated zest of 2 lemons to 450 g (1 lb) of clear honey. The flavour will infuse, becoming stronger as it ages. This will keep until the use-by date on the honey. For a quicker version or a smaller quantity, combine 3 tablespoons of clear honey with 1 heaped teaspoon of grated lemon zest. Warm gently to help the infusion of the two flavours before using.*

Crusted Lamb with Creamy Ham and Red-pepper Potatoes

Serves 4

2 racks of lamb, French trimmed (page 109) and fat removed from meat

1 tablespoon cooking oil

salt and pepper

Dijon mustard, for spreading

For the Sauce (makes about 600 ml/1 pint)

knob of butter

2 English onions, sliced

1 teaspoon demerara sugar

1 garlic clove, crushed

4 tomatoes, chopped

150 ml (5 fl oz) Noilly Prat or white vermouth

150 ml (5 fl oz) white wine

600 ml (1 pint) Veal or Beef *Jus* (page 203) or alternative

salt and pepper

For the Potatoes

2 large red peppers

olive oil, for brushing

175 g (6 oz) thick-cut ham (purchased from the butcher) in 5 mm (¼ in) slices cut into 5 mm (¼ in) dice

knob of butter

675 g (1½ lb) Mashed potatoes (page 142)

For the Herb Crust

4 slices of white bread, crusts removed

25 g (1 oz) picked fresh curly parsley

knob of butter

2 shallots or ½ onion, very finely diced

2 large garlic cloves, crushed

1 teaspoon chopped fresh thyme

1 teaspoon chopped fresh rosemary

salt and pepper

Introduction This lamb dish is very similar in concept to the French classic *carré d'agneau à la provençale*, which has a fresh herb crust cooked on top of the best ends (racks). The short best ends of lamb are found between the saddle and middle neck of lamb. These are chined to remove the central bone, leaving two racks. The short cuts will have an average of seven bones each which, when carved, will result in three cutlets per portion (one bone close to the end will be removed).

It's also important to ask for French-trimmed racks (see the introduction on page 109). When topping with any crust, it's best to have all fat removed from the meat, leaving only the trimmed loins attached to the bones.

I've included a recipe for a sauce, the flavours of which work wonderfully with the herby crust; it's also very *provençale*, with tomatoes, onions and garlic puréed into the sauce itself. A simple alternative to this, if you prefer, is to make a gravy in the lamb roasting pan while the racks are resting.

The creamy potatoes are a French classic, known as *pommes Biarritz*; the mash contains sweet red peppers and soft ham, a perfect accompaniment to the herby lamb.

Method First, make the sauce. Heat a large frying pan with the butter. Once bubbling, add the sliced onions. Increase the heat, allowing the onions to fry quickly and take on a deep colour. Add the demerara sugar and, once dissolved into the onions, add the garlic and tomatoes. Reduce the heat, cooking the tomatoes to a pulp. Pour in the Noilly Prat or vermouth, boiling and reducing by three-quarters. The white wine can now also be added, cooking to the same stage. Add the *jus* and bring to the simmer, cooking for 15–20 minutes.

Blitz in a liquidizer and strain through a sieve for a smooth finish. The sauce will have thickened; if too thick, loosen with chicken stock or water. Season with salt and pepper and the sauce is ready (this sauce also freezes well).

For the potatoes, rub the red peppers with a little olive oil and place on a baking tray. Sit the peppers under a pre-heated medium–hot grill, not too close to the heat. The peppers will colour and cook, slightly burning. As they do, turn them and continue until coloured all round. Once cooked, remove from the heat and allow to cool for a few minutes before peeling away the skin. Once peeled, split in half, removing the stalk and seeds. The pepper flesh can now be cut into a small dice.

Place the diced ham in a small saucepan with a knob of butter and tablespoon or two of water and bring to a soft simmer. This will create steam, warming the ham through (the ham can also be gently microwaved). Prepare the Mashed Potatoes as described. The sweet peppers and ham can be added when ready to serve.

To make the herb crust, place the white bread slices and picked curly parsley in a food processor and blitz to fine crumbs. The parsley will spread its lovely flavour and colour into the crumbs.

Roast Turkey Ballotine with a Ham and Armagnac Stuffing

Melt a knob of butter in a saucepan, adding the chopped shallots or onion and garlic and cooking for a few minutes until tender. Remove from the heat and leave to cool. The parsleyed breadcrumbs, shallots, thyme and rosemary can now all be mixed together, seasoning with salt and pepper. Spread this into two rectangular shapes on butter papers or cling film, ready to place on the loins of the two racks.

Pre-heat the oven to 200°C/400°F/ Gas 6. Season the racks with salt and pepper. Heat a roasting tray with a tablespoon of cooking oil on top of the stove. Once hot, place the racks in, meat-side first, sealing the loin to a deep golden brown. Each end of the lamb can now also be sealed. Remove the racks from the pan before brushing the mustard over the loins. Cover each loin with the herb crust mix, approximately 5–6 mm (¼ in) thick, pressing on firmly for a neat finish.

Return the racks to the roasting tray and place in the pre-heated oven, roasting for 10–12 minutes for a pink finish. Once cooked and well coloured to a golden brown, allow to rest for 5–6 minutes before carving into cutlets.

Should the crust not have taken on a rich roasted colour, simply finish under a pre-heated grill. The rack cutlets are now ready to serve, with the creamy potatoes and lamb gravy/sauce.

Notes: *Nutmeg Spring Greens (page 154) or English Spinach (page 142) will both eat well with this dish.*

A tasty alternative is to grill courgettes, aubergines, leeks, asparagus and mushrooms, brushed with olive oil, to complete a provençale-style meal.

Serves 6–8, generously

3.5–4.5 kg (8–10 lb) turkey, boned (see overleaf), saving the carcass

4 rashers of streaky bacon

watercress, to garnish (optional)

For the Stuffing

100 g (4 oz) chicken livers, soaked in milk for several hours

cooking oil

2 heaped tablespoons finely chopped shallots or onions

75 ml (3 fl oz) armagnac (a splash or two more may be needed)

225 g (8 oz) boned turkey thigh meat, cut into small dice

100 g (4 oz) lean pork meat, finely minced, plus 50 g (2 oz) pork fat, finely minced, or 175 g (6 oz) belly of pork, which provides its own fat content

1 egg

200 ml (7 fl oz) double cream

100 g (4 oz) cooked ham, cut into 5 mm (¼ in) dice

finely grated zest of 1 lemon

salt and pepper

For the Stock

knob of butter

turkey carcass chopped, plus trimmings and drumsticks from boned bird

1 large onion, chopped

2 celery sticks, chopped

1 leek, chopped

few black peppercorns

1 bay leaf

fresh thyme sprig

300 ml (10 fl oz) white wine

salt

For the Sauce

reduced cooking liquor (see method)

150–300 ml (5–10 fl oz) double or whipping cream

armagnac

75 g (3 oz) ready-to-eat prunes, cut into strips or small dice, plus extra to garnish, if liked

salt and pepper

'What a shocking fraud the turkey is. In life preposterous, insulting – that foolish noise they make... In death – unpalatable... practically no taste except a dry, fibrous flavour reminiscent of a mixture of warmed-up plaster of Paris and horsehair. The texture is like wet sawdust and the whole vast feathered swindle has the piquancy of a boiled mattress.'

Cassandra (William Connor)
'Talking Turkey' (1953)

Introduction Quite a statement from Cassandra, but how near is it to the truth? Turkey is quite a delicate meat, and it needs care and attention during cooking. If it is ever over-roasted, for 4–6 hours perhaps, the statement starts to become quite close to the truth.

Ballotine is a French culinary term describing a large piece of meat, usually poultry, that has been boned, stuffed and rolled before braising or roasting. Boning a whole turkey may seem quite a challenge and chore, but I'm sure your butcher will be 'happy' to prepare it for you. If not, I've included with this recipe a step-by-step guide to help you through the boning process. This recipe is perfect for Christmas Day, and one advantage is that the boning and stuffing can be done a day or two in advance, so long as the bird is kept chilled. When carving through the stuffed bird (with no bones to worry about), the stuffing is revealed, showing the pieces of ham encased in a smooth armagnac pork mixture. And the sauce to go with the dish is a simple creamed reduction of the pot-roast cooking liquor, making a change from gravy. The Mousseline Mashed Potatoes (page 142) and the English Spinach (page 142) are both perfect accompaniments to this dish.

Boning the turkey

1. Turn the turkey breast side down, with the neck end away from you. Cut through the skin from top to tail along the central point.
2. The legs can now be lifted and snapped towards you, loosening the ball joint connecting them to the carcass. From the neck end, cut through the flesh, following the carcass bones towards the thigh, placing the point of the knife in the ball joint and twisting to separate. The leg can now be pulled and simply cut loose from the carcass.
3. Return the knife towards the wing (the wings can be shortened by cutting at the second joint, keeping them for the stock), cutting close to the carcass until it is loosened. The wing can now be separated from the carcass.
4. Once you have cut through the wing joint, continue to cut carefully, feeling along the carcass and wishbone until you reach the breast bone.
5. Cut close to the bones and the breast will now fall away quite easily. Cut to the top point of the breast. Half of the turkey is now completely free.
6. Turn the bird around and follow the same directions on the opposite side.
7. Once the breasts are totally free, the central carcass can simply be pulled or cut away.
8. The legs can now be released by turning them inside out of their skin, then either cutting or pulling completely away between thigh and drumstick. The drumstick can now be cooked in the stock, and its meat removed from the bone once cooked. This can be used to garnish a home-made turkey soup or other snack. Remove the thigh bone (adding it to the stock), and trim all the sinews from the thigh meat. This can now be cut into a small dice ready for the stuffing. A total of 225 g (8 oz) is needed from both thighs; any left over can be used as per the drumstick. Return the skin outside in again.
9. The wing joints need to be cut around before also turning inside out as above. The wing bones and meat can be used for the stock.
10. Pull the breasts away from the skin, separating them to remove any central sinews. Now the skin can be stretched open, cutting away excess fats, meats and any remaining bones. A square of skin can now be formed on top of a sheet of cling film.
11. Replace the breasts on the skin, pulling away their fillets. These can now be laid at the pointed ends of the breasts, facing the fillet points towards them. This now creates quite an even rectangle of white meat in which to spoon the turkey, pork and ham stuffing.

Method To make the stuffing, remove the livers from the milk, this soaking will have helped remove the blood content and bitterness. Dry on kitchen paper before cutting into rough 1 cm (½ in) dice. Heat a frying pan with a drop of cooking oil and toss the livers very quickly to seal.

Remove them from the pan and leave to cool. Place the chopped shallots or onions in a saucepan with the armagnac and bring to the boil. Continue to boil and reduce until almost dry. Leave to one side to cool.

For the smoothest of finishes place the diced thigh meat and sautéd livers in a food processor and blitz to a purée. Add the minced pork and fat, re-blitzing for a minute. Season with salt and pepper.
Add the egg and blitz while pouring the cream in slowly. Once all mixed, place in a

stainless steel bowl, preferably sitting over ice. Check it for seasoning with salt and pepper.

Add the diced ham, armagnac shallots and lemon zest to the stuffing mix. It's important the stuffing is kept well chilled and firm before it is spooned into the boned turkey.

To stuff the turkey, first season the breast meat with salt and pepper. Spoon the stuffing along the central channel between the breasts and fillets. Continue to spoon, beginning to form a dome shape between the meats. Use a palette knife to smooth the stuffing into a cylinder shape.
To protect the soft texture while cooking, lay the four rashers of bacon lengthways over the stuffing.

Pull one side of the skin totally over the stuffing, reasonably tight, to hold its shape. Follow with the other side, folding in each end to complete the wrap.

Wrap fairly tightly in cling film and refrigerate for 2–3 hours (or overnight). This will set and firm the stuffing, holding the 'joint' together while being tied.
Remove the cling film and tie reasonably firmly every 2–3 cm (1 in or so), starting in the centre and completing the process towards either end of the rolled bird. This

will help keep an even shape and not push the suffing towards one end. Wrap in buttered and seasoned foil and refrigerate. This whole boning, stuffing and rolling process can be completed up to 2–3 days in advance.

Once the turkey has been stuffed, rolled and is resting and firming, the turkey stock can be made. Melt a knob of butter in a large saucepan. Add the chopped carcass and trimmings and fry for a few minutes to seal and take on a little colour. Add the vegetables and herbs, cooking for a further 10 minutes. Add the white wine, then boil and reduce by half. Pour 2.25–2.75 litres (4–5 pints) water into the pan and bring to the simmer, skimming away any impurities. Cook for 1–2 hours.

Strain the stock through a sieve. Use 1.2 litres (2 pints) of this to pot-roast the turkey, with the remainder providing the stock base for a Boxing Day roast turkey soup (following Creamy Roast Chicken Soup, page 57), or simply freeze for later use.

To pot-roast, place the foil-wrapped turkey in a suitable roasting tray. Pour in the measured 1.2 litres (2 pints) of stock and bring to the simmer. Place in the oven pre-heated to 190°C/375°F/Gas 5 and cook for 1 hour. This cooking method is self-basting, the buttered foil creating steam to provide a moist finish. After 1 hour, pierce through the foil and bird with a skewer or small knife. If it comes out completely hot, the bird is cooked. If not, return the bird to the oven and cook for a further 15–30 minutes. After 1½ hours the turkey will be cooked. Remove from the pan and leave to rest for 10 minutes. The foil wrapping will retain the heat in the bird.

To make the sauce, boil and reduce the cooking liquor to 300–400 ml (10–14 fl oz). Pour 150 ml (5 fl oz) into a separate pan and continue to reduce by half to two-thirds, creating a savoury syrup glaze to brush over the finished roast. Set aside. Add 150 ml (5 fl oz) of the cream to the remaining 275 ml (9 fl oz) of stock. Bring to the simmer, cooking for a few minutes. For a creamier finish, add more of the remaining cream. Once at a good sauce stage, add a splash of armagnac, then, just before serving, the diced prunes.

To create the roasted finish, unwrap the bird and dry it on kitchen paper. Heat a large frying pan or roasting tray with a little cooking oil and place the turkey in it, presentation-side down. With the moisture leaking, the pan will spit quite a lot of oil, so it's best to carry out this job using a large spatula or fork to hold and turn the joint, colouring it on all sides. I suggest that you keep children away from the stove during this process. (I also suggest you wear a bibbed apron to avoid splashing your new Christmas present!) Although this part of the cooking is messy, the flavour and total presentation of the ballotine will convince your guests that the turkey has been roasted. For an alternative (and cleaner) method, see Notes below. The roast turkey ballotine is now ready to serve: simply carve straight through the rolled joint, leaving the moist ham and armagnac stuffing. Place each slice on a plate before finishing with the sauce, and a few pieces of diced prunes and watercress, if using. Slicing into the turkey is almost like pulling your first Christmas cracker, with the tastiest of presents inside.

Notes: *When making the turkey stock, any of the meat trimmings – drumsticks, excess thigh meat and suchlike – can be poached in the stock during its cooking time. This meat can now be flaked and used as a garnish for home-made turkey soup.*

Cooking the bird in foil guarantees that its moistness is maintained, but the skin remains pale. It can be browned by frying (as described earlier), or alternatively, remove the foil after 45 minutes of pot-roasting and continue to roast, uncovered, for the remaining cooking time. This will give a lovely golden brown colour.

Roast chestnut shavings are an excellent accompaniment to the English Spinach. One or two chestnuts per portion of spinach will probably be enough, but I suggest a few extra are roasted (there are always one or two duds), providing a nuttier finish for chestnut lovers.

To roast and cook completely, arrange on a baking sheet, sprinkle with a little water and cook for 15 minutes in a pre-heated oven, 200°C/400°F/ Gas 6. Or cook under a hot grill, also for 15 minutes. Peeling roasted chestnuts is very easy if they are still warm. The skin surrounding the fresh nut must also be removed. Now they are ready to slice/grate over the cooked spinach.

It's not essential to pre-roast the chestnuts: peeled raw or frozen nuts can also be used. Slice the chestnuts with a sharp knife. Melt a knob of butter in a frying pan, adding a tablespoon or two of the slices. Cook on a medium heat, not allowing the butter to burn, and fry to a golden brown. Turn the slices and continue to cook for 1–2 minutes before removing from the pan and sprinkling over the cooked spinach. The chestnuts will now have become very crispy, almost like a vegetarian crackling. These can be cooked in advance and warmed in butter just before serving.

Pot-roast Riesling Chicken with Fresh Herbs and Cream Cheese

Serves 4

50 g (2 oz) cream cheese

50 g (2 oz) butter

1 heaped tablespoon chopped shallots

2 tablespoons chopped fresh parsley

1 tablespoon chopped fresh chervil

1 tablespoon chopped fresh chives

1 tablespoon chopped fresh tarragon

1.6–1.8 kg (3½–4 lb) free-range chicken

2 tablespoons cooking oil

600 ml (1 pint) Riesling (see Notes)

300 ml (10 fl oz) Chicken Stock (page 201) or alternative, or water

8–12 baby turnips, peeled (optional)

3 carrots, peeled and cut into 1 cm (½ in) slices (optional)

100 ml (3½ fl oz) single cream or crème fraîche

salt and pepper

Introduction This dish is heavily influenced by a *nouvelle cuisine* classic created in the late 1970s by Michel Guérard, one of the most famous French chefs. His recipe for a roast chicken, its skin lined with *fromage blanc* and parsley, was a very simple concept, but had a quite exquisite flavour. Here I am using cream cheese mixed with lots of herbs and chopped shallots. The cream cheese can be replaced by *fromage frais* or *blanc*, an unripened soft cheese which contains from 0–8 per cent fat. Reduced-fat cream cheese is also available.

The chicken is pot-roasted in a dry Riesling wine, which results in a very flavourful sauce. Baby turnips and thick slices of carrot can also be cooked in the wine and stock surrounding the chicken. English Spinach (page 142) is a suitable accompanying vegetable, as is a dish of Jersey Royal potatoes (page 147).

Method Pre-heat the oven to 200°C/400°F/Gas 6. Mix together the cream cheese, 25 g (1 oz) of the butter, the chopped shallots and mixed herbs (some of the herbs can be kept to serve in the pot-roast sauce). Season with salt and pepper. The mixing can be done in a food processor; this will result in a rich green filling.

Release the skin carefully from the chicken breasts, starting at the neck end. This is very easy but it is important not to split the skin. Spoon the cheese mix underneath, dividing between the two sides. Pull the skin over and press gently to spread the cheese across the breasts. Pull the excess skin underneath the bird and pierce with one or two cocktail sticks to hold in place. To maintain a good chicken shape, tie the legs together.

Heat a large frying pan with the cooking oil. Season the chicken with salt and pepper and fry until coloured all over to a rich golden brown. Once coloured, sit the bird in a deep braising pan. Pour in 300 ml (10 fl oz) of the Riesling plus the chicken stock or water. Bring to the simmer before covering with a lid and placing in the pre-heated oven. Pot-roast for 20 minutes before removing the lid and basting the bird with all the juices. If including the turnips and carrots, add to the dish now, replace the lid and continue to pot-roast for a further 20 minutes. Repeat the same basting process, this time not replacing the lid, and cook for the final 20 minutes. During this last period of cooking, baste two or three more times. After a total of 1 hour the chicken will have roasted through, along with the tasty, slightly overcooked vegetables. Remove the chicken and vegetables, keeping covered and warm.

Skim any excess fat from the liquor before reducing to 150 ml (5 fl oz). The remaining 300 ml (10 fl oz) of Riesling can be boiled and reduced separately by three-quarters. This, once added to the stock, will lift the total wine flavour. Add the single cream or crème fraîche and return to the boil. Whisk in the remaining 25 g (1 oz) of butter and season with salt and pepper, before straining through a fine sieve. Any saved herbs can now be added to the Riesling pot-roast sauce.

The chicken legs and breasts can now be removed, offering either a thigh or drumstick with half a breast per portion. Once you cut into the breast you will capture the flavours of the cream cheese melting with the butter into the complete dish. Present with the vegetables (if using) and any accompaniments (one of my favourites is Mousseline Mashed Potatoes, page 142) before spooning the sauce over the chicken.

Notes: *Instead of the wine you can add a dozen grapes to the pot-roast. As the chicken cooks, the grapes become tender, releasing their flavour into the liquor. To garnish, peel and halve 4–5 grapes per portion and warm in the finished sauce.*

Roast Rump of Lamb with Redcurrant Jelly and Lyonnaise Potatoes

Serves 4

2 tablespoons cooking oil

4 rumps/chumps of lamb, trimmed

150–300 ml (5–10 fl oz) Chicken Stock (page 201) or water

knob of butter (optional)

salt and pepper

Redcurrant Jelly (page 214) or bought ready-made, to serve

For the Lyonnaise Potatoes

750–900 g (1½–2 lb) new potatoes or medium-sized baking potatoes, unpeeled

2 tablespoons olive oil

50 g (2 oz) butter

2 large or 3 medium onions, sliced

salt and pepper

> Cooks are made, meat-roasting experts are born.
>
> Brillat-Savarin

Introduction The rump of lamb is also known as the chump. It's from this joint, found at the leg end of a long-cut saddle of lamb, that chump chops are cut. Two rumps/chumps, usually weighing 275–350 g (10–12 oz) before trimming, are cut from each lamb. When purchasing these from your butcher, it's best to ask for them to be trimmed of all sinews (from where the meat is attached to the bone) and excess fat, leaving only a 2–3 mm (⅛ in) covering.

For this dish, a quick red-wine gravy can be made, swilling the roasting tray with the wine to draw up all of the juices, and adding lamb or veal/beef *jus*. Or you can use a simple cooking liquor to trickle over the meat: the choice is yours.

Redcurrant jelly, a classic British accompaniment to lamb is recommended. Lyonnaise potatoes are a variation of the French *pommes sautées*, the *à la lyonnaise* indicating the addition of fried onions. Classic sauté potatoes are made from raw slices, but here I'm using pre-cooked. Once sliced and sautéd, they are crisp on the outside and creamy inside.

Method First, cook the potatoes by boiling or steaming until tender. Peel the potatoes while still warm. For new potatoes peeling is not essential but will give a more crumbled finish. Once peeled, cut into 5 mm (¼ in) slices; new potatoes can simply be halved lengthways, the bowl they are in being lightly shaken to give a slightly broken edge. Heat a frying pan or wok with a tablespoon of the olive oil. For this quantity of potatoes, it's best to fry in two lots; this will leave more room for them to colour and not just steam. Add half the sliced potatoes to the pan and fry on a medium heat until golden brown on both sides. Many will break during the cooking time, these 'crumbles' will become crispy, creating an even better texture. Season with salt and pepper before removing and keeping warm. Repeat the same process with the remaining half, also keeping warm.

Re-heat the pan with a trickle more olive oil and a knob of butter. Add the sliced onions and fry on a medium heat until softened and a rich golden brown. Add the potatoes, along with the remaining butter, mixing together and checking for seasoning with salt and pepper. The potatoes and onions can be fried in advance and kept separate until needed. The potatoes can then be warmed through in a hot oven while the onions are heated in a pan on top of the stove. Mix together and season as described above.

To cook the lamb, pre-heat the oven to 200°C/400°F/Gas 6. Heat a roasting pan with the oil. Season the lamb with salt and pepper. Place in the tray, fat-side down, and cook for several minutes to colour and release excess fats. Turn in the pan until each side is sealed and browned. Then cook in the pre-heated oven for 10–12 minutes for a medium-rare finish. For a good medium finish, 12–15 minutes will be needed, depending on the size of the joint. The lamb will need an equal resting time to cooking time. This will then give the meat enough time to relax, resulting in a more tender finish.

While the lamb is resting, the cooking liquor can be finished. Pour away any excess fats from the pan. Re-heat the pan on top of the stove, adding the stock or water to lift all the flavours. Reduce a little, adding a good knob of butter (if you like), before straining through a tea strainer for a smooth finish. This liquor will have just the natural flavour of the lamb.

To serve, carve the lamb trickling with the roast liquor. The lyonnaise potatoes can be plated with the lamb or offered separately with the redcurrant jelly.

Notes: *When making the roasting liquor with the stock or water, 150 ml (5 fl oz) of red wine can be used and reduced in the pan to lift the flavours before adding the stock. The red-wine flavour will complement the lamb.*

When pre-cooking the fat side of the lamb in a frying pan, cooking to a burnt tinge (almost black) will create a barbecued bitterness that works with the sweetness of the lamb meat.

Chopped parsley can be sprinkled over the potatoes, creating an extra flavour and colour in the dish.

Chicken Sauté with Mushrooms and Tarragon

Serves 4

1.6–1.8 kg (3½–4 lb) chicken, preferably free-range

1 tablespoon of picked tarragon leaves, stripped, saving stalks for the sauce

2 tablespoons olive oil

25 g (1 oz) butter

225 g (8 oz) chestnut or button mushrooms, trimmed and wiped

150 ml (5 fl oz) dry sherry (optional)

150 ml (5 fl oz) white wine (300 ml/ 10 fl oz if sherry not used)

150–300 ml (5–10 fl oz) double or whipping cream

salt, pepper and a squeeze of lemon juice

Introduction The culinary term 'sauté' comes from the French *sauter*, to jump. Jumping in the pan here are chicken pieces, which colour all over in a foamy butter that turns an appetizing nut brown. The chicken is then roasted in the oven, and the sauce is made in the dish once the chicken is taken out. The French *fricassée* method is very similar, but the chicken pieces are cooked in the stock. This dish can be made either way, but the advantage of sautéing is that the sauce garnishes can be prepared while the chicken roasts.

The mushrooms used can be almost any variety – button, cup, flats, chestnuts, mixed wild (pleurottes, girolles, and so on) or, for the ultimate flavour, morels. The latter have a short season, but can be bought dried. Once soaked for several hours, the water they've softened in becomes a mushroom stock with which to make the sauce. I'm making this dish with simple button and chestnut mushrooms, but if you ever have the chance, try the morels – you won't be disappointed. Fresh (or dried) buttered pasta (page 208) will be a perfect accompaniment, or braised rice (page 95), using Patna or basmati rice.

Method Pre-heat the oven to 200°C/400°F/ Gas 6.

Cut the chicken into eight pieces, splitting the legs into drumsticks and thighs, and cutting each breast with the wings off the bone and splitting each in two. (Classically, the breasts should be left on, but this way is easier for eating.) The carcass can now be chopped quite small before being rinsed of any excess blood.

Now make a quick chicken stock. Place the carcass in a saucepan, top with 600 ml (1 pint) of water, add the tarragon stalks and bring to the simmer. Cook for 20–30 minutes before increasing the heat and reducing by half. Strain and the quick stock is made.

Heat a flameproof braising dish with the olive oil. Season the chicken pieces with salt and pepper. Add the butter to the dish and, once foamy, insert the chicken pieces. Sauté on a reasonably high heat, turning and allowing the pieces to become a rich golden brown. Add the mushrooms and allow to colour before covering with a lid and baking in the pre-heated oven for 15–20 minutes.

Remove the chicken and mushrooms from the pan, cover and keep warm. Pour off any excess fat, then place the dish back on the stove top. Add the dry sherry (if using), bringing almost instantly to the boil and reduce by three-quarters. Add the white wine, reducing to the same quantity. Pour on the quick stock, cooking until reduced by half. Add 150 ml (5 fl oz) of the cream, bring to the simmer and cook for a few minutes to a loose sauce consistency. For a creamier finish add the remaining cream.

Season the sauce with salt and pepper, adding a squeeze of lemon juice to enrich the total flavour. Strain through a fine sieve for a smooth finish. The chicken pieces and mushrooms can be quickly warmed through in the oven, before being presented in a suitable dish. Add the tarragon leaves to the sauce and pour over before serving.

Note: *A dry chicken sauté can also be made, omitting the stock, wines and cream. Follow the recipe, cooking the chicken in the oven with the mushrooms. Once cooked, add the tarragon leaves and a squeeze of lemon juice. The sauté is now ready to serve. Eating a dry sauté is equally good and, obviously, omitting the double cream makes it a reasonably healthy option. (The butter can also be omitted: simply fry the chicken in cooking or olive oil.)*

Beef Goulash with Sweet Red Pepper and Parsley Gnocchi

Serve 4–6

1 kg (2¼ lb) lean chuck steak, cut into large dice

1 heaped tablespoon paprika

olive oil or beef fat, for frying

knob of butter

3 large onions, cut into 1 cm (½ in) dice

2 garlic cloves, crushed

1 tablespoon plain flour

6 large tomatoes, blanched (page 209) and diced

1 teaspoon tomato purée

1.2 litres (2 pints) Beef or Chicken Stock (page 203 or 201) or alternative

salt and pepper

4–5 tablespoons soured cream, crème fraîche or double cream, to serve (optional)

For the Gnocchi

1 kg (2¼ lb) large potatoes, unpeeled

1 large sweet red pepper

1 tablespoon chopped fresh parsley

1 tablespoon Parmesan cheese

175 g (6 oz) plain flour

25 g (1 oz) butter or 2 teaspoons olive oil

1 egg

1 egg yolk

salt and pepper

butter, for frying

Introduction Beef goulash has a surprising history. The diced beef and potato stew, flavoured with the characteristic Hungarian spice, paprika, is generally considered a great historic and classic dish of Hungary. A meat and potato stew-soup would have been a basic, and it would have been spiced, but the introduction of paprika entirely changed the Hungarian way of eating. The interesting flavour gained when paprika is fried with meat – creating an almost burnt, barbecued touch – was what made it so popular, and it is this that distinguishes the best goulashes. Another, possibly strange, edge to this dish is its accompaniment, usually a form of dumpling made from potato and flour, very similar to Italian gnocchi. So instead of cooking potatoes in the stew, I'm making potato gnocchi, offering both possible goulash garnishes in one. Another vegetable sometimes included in the Hungarian stew is red peppers, and these I'm incorporating into the gnocchi, along with parsley.

Method Season the beef with salt, pepper and a quarter of the paprika. Heat a frying pan with the olive oil or fat: once smoking, add a handful of the beef. Fry until well coloured on all sides before transferring to a colander. Repeat the same process until all the beef has been coloured.

In a saucepan, melt a knob of butter; once bubbling, add the chopped onions. Cook on a fairly fast heat to colour to a rich golden brown as they soften. Add the garlic and remaining paprika and continue to cook for a few minutes before adding the beef. Sprinkle over the flour and stir into the mix, cooking for 2–3 minutes. Add half the diced tomatoes, stirring them in before adding the tomato purée and stock. Bring to a simmer, skimming away any excess fat. The beef can now be cooked over a gentle simmer for 2–2½ hours, until tender. It's best to skim from time to time, ensuring the sauce stays fat-free. The sour cream, crème fraîche or double cream, if using, can now be added, returning to the simmer for 2–3 minutes. Add the remaining tomato dice and the goulash is ready.

The gnocchi can be made while the goulash is cooking. To do so, cook the potatoes in boiling, salted water until tender. While they are cooking, place the red pepper under a heated grill and colour towards burnt on all sides. This, once cooled slightly, can be peeled, halved and seeded. Cut the pepper into small dice.

Drain the potatoes and leave to cool slightly. When warm, peel and mash to a smooth consistency. Add the sweet pepper, chopped parsley and Parmesan, seasoning with salt and pepper. Mix in the flour, butter or olive oil, egg and egg yolk. Roll the mixture on a floured surface into small 1–2 cm (½–¾ in) balls. These can be left as they are or slightly pressed with a fork to leave a corrugated edge.

The gnocchi are now ready to poach in simmering water for 3–4 minutes, 5 minutes being the maximum they will need. If using immediately, remove from the water, then roll them in butter or gently pan-fry in bubbling butter for a light golden edge.

They can also be refreshed in iced water to re-heat when needed, either by pan-frying to a rich golden colour or dropping back into simmering water for a few minutes and then rolling in butter.

The Hungarian beef goulash is now ready to serve with its sweet red pepper and parsley gnocchi. A little extra paprika can be sprinkled over the meat, if you wish.

Notes: *Extra Parmesan cheese can be sprinkled over the gnocchi and toasted before serving.*

The sweet red peppers can be peeled and cut into small dice while raw rather than first grilling.

A quarter of the diced peppers can be saved to cook in melted butter or olive oil and sprinkle over the finished gnocchi.

Soured cream or crème fraîche can accompany the dish as an alternative to adding to the goulash.

A very quick stir-fry goulash can also be made. Cut fillet beef tails into strips and dust well with paprika and salt. Quickly stir-fry in a very hot wok with sliced onions and red peppers. Once all seared, add two diced tomatoes (seeds removed), a splash of white wine and few tablespoons of soured cream. The goulash is now ready to serve and will eat best with braised rice.

Steamed Rabbit, Fennel and Tarragon Suet Pudding

Serves 4–6

6–8 rabbit legs, boned

1 large onion or two medium, sliced

finely grated zest of 1 lemon

1 tablespoon of tarragon leaves, snipped (saving stalks and a sprig for the sauce)

100 ml (3½ fl oz) white wine

3 tablespoons olive oil

coarse sea salt and white pepper

1–2 heads of fennel (1 large will be plenty)

1 quantity Suet Pastry (page 128), replacing vegetarian suet with beef suet

150 ml (5 fl oz) Chicken Stock (page 201) or alternative, or water

For the Sauce

knob of butter

rabbit leg bones, chopped

fennel trimmings, chopped

1 onion, finely chopped

sprig of tarragon and stalks

1 star anise

150 ml (5 fl oz) white wine

450 ml (15 fl oz) Chicken Stock (page 201) or alternative

150 ml (5 fl oz) double or whipping cream

salt, pepper and a squeeze of lemon juice

Introduction Cooking rabbit in suet pastry is classically British, and pastry-topped rabbit pies have an even longer history. Farmed or wild rabbits can be used for this recipe; the wild will obviously have a stronger, gamier flavour. Only the legs are being used and, depending on their size, 6–8 should be plenty to fill the pudding basin. I'm sure your butcher will be more than happy to bone the legs for you, but make sure he gives you the bones with which to make the sauce.

It's best to plan a day ahead, as this will give plenty of time for the meat to marinate and absorb all the interesting flavours. The meat and all the vegetables are placed in the suet crust absolutely raw, allowing the long cooking time to blend them all together. For a vegetable accompaniment, I recommend some buttered English Spinach (page 142).

Method Separate the thigh and drumstick meat from the rabbit legs. Mix with the sliced onions, lemon zest, snipped tarragon, white wine and olive oil, seasoning with a small sprinkling of sea salt and white pepper. Mix well, cover with cling film and leave to marinade for several hours preferably overnight.

The fennel has not been included in the marinade as it tends to discolour. Once the other ingredients have marinated, split the fennel heads in half, removing the outside layer: this can be used in the sauce. Finely shred and mix with the rabbit.

Grease a 1.2 litre (2 pint) pudding basin and line it with suet pastry, as described on page 128, replacing vegetarian suet with beef suet. Pack it with the rabbit and fennel mixture, adding the chicken stock. Cover as instructed in the suet-pastry recipe and top with buttered and floured foil.

Place in a steamer (or colander in a large saucepan) and cook for 2–2½ hours. During this time, the rabbit will have cooked through completely, now eating like butter. While the pudding is steaming, the sauce can be made.

Melt a knob of butter in a saucepan and add the chopped rabbit bones. Cook for a few minutes to seal but not colour the bones. Chop the fennel trimmings and add to the bones, along with the onion, tarragon and star anise. Continue to cook for 10–15 minutes, allowing the vegetables to take on a gentle golden colour. Add the white wine and bring to the boil, reducing until almost dry. Add the chicken stock and bring to the simmer, cooking until the stock has reduced by at least half to two-thirds.

Add the cream, return to the simmer and cook gently for 7–8 minutes before straining though a sieve. Check the sauce for seasoning with salt and pepper, adding a squeeze or two of lemon juice. If the sauce is too thin, reduce a little, but not allowing to become coating consistency. This will be too thick to enjoy with suet, which absorbs the sauce quite easily.

Before serving, the sauce can be blitzed with an electric hand blender to a frothy 'milkshake' consistency, for a lighter finish.

To serve, the pudding can be either turned out or simply spooned into bowls, treating it like a pastry-topped pie. Finish the portions with the frothy rabbit sauce.

Note: *Sliced button mushrooms can also be added to the pudding.*

Calf's Liver with Roasted Apples, Onions and Turnips

Serves 4

2–3 tablespoons cooking oil or olive oil

flour, for dusting

4 × 175–225 g (6–8 oz) calf's liver steaks, approximately 1.5–2 cm/⅝–¾ in thick)

knob of butter

salt and pepper

For the Garnishes

12–16 button onions, peeled

cooking oil

butter

12–16 baby turnips, peeled

2 apples, peeled and each cut into 8–12 wedges, removing core

100–150 ml (3½–5 fl oz) Chicken Stock (page 201) or alternative, or water

1–2 teaspoons clear honey

squeeze of lemon juice (optional – this helps create a sweet-and-sour flavour)

salt and pepper

For the Red-wine Sauce

2 glasses of red wine

150 ml (5 fl oz) Veal or Beef *Jus* (page 203) or alternative

salt and pepper

Introduction Regular thinly sliced escalopes of liver, quickly pan-fried or grilled, will work perfectly in this dish, but a more interesting and unusual method is to roast thick 'steaks' that are first sealed and then roasted in the oven, or very gently poached in their own sauce. Once rested and carved, you have very tender and sweet, medium-rare slices. This changes the texture of the meat, adding more, I feel, to its character.

Method Make the garnishes first. Cover the button onions with cold water and bring to the boil. Cook for 2 minutes before draining the onions from the pan. Heat a tablespoon of cooking oil in a frying pan and add the onions. Cook on a medium–high heat until the onions have a rich golden brown colour with one or two burnt tinges. Add a knob of butter, reduce the temperature of the pan, and continue to fry in bubbling butter until tender. This should take only 6–8 minutes. Remove the onions and keep to one side. The turnips can be cooked in boiling, salted water for 5–6 minutes until tender. Remove from the pan, allowing their steam to release excess water; keep to one side.

The apple wedges can be placed in the chicken stock or water. Bring quickly to the boil and remove the apples immediately, saving the chicken stock. This will have taken away the apples' rawness, leaving them with a slight bite.

To finish the garnishes, heat a frying pan with a knob of butter. Quickly shallow-fry the turnips before adding the button onions, honey and lemon juice. Add 100 ml (3½ fl oz) of the stock and bring to the simmer. As this reduces, it will develop a syrupy consistency, forming a glaze around the vegetables. The apple can quickly be coloured in a hot frying pan – this will take just 30 seconds if the pan is hot enough – before adding to the onions and turnips, seasoning them with salt and pepper. Add the remaining chicken stock, if needed, to loosen the syrup. The vegetables are ready to serve.

For the liver, heat a frying pan with 2–3 tablespoons of cooking oil or olive oil. Lightly dust the liver steaks with flour, shaking off any excess, before placing them in the hot pan. You will notice I haven't seasoned the liver at this point. With raw liver, salt tends to draw the blood from the meat, leaving a burnt, bitter taste. If cooking on top of the stove, pan-fry for 3–4 minutes before turning over, adding a knob of butter before seasoning the sealed side and continuing for the same cooking time. The steaks will now be medium-rare to medium. Make sure both sides of the steaks have been seasoned. Remove from the pan and allow to rest for a minute or two before presenting on plates with the vegetables and apple, or carve into 4–5 slices before presenting.

To make the sauce, boil and reduce the red wine by three-quarters. Add the *jus* and simmer for a few minutes, checking the seasoning with salt and pepper. Strain through a tea strainer/sieve and the sauce is ready.

If you prefer to poach the livers, once seared on both sides in the pan, the steaks can be finished in the red-wine sauce. To achieve this, I suggest the quantity of sauce in the recipe is doubled.

Warm the sauce not quite to simmering point. Add the seared livers and leave at the same temperature for 7–8 minutes. This will give you a medium-rare stage. Remove the livers and rest for 1–2 minutes while the sauce is skimmed and strained through a sieve, ready to serve. The liver steaks can now be carved, if wished, before serving.

Notes: *A few tablespoons of the red-wine sauce can be reduced to a syrupy consistency to brush and shine the livers.*

Roast Rib of Beef with Steamed Savoury Red-onion Jam Roly-poly

Serves 8, generously

2–3 tablespoons cooking oil

3-bone forerib of beef, oven-ready, approximate weight 3.5 kg (8 lb), or a boned and rolled rib from the same sized cut, approximate weight 2–2.5kg (4½–5½ lb)

4 shallots, peeled and roughly chopped

2 garlic cloves, halved

fresh thyme sprig

½ bottle of red wine

300 ml (10 fl oz) Veal *Jus* (page 203) or alternative

salt and pepper

For the Red-onion Jam

knob of butter

450 g (1 lb) red onions, finely chopped

25 g (1 oz) demerara sugar

100 ml (3½ fl oz) red-wine vinegar

300 ml (10 fl oz) red wine

salt and pepper

For the Suet Pastry

225 g (8 oz) self-raising flour

1 teaspoon baking powder

pinch of salt

100 g (4 oz) beef suet

100–150 ml (3–5 fl oz) milk or water

Introduction The roast rib of beef recipe is from *New British Classics*, and, if followed meticulously, the beef will be cooked to your liking every time. But the accompaniment is completely different. Jam roly-poly is a favourite British pudding, the jam steaming into the suet roll as the 'sponge' begins to soufflé and lighten. Here, though, I'm making a savoury version, which works in exactly the same way, but with a rich red-onion jam replacing the usual strawberry jam. The red wine and vinegar in the onion jam not only help the onions but, at the same time, complement the red-wine-flavoured gravy accompanying the beef. The idea is that the suet roll can replace the traditional Yorkshire pudding; I know the latter is a long-time favourite, but there's certainly no harm in trying something new. The gravy is absorbed quite quickly by the suet sponge, which makes it even more enjoyable to eat.

Always choose good Scottish beef: the best part of the rib to buy for roasting is the forerib. When buying on the bone (if allowed), you want three ribs, which will weigh approximately 3.5 kg (8 lb), including bones. The same rib piece can be bought off the bone. Buy it 'oven-ready' (this means the beef will be chined, leaving the rib bones just attached; any bone trimmings can be kept to roast the meat on).

Method For the red-onion jam, melt a knob of butter in a saucepan and add the chopped red onions, cooking for a few minutes without colouring until they begin to soften. Add the sugar and red-wine vinegar and boil until almost dry. Add the red wine and return to the boil, also reducing until just moist. Season with salt and pepper. Remove from the stove and leave to cool. This can be made several days in advance, keeping refrigerated.

To make the suet pastry, sift together the self-raising flour, baking powder and pinch of salt. Add the suet and work to a breadcrumb consistency. The milk or water can now be added a little at a time, until a soft texture has formed, not allowing it to become sticky. Wrap in cling film and rest for 30 minutes.

The suet dough can now be rolled into a rectangle, approximately 30 × 20 cm (12 × 8 in). Spread the red-onion jam on the pastry, leaving a clear1 cm (½ in) border. Brush the border with water or milk, then roll into a cylinder from the long side, pinching at either end to seal the jam inside. The roly-poly can now be wrapped very loosely in greaseproof paper, followed by loose foil. Tie at either end.

Steam the pudding for 1½–2 hours, topping up with water during the cooking time. (Make sure you calculate the beef cooking time first. The joint suggested here needs 2 hours plus a good 20–30 minutes' resting time, so don't start steaming the pudding too soon.)

To cook the beef, pre-heat the oven to 190°C/375°F/Gas 5. Heat a roasting pan with 2–3 tablespoons of cooking oil. Season the beef rib generously with salt and pepper. Place in the hot pan and colour and seal on all sides. Any bone trimmings, if available, can now be placed in the pan, sitting the beef on top. Roast in the pre-heated oven, allowing 15 minutes per 450 g (1 lb) whether on or off the bone, for a medium-rare finish.

It is important to baste the beef every 15 minutes, to ensure all-round flavour and seasoning. Halfway through the cooking time, turn the joint over, sprinkling the shallots, garlic and thyme around the pan.

Once the cooking time is complete, remove the beef from the oven and roasting pan. Cover with foil and leave to rest for 20–30 minutes before carving.

Pour any excess fat from the roasting pan, leaving in the shallots, garlic and thyme, which will have collected a lot of beef juices as flavour. Heat the pan on top of the stove and add a third of the wine. This will instantly lift the residue from the pan. Reduce until almost dry. Add another third of the wine, also boiling and reducing until almost dry. Repeat this process with the remaining wine. Add the *jus* and return to the simmer. Cook for 5–10 minutes before pushing through a sieve, extracting the juices from the shallots, garlic and thyme. The red-wine gravy is now ready. Adjust the seasoning with salt and pepper.

So now the roast beef and red-onion roly-poly are ready to carve and serve together. The roly-poly can be cut into one thick or two thinner slices, and the same with the beef. A good sprig of watercress will be a nice garnish on the plate. For potato and vegetable accompaniments, I suggest the Mousseline Mashed Potatoes or Baked Mashed Potatoes (*Pommes Macaire*), page 142 or 141 (although the suet can replace potatoes), along with Red-wine Baby Carrots (page 150), Roast (or Braised) Onions (page 144) and English Spinach (page 142).

Note: *Chicken or beef stock or water can be used in place of the jus to create the gravy. A sprinkling of flour in the roasting pan before adding the liquor will help to thicken the sauce.*

If a large steamer for the roly-poly is available, cut the latter into two and steam together in the same pan.

Hotchpot

Serves at least 6

1 kg (2¼ lb) brisket of beef, unrolled and trimmed

2 large onions, quartered

few black peppercorns

2 bay leaves

fresh thyme sprig

2 garlic cloves

zest from ½ orange

1 kg (2¼ lb) shank of lamb (half leg)

1 kg (2¼ lb) boned and rolled hand or chump of pork

cooking oil

6 whole potatoes, peeled

6 medium turnips, peeled

6 large carrots, peeled

1–2 glasses of red wine (optional)

1 tablespoon chopped fresh flatleaf parsley

knob of butter (optional)

150 ml (5 fl oz) Veal or Beef *Jus* (page 203) or alternative, for glazing (optional)

salt and pepper

For the Cabbage

1 medium savoy cabbage, cut into 6 wedges

butter

salt and black pepper

4 tablespoons crème fraîche (optional)

Introduction 'Hotchpot, 'hotch-potch' or 'hodge-podge', as it's variously known, is a British stew of mixed meats dating back to the sixteenth century. The name is derived from the French *hocher*, to shake about, and the stew itself can be compared to the Italian *bollito misto*, the Spanish *cocido*, and many French dishes, among them *cassoulet*. All the meats and vegetables are braised under one roof, creating a strong broth to serve with the finished results.

We are using three large joints, one each of beef, lamb and pork, and the vegetables include whole potatoes, carrots and turnips, with steamed peppered cabbage wedges served separately. This recipe is in keeping with its traditions, which makes it quite an awesome dish to take on – awesome only in its pure size, as the cooking needs very little help. A complete meal, all cooked in one pot. The beef joint, brisket, comes from the belly and is superb for boiling or pot-roasting. It usually comes boned and rolled, which I dislike as it tends to tie in the salt content (most brisket comes salted), so with this recipe it comes unrolled. For the lamb, I'd use a shank, a joint from the end of the leg, but you may find you need a half leg to guarantee enough meat for all. As for the pork, two cuts of meat can be chosen, from almost opposite ends of the carcass. One is a boned and rolled hand, taken from the front leg; the other is a boned and rolled chump, a cut from which pork chops are taken, which is next to the back leg.

It's important to remember a large saucepan or braising pan will be needed. A large deep roasting tray could also be used. The meats can be cooked on top of the stove or in the oven, but there is no way of rushing this dish: the liquor should barely murmur, treating each piece of meat with the respect it deserves. The complete dish will take between 4 and 5 hours, with different items added to the pot as the cooking progresses.

Method Place the brisket in a saucepan of cold water and bring to the boil. Cook for 2 minutes before removing from the stove and rinsing under cold water. This will remove any excess salt content. Place in a large suitable pot and cover with water, adding the onion quarters, peppercorns, bay leaves, thyme, garlic and orange zest. Bring to a very gentle simmer, cover with a lid and cook with a slight murmur of movement on top of the stove, or in a pre-heated oven (170°/325°F/Gas 3) for 1 hour.

While the beef is cooking, season both the lamb and pork, These can now be coloured separately in cooking oil on top of the stove. It's important to give them a really roasted flavour and look, so cook only on a medium heat, not allowing them to overcolour too quickly. It can take 20–30 minutes to colour all around. Add both of these joints to the same pot. They will not be totally submerged: this is a pot-roasting method. Continue to cook for a further 2 hours without a lid.

Add to the pot the whole potatoes, carrots and turnips (see Notes). Replace the lid and cook for a further 1¼–1½ hours. Everything inside the pot will now be cooked and very tender. Remove the pot from the top of the stove or oven, ladling away and saving 1.2 litres (2 pints) of the cooking liquor, plus a few tablespoons for the crème fraîche butter. Replace the lid and leave the meats to relax for 20–30 minutes.

Meanwhile, make the sauce. Boil and reduce the saved stock by half, leaving a rich, flavoursome cooking liquor. (This is not essential: the cooking liquor can be strained and spooned straight over the

meats, but wine does lift its flavour.) For an even richer finish, boil and reduce the red wine, if using, by three-quarters before adding to the liquor. The butter can also be whisked in for a more velvety sauce consistency. Finish the sauce with the chopped parsley just before serving.

The *jus* is also optional, but if reduced by at least two-thirds to a sticky stage, it can be painted over the shank of lamb to give it a glossy roasted look and flavour.

While the hotchpot is cooking, the cabbage wedges can be prepared. If steamed, these will need to be cooked at the last moment, taking between 5–6 minutes in a rapid steamer. Here is an alternative method that can be prepared many hours before eating. Boil a large pan of salted water, add the wedges of cabbage and cook uncovered for 4–5 minutes until tender. Once cooked, refresh in iced water for just a minute or two. Place the drained wedges on kitchen paper or cloth to dry further. Melt a knob of butter and pour over the cabbage, allowing it to drizzle between the layers. Season with salt and plenty of black pepper, also between the layers. These can now be transferred to a serving plate, cling filmed and refrigerated until needed. To re-heat, simply microwave and the cabbage is ready to serve.

A crème fraîche butter sauce can be made to spoon over the wedges. Heat a few tablespoons of the stock or water and bring to a simmer. Whisk in 25 g (1 oz) of butter, before also whisking in the crème fraîche. Season with salt and pepper, blitzing with an electric hand blender for a smoother finish, and spoon over the cabbage before serving.

To serve the dish: the whole potatoes can be served straight from the pot. An alternative is to brush well with butter, place them on a baking tray and colour to a golden brown under a medium-hot grill. The meats can now be carved (or broken into pieces), offering a piece of each per plate. Serve with a potato, a carrot and turnip, spooning over the finished wine sauce. The cabbage wedges can be placed on the plates or presented in a serving dish.

That's a real family hotchpot you have created – worth every minute of slow cooking.

Notes: *All three meats can be placed in the pan together, adding the potatoes and vegetables 1½ hours before the end of the cooking time. The total cooking should be at least 3½–4 hours. The meats will now just carve with a spoon.*

The turnips, like the cabbage, can be cooked separately in boiling salted water to help maintain their distinctive colour. Refresh in iced water, ready to microwave, or steam or re-heat in the cooking liquor later.

Boiled Gammon and Broad Beans with a Crunchy Mustard and Marjoram Mash

Serves 4–6

1.8–2 kg (4–4½ lb) middle-cut gammon joint, soaked as in method (see introduction for number of servings)

fresh marjoram sprig

2 carrots, peeled (optional)

2–3 celery sticks (optional)

1 large onion, peeled (optional)

few black peppercorns

1 bay leaf

For the Potatoes

1 quantity Mashed Potatoes (page 142)

3 slices of white bread, crusts removed, crumbed

knob of butter

1–2 tablespoons English mustard (personal choice for strength)

1 dessertspoon picked and snipped (if large) fresh marjoram leaves

salt and pepper

For the Beans

450 g (1 lb) podded broad beans

knob of butter

salt and pepper

Introduction Fresh broad beans, ham (or gammon) and mashed potatoes go back a long way in our eating history. This is one of the longest-lasting culinary relationships we know, working together so well. I felt I just had to include this complete recipe.

The difference between ham and gammon is quite simple to explain. Ham is the hind leg of the pig, cut immediately from the carcass and salted, cured and matured over several months. Gammon, although the same cut of meat, is left on the carcass and taken through a quick curing method, finishing with a milder flavour.

The best gammon to buy is the middle cut, taken from the lean middle part of the whole leg. A good 1.8–2 kg (4–4½ lb) piece will be just perfect for this dish. Gammon is also cheaper to buy than ham, eating equally well.

Whenever purchasing gammon or ham, also remember that it should be soaked in cold water for 24 hours, changing the water at least once to help draw out the excess salt.

Green, kidney-shaped broad beans have quite a short summer season, so it's important to take advantage of this time and enjoy the fresh flavour they hold and lend to so many other tastes. I always insist on removing the grey outer skin surrounding each bean before eating. The rich green is now on show, with the beans' complete tenderness waiting to be enjoyed.

The mashed potatoes are flavoured with English mustard to provide a bite, with marjoram offering its distinctive herby edge to the complete dish. The crunch is supplied by fresh white breadcrumbs pan-fried in butter and sprinkled over the mustard and marjoram-flavoured potatoes. There is no actual sauce offered with the gammon; instead, it is served with a more natural accompaniment of reduced cooking liquor, strengthening the gammon flavour.

The piece of gammon listed is enough for 4–6 portions, with extra for second helpings, salads or sandwiches.

Method Place the soaked gammon in a saucepan, along with all of its flavouring ingredients. Bring to a gentle simmer and cook, skimming from time to time, allowing 20–25 minutes per 450 g (1 lb) of meat. Once cooked, allow to sit and rest in the stock for 20 minutes before serving.

During this resting time 600 ml–1.2 litres (1–2 pints) of the cooking liquor can be boiled and reduced by half, creating the 'sauce' to serve with the finished dish.

Prepare the mashed potatoes as described on page 142. The breadcrumbs, which can be prepared in advance, are pan-fried in butter to a crisp golden brown and can be re-warmed when needed. Before serving, stir the mustard and marjoram into the mashed potatoes and sprinkle the warm crumbs over them.

To cook the beans, bring a large pan of salted water to the boil. Remove the lid and add the broad beans; it's important the lid stays off to maintain the colour of the vegetable. Cook medium-sized beans for just 1–2 minutes, with 5 minutes being the absolute maximum. Once tender, lift from the pan and remove the skins. If serving immediately, add the butter and season with salt and pepper. If cooking in advance, plunge into iced water. Once cold, remove the skins. The beans can be microwaved to order or plunged into hot melted butter with a tablespoon or two of water. Season with salt and pepper and, once hot, serve.

Slice the gammon and serve with the potatoes, beans and a drizzle of the reduced stock. The dish, with its two accompaniments, has now become a complete meal.

Note: *The mustard and marjoram can both be excluded from the recipe; just offer simple mashed potatoes.*

Pork Cutlet Hotpot

Serves 4

4 large potatoes, peeled

450 g (1 lb) onions, sliced

1 teaspoon picked fresh marjoram leaves

400 g (14 oz) cup or button mushrooms, wiped and thickly sliced

50 g (2 oz) butter, diced

4 thick pork cutlets or chops, French trimmed (page 109)

850 ml (1½ pints) Chicken Stock (page 201) or alternative, or water (see Notes)

salt and pepper

Introduction The classic relation to this dish is, of course, the Lancashire hotpot, a cousin of the great Irish stew. Lancashire hotpot consists of lamb (using the cheaper middle neck rather than lamb cutlets) layered with onions, often mushrooms, and always potatoes. This 'tougher' cut of meat required long, slow cooking, which allowed the lamb to become tender enough to carve with a spoon. At one time a hotpot – named after the tall pot in which the stew was made – would be cooked in the cooling oven after a morning's baking, ready for the evening meal.

So why a pork hotpot? Pork is usually roasted, grilled or pan-fried, and the meat can often become 'dry' in texture. If it is slowly braised, this will not happen; instead the gentle stewing of the meat in stock with vegetables will allow it to absorb liquid and flavour and have a tender, moist finish. Pork also relies quite heavily on its fat content to help with any form of tenderizing, and this can result in a fatty cooking liquor. In a hotpot, the layered potatoes absorb this fat and take on all its rich flavours.

Method Pre-heat the oven to 180°C/350°F/Gas 4. You will need a 2.5 litre (approximately 4 pint) flameproof casserole, lightly buttered.

Cut two of the large potatoes into 5 mm (¼ in) thick slices and arrange in the base of the dish. Sprinkle over half the sliced onions, along with half the marjoram. The mushrooms can be used raw or quickly pan-fried in a knob of butter to colour slightly, giving a nutty edge to their flavour. Either way, lay half of them over the onions. Season with salt and pepper and dot with half the butter. The pork cutlets or chops can now be placed in the dish. Pour the chicken stock or water over, just covering the meat. Now repeat the layers of onions, marjoram and mushrooms, seasoning with salt and pepper. The remaining two potatoes can now be cut into 2–3 mm (⅛ in) slices and neatly arranged, overlapping, to finish the presentation of the dish. Dot with the remaining butter.

Bring the pot to the simmer, cover with a lid and place in the pre-heated oven. The hotpot can now be slowly braised for 2–2¼ hours, checking to ensure a reasonable moistness is maintained and topping with any remaining stock if needed. Once tender – this can be checked by piercing through the potato and meat with a trussing needle or thin, sharp knife – remove the lid, increase the oven temperature to 200°C/400°F/Gas 6 and continue to bake for 30–40 minutes until the potatoes have achieved a golden brown finish.

The hotpot can now be served; however, I prefer to remove it from the oven, cover it again and allow it to relax.

After a resting time of 10–15 minutes, the cutlets will be at their best for eating. The potatoes, onions and mushrooms will all have taken on the flavour of the stock, the potatoes thickening the cooking liquor and becoming almost puréed at the base of the dish. Although it has a very simple plain finish, this dish is packed with flavours.

For a vegetable accompaniment, I suggest English Spinach (page 142) or Nutmeg Spring Greens (page 154). Both of these offer the right flavour, carrying the bonus of a good distinctive colour to help with the final presentation.

Notes: *Thick slices of boned pork loin can be used in place of the chops, giving you more space in the dish.*

Chicken stock or water has been listed as the cooking liquor. Water will take on the flavour from the pork and vegetables but will not hold the strength of the chicken stock. A good-quality stock cube (half a cube will be sufficient) can be used. Another alternative is to use one tin of condensed chicken consommé and add water to make up the quantity.

Roast and Poached Beef Fillets with Guinness Onions, Crispy Bacon and Butter-fried Carrots

Serves 4

knob of beef dripping or cooking oil

4 × 175 g (6 oz) fillet steaks

salt and pepper

For the Onions

knob of butter

5 large onions, sliced

25 g (1 oz) demerara sugar

300 ml (10 fl oz) Guinness

9 rashers of rindless streaky bacon

1 garlic clove

few black peppercorns

1 bay leaf

400 ml (14 fl oz) Veal or Beef *Jus* (page 203) or alternative

200 ml (7 fl oz) Chicken Stock (page 201) or alternative, or water

salt and pepper

For the Carrots

8–12 medium carrots, peeled

pinch of salt

pinch of sugar

knob of butter

salt and pepper

Introduction Beef cooked in beer has been popular in Europe for centuries, but this recipe turns the dish into a new twenty-first-century classic. The first part of the beef fillets' cooking process happens on top of the stove, the meat seared in a hot pan to give a 'roasted' flavour. The fillets are then gently poached in the Guinness and onion sauce, which cooks and tenderizes the meat.

Method Melt a knob of butter in a frying pan and add the onions. With this quantity, it may be best to cook in 2–3 batches. Allow the onions to fry rapidly, taking on a deep colour with tinges of burnt while becoming tender. As onions cook, the natural sugar content almost caramelizes. English onions generally give the best results. Once all are fried, place in one pan, adding the sugar and seasoning with salt and pepper. Continue to cook the onions until the sugar has dissolved into them. Add a third of the Guinness and bring to a rapid simmer, cooking and reducing until almost dry. Three-quarters of the onions can be removed from the pan and kept to one side.

To the remaining quarter of onions add one chopped rasher of bacon, the garlic, peppercorns and bay leaf, continuing to cook for a few minutes before adding the remaining Guinness. Bring to the boil and reduce by three-quarters before adding the *jus* and stock. Bring to the simmer and cook for 10–15 minutes on a gentle heat. The cooking liquor/sauce is now ready to use.

Grill the remaining rashers of bacon until crispy, as described on page 64.

To cook the carrots, place them in a saucepan with enough water just to cover, adding the salt and sugar. Bring to the simmer before covering with a lid and cooking for approximately 15 minutes, until tender. Drain into a colander.

Heat a frying pan or saucepan with a knob of butter. Once bubbling, add the carrots and pan-fry on a medium heat, allowing them to take on a golden edge. Season with salt and pepper and the carrots are ready.

To cook the fillet steaks, heat a large frying-pan. Once hot, add a knob of beef dripping or cooking oil. Season the fillets with salt and pepper and pan fry, colouring well on all sides. Transfer the steaks to the cooking liquor. It's important that this, although hot, is not even at simmering point. It's quite a fine line, but if simmering, the steaks take on a boiled texture, rather than poached.

Cook for 7–8 minutes for medium-rare, adding an extra 2–3 minutes for every next stage preferred. Remove the steaks from the liquor and keep warm, allowing them to relax for 4–5 minutes. Bring the liquor to the boil, skimming away any impurities, and quickly reduce to a sauce consistency before straining through a sieve.

For a shiny finish to the steaks, place them back in the pan with a few tablespoons of this sauce. Cook on a high heat for a minute or two, reducing the sauce to a syrup. Turn the steaks in the sauce and they will have a very shiny look. Re-heat the Guinness onions, dividing them between plates or bowls. Place the steaks on top of each pile of onions, topping with two strips of bacon per portion. The carrots can now also be plated with the beef, offering the sauce separately.

Note: *A scroll of soured cream can be placed on top of the beef fillets before serving. The sour flavour eats well with the bitter-sweet onions.*

Layered Mushroom and Onion Suet Pudding with 'Truffle' Cream Sauce

Serves 4–6

For the Suet Pastry

300 g (10 oz) self-raising flour

150 g (5 oz) shredded vegetarian suet

200 ml (7 fl oz) water

pinch of salt

For the Filling

4–6 large onions, depending on size, sliced

50 g (2 oz) butter

1 dessertspoon demerara sugar

8–10 large flat mushrooms, preferably 7–12 cm (3–4½ in) diameter), stalks removed (these can be used in the sauce reduction)

olive oil

1 teaspoon lemon thyme leaves, picked and chopped

salt and pepper

For the 'Truffle' Sauce

large knob of butter

4 large shallots or 1 onion, finely sliced

juice of ½ lemon

175 g (6 oz) button mushrooms, finely sliced

300 ml (10 fl oz) Noilly Prat

300 ml (10 fl oz) white wine, preferably Gewürztraminer

150 ml (5 fl oz) double cream

salt and pepper

Introduction After making (now several times) the layered steak and onion pudding from *New British Classics*, I was inspired to create a vegetarian version, and that's exactly what I have for you here. A vegetarian suet dough is used to line a 1.2 litre (2 pint) pudding basin (preferably plastic), then onions and large flat mushrooms – these becoming the 'meat' of the dish – are layered in, along with a touch of lemon thyme. After 1½ hours of steaming, the mushrooms and onions have braised in their own liquor, spreading flavours from one to the other. The truffle sauce doesn't actually contain any truffle, but the combination of flavours working together in it creates more than a hint of truffle. To guarantee real truffle flavours, a few drops of truffle oil can be sprinkled on top just before serving.

Method First make the pastry. Sieve the flour and salt together into a mixing bowl. Add the suet, breaking it into the flour as it is mixed in. Stir in the water to form a fairly firm dough. Wrap in cling film and allow to rest for 20 minutes.

The pastry is now ready to use. Lightly flour your work-surface and roll out the pastry to a circle about 0.5–1 cm (¼–½ in) thick. Cut a one-third triangular wedge and from this cut a circle using the pudding basin top. This circle forms a lid for the pudding. Lift the remaining two-thirds of pastry and shape into a cone. Fit it into the pudding basin, leaving 1–2 cm (½–½ in) hanging over the edge. (When the basin has been filled, this can be folded in to create a border base to sit the lid on.)

To make the filling, the onions can be fried in batches in the butter. It's important to fry them well, allowing the onions almost to burn in parts; this will create a natural bitter caramelizing. As each 'lot' comes to that stage, season with salt and pepper, adding a sprinkling of the sugar for a slightly sweet finish. Leave to cool.

Rather than washing the mushrooms, wipe them clean with a damp cloth. Heat a large frying pan with a drop of olive oil. Season the mushrooms with salt and pepper and sear very quickly in the oil to colour a deep golden brown. This will need to be carried out with just 2–3 mushrooms at a time, due to their size, maintaining the heat in the pan. Once all are coloured, leave to cool.

Add the lemon thyme to the fried onions just before filling the basin. Spoon some onions into the basin before topping with one of the mushrooms. Add more onions, spreading them across the mushroom to achieve even layers. Repeat the same process until all the onions and mushrooms have been used (two mushrooms per layer may be needed towards the top of the basin). The filling has come above the pudding mould into a dome shape. Brush the hanging edges with water and fold in. Top with the pastry lid. (Alternatively, sit the lid directly on top of the filling, moisten the edge with water, then fold the border in to secure the base.)

Cover with buttered and floured foil, wrapping around the edge of the basin. The pudding can now be cooked in a steamer (or colander inside a large saucepan) for 1½ hours.

Meanwhile, make the sauce. Melt the knob of butter in a saucepan and, once bubbling, add the sliced shallots/onion. Cook without colouring for a few minutes, until beginning to soften. Squeeze the lemon juice over the mushrooms before adding them to the pan. Continue to cook for a few minutes until the mushrooms have also softened. Add the Noilly Prat and white wine and bring to the simmer. Cook to reduce by half. The double cream can now be added and cooked into the reduction for a few minutes before removing from the heat and straining through a sieve.

This is a very important stage. The juice must be completely squeezed from the shallots and mushrooms so that every last drop of juice and flavour is extracted. Season the sauce with salt and pepper. The taste now has an amazing truffle edge.

Once cooked, remove the pudding from the steamer and leave to rest for 10–15 minutes before turning out.

The sauce can be offered separately, or, for a lighter finish, blitz with an electric hand blender to a frothy 'milkshake' stage. Spoon over the pudding, just rolling down the sides like a soft waterfall.

The pudding is now ready to be cut and served, revealing the 'meaty' mushroom and onion layers.

Notes: *Whichever basin you use, it must always be well buttered. Heatproof plastic bowls work perfectly with steamed puddings. Butter well and, when cooked, just invert, squeeze and the pudding will fall out – gently.*

The sauce can be loosened with 150 ml (5 fl oz) vegetable stock, adding it once the wines have reduced. Continue as per the recipe. This loosening will result in a greater yield.

vegetables

Baked Mashed Potatoes (*Pommes Macaire*)

Serves 4

900 g (2 lb) large baking potatoes

75 g (3 oz) butter

cooking oil

salt and pepper

Introduction *Pommes macaire* is a French classic, one of the recipes published by Auguste Escoffier (executive chef at the Savoy Hotel in the early 1900s). Endless potato dishes were created at this time. Escoffier's version fries the flesh of a baked potato in butter and seasonings, then piles it back into the skin. Other versions fry the potato flesh as a sort of potato cake. Mine is a little more elaborate, baking the potato mixture in a mould.

This potato dish has many advantages. It can be made well in advance, just waiting to be baked when needed, and endless additions – onion, garlic, herbs and so on – are possible.

Method Pre-heat the oven to 200°C/400°F/Gas 6. Place the potatoes on a baking tray and cook in the pre-heated oven for approximately 1 hour, turning them halfway through the cooking time. Check for readiness by gently squeezing each in a cloth: once slightly 'giving' and feeling tender, remove from the oven.

Split lengthways, scooping all the potato from the centre. Season with salt and pepper, mashing as lightly as possible with a fork. Add the butter and the potatoes are ready for moulding.

Individual *macaires* can be made or a single large one. Classically, they are pressed into a copper 'anna' mould. This is a round metal dish with straight 6 cm (2¼ in) deep sides. Cake rings can also be used, or an ovenproof vegetable dish brushed with butter. With the latter, it's best to finish the baked dish with lots of grated cheese on top and gratinate under a hot grill.

I prefer to use one 12–15 cm (5–6 in) metal ring. For this, heat a suitable non-stick ovenproof frying pan with 2 tablespoons of cooking oil. Once warmed, remove from the heat. Butter the metal ring and place in the heated frying pan. Spoon the potatoes into the ring, smoothing the top. Return to the heat and pan-fry for a few minutes until a golden-brown, crisp base is forming. Brush with butter and place in the oven, increasing the temperature to 230°C/450°F/Gas 8. Bake for 20–25 minutes.

Remove from the oven and rest for 5 minutes before placing a serving plate on top and turning the pan over. The golden-brown *macaire* potatoes are now ready to serve. Before presenting, a knob of butter melting on top along with a sprig of curly parsley gives you a real classic finish.

Notes: *It's not essential to turn the potatoes out of the ring: simply transfer to a serving plate with a fish slice and lift away the mould. The potatoes can now be coloured under a hot grill or topped with lots of grated Cheddar cheese (one of my favourite versions) and garnished as above. (Try adding some shredded spring onions to the cheese.)*

For a golden glaze on top of the cheese, spoon 3–4 tablespoons of double cream over. This will create an almost sauce-like glaze to the dish.

Once mashed and moulded, the potato cake can be refrigerated until you're ready to pan-fry and bake it when needed.

This dish is a good accompaniment to roast dishes, and goes well with Chicken Sauté with Mushrooms and Tarragon (page 120), Braised Pork 'Daube' with Parsnip and Bramley Apple Purée (page 125), Boneless Potato Oxtail (page 102) and Steak and Kidney Sausages (page 98).

Mashed or Mousseline Mashed Potatoes

Serves 4–6

900 g (2 lb) large floury potatoes, preferably Maris Piper, peeled and quartered

75–100 g (3–4 oz) unsalted butter

100 ml (3½ fl oz) milk

salt, pepper and freshly grated nutmeg

For Mousseline Mashed Potatoes

100–150 ml (3½–5 fl oz) whipping cream

Introduction I don't think I've written a book yet without including mashed potatoes, and I don't think I ever will. It's probably my favourite potato dish of all time, although another that I like to make regularly at home is simply boiled potatoes, finished with an 'Irish' touch. The potatoes are quartered, boiled to tender, then drained in a colander, covered with a tea towel and left to rest for 5 minutes before shaking slightly, to crumble the edges. A sprinkling of salt and butter melting on top, and you have an amazing potato experience.

The first stage of this recipe is a simple mash, then it is followed by the *mousseline*, a French influence. The potatoes are finished with whipped cream, providing a soft lightness that no other mashed potato recipe can bring you. This eats beautifully with almost any of the main-course dishes.

Method Boil the potatoes in salted water until tender, approximately 20–25 minutes, depending on size. Drain off all the water and replace the lid. Shake the pan vigorously, which will start to break up the boiled potatoes. Add the butter and milk, a little at a time, while mashing the potatoes. Season with salt and pepper and some freshly grated nutmeg, according to taste. The mashed potatoes are now ready to eat.

Note: *For creamier mashed potatoes, add 75–100 ml (2–3½ fl oz) of warmed whipping (or single) cream.*

Mousseline Mashed Potatoes

Lightly whip 100 ml (3½ fl oz) of the cream to a soft peak, then fold into the hot potatoes; this will lighten the texture, giving a very soft and creamy finish. Check the seasoning. For even lighter potato, whip the remaining cream and fold in.

English Spinach

Serves 4

900 g (2 lb) spinach

25 g (1 oz) butter

salt, pepper and freshly grated nutmeg

Introduction Spinach is probably every chef's favourite vegetable as it is so versatile, lending its delicate texture and slight bitter-sweetness to almost any dish. However, when spinach is cooked, it reduces in volume by at least half. So for every portion as a vegetable, you will need 225 g (8 oz) of the raw item.

Home-grown spinach has a very mixed season. The best times to enjoy this vegetable are during May and June, September and October. In July and August the leaves are weak in texture and flavour.

When buying, look for a crisp and bouncy leaf, with a very deep green colour, all of which will guarantee success in those few minutes of buttery bubbling.

People often ask why nutmeg is so frequently associated with spinach. From the sixteenth to the eighteenth century, spinach was often served in a sweet tart flavoured with many spices, one of which was nutmeg. Obviously, old friendships never die.

Method Discard any bruised spinach leaves and remove the central stalks. To wash, gently turn the leaves through a bowl of cold water and drain in a colander, repeating this process at least twice more. This will remove any fine grit deposited by rainfall. Now leave the picked leaves to drain.

When ready to cook, melt the butter in a large saucepan and, once bubbling, add the spinach. Cook on a medium-high heat, drawing the excess water from the leaves, which, in turn, will create a cooking steam. Stir with a spatula for a minute or two, season with salt, pepper and nutmeg before draining in a colander and serving.

Note: *The butter and seasonings can be omitted, and the washed leaves cooked on a slightly reduced heat. The spinach water will steam the vegetable, leaving a totally natural flavour.*

Sautéd Butternut Squash

Serves 4

1 small butternut squash

olive oil

flour, for dusting (optional)

25 g (1 oz) butter

salt and pepper

Introduction Almost any form of squash can be used in this recipe, and there is a huge variety now available to us, imported from all over the world. Pumpkin would be good, as would onion squash, Kabocha and other winter varieties. These are the squashes that are left to mature; their skins harden and become inedible, but the flesh acquires good flavour. Summer squashes, such as marrow and courgette, can be used as well, and do not usually need to be peeled. Butternut squash will lend itself to most cooking techniques, particularly roasting, grilling and sautéing or pan-frying.

Method Split the squash lengthways, then cut each half into 2–3 cm (¾–1¼ in) wedges. Remove all the seeds and use a sharp knife to remove the skin as you would from a wedge of melon. Each strip can now be divided into chunks also 2–3 cm (¾–1¼ in) thick.

Heat a large frying pan or wok with a tablespoon of the olive oil. For a crisper edge, the butternut pieces can be lightly rolled in the flour. Fry a suitable quantity of the pieces on a medium–hot heat, allowing the wedges to colour to a golden brown and become tender. Remove from the pan and keep to one side. Repeat the same process until all have been fried.

To finish, melt the butter in the frying pan (an extra 25 g/1 oz can be added for a richer finish), returning all the sautéd butternut. Season with salt and pepper and turn in the pan to give the vegetable a buttery finish.

Note: *Other flavours can also be added. Try the following:*

- *chopped, toasted pine nuts*
- *fresh breadcrumbs*
- *chopped fresh parsley or mixed herbs.*

Roast (or Braised) Onions

Serves 4

8–12 medium onions, unpeeled

butter

salt and pepper

Introduction Probably the oldest vegetable known to mankind, the onion has a place in every type of cuisine throughout the world. There are many types, and close relations include shallots, leeks and garlic. Many onions can be eaten raw, but it is in cooking that their pungency and natural sweetness is most appreciated. Onions were introduced to Britain by the Romans, and have been valued ever since – as a pot-herb, as a basis for a soup, or as an ingredient in other dishes. Rarely are they cooked by themselves, but as a complete vegetable, they are probably one of the cheapest to produce. And if slowly cooked, they are certainly one of the tastiest, holding natural sugars that caramelize so well. Roast onions can be cooked in or out of the skin. Here I give both options, along with a braising method as well.

Method Pre-heat the oven to 200°C/400°F/Gas 4.

There are two options with this dish: the onions can first be boiled for 10 minutes, removed from the water and wiped dry before being placed in a roasting tray and cooked in the oven for 1–1½ hours. Alternatively, the raw onions can be placed in the tray and roasted for 2½ hours. Once cooked, remove from the oven and serve. It's almost like eating an onion pie: the skin comes away to reveal the most tender of fillings. Add butter, season with salt and pepper and they are ready to enjoy.

To roast peeled onions, boil for 5 minutes before draining and drying. Melt a knob of butter in a roasting tray or frying pan and colour the tops only. Lightly season with salt.

These can now be roasted, coloured-side up, in the pre-heated oven, for 40–45 minutes; they will eat at their best if cooked around a roast joint, the onions collecting a lot of its juices and flavour.

Note: *Each onion can be wrapped in foil. This steams rather than roasts them, but does work well.*

Braised Onions

2–3 medium onions per portion

25 g (1 oz) butter

300 ml (10 fl oz) Chicken or Vegetable Stock (page 201 or 204) or alternative

salt and pepper

Method Pre-heat the oven to 200°C/400°F/Gas 6. Peel the onions. Melt the butter in a roasting tray or shallow braising dish. Once bubbling, colour the onions on top, presentation-side only, until deep golden brown. Turn the onions over and season with salt and pepper. Pour the stock into the pan, place in the pre-heated oven and braise for 35–40 minutes, until tender. These can now be kept warm in the stock until ready to serve.

Before serving, lift the onions from the tray, boiling and reducing the liquor to an almost syrup-like consistency. Roll the onions in the syrup or gently brush to finish with a rich glaze.

'Braised' Blue Cheese Leeks

Serves 4

4 medium leeks or 8–12 small baby leeks

25 g (1 oz) butter

75–100 ml (2–3½ fl oz) single cream

50–75 g (2–3 oz) blue cheese e.g. Stilton, Cashel blue, crumbled

salt and pepper

Introduction The leek, the poor man's asparagus, is a member of the onion family. It has an amazingly long history, as leeks were grown by the ancient Egyptians. Over the centuries since then, leeks became recognized and appreciated throughout Europe and Asia. In Britain it is viewed more as a pot-herb, a vegetable useful only in soups and stews, but it has returned in the last 50 years to its true position as a fine vegetable in its own right.

Leeks and cheese make a tasty combination, especially if you use Cheddar, Parmesan or Swiss cheese. In this recipe I'm using a blue cheese, with Stilton or the Irish Cashel blue as first choice, but Roquefort or Gorgonzola following quite closely behind. Although the recipe title uses the word 'braised', over-cooking leeks, as long braising would do, gives them a very 'stewy', stale flavour, and texture is lost. The leeks here will look as if they have been braised, but will carry the freshest of flavours.

Method Split the leeks lengthways, keeping the base intact, and wash well. If using baby leeks, keep them whole. The outside 'leaf' is best removed, as this is usually too stringy. Boil a large saucepan of salted water, add the leeks and cook until tender. Depending on their size, this will take 2–5 minutes. Once tender, drain and use a cloth to carefully squeeze away any excess water. If you wish to have the leeks prepared well in advance, refresh in iced water before drying. Now the leeks can have the root base cut away (this has kept the vegetable together during its boiling). Brush with butter and season with salt and pepper. (If the leeks are refreshed, butter and season them ready to be microwaved or baked when needed.) To give the leeks some colour, place them in an ovenproof vegetable dish, alternating the white and green. Place under a pre-heated grill and colour to a gentle golden brown on top only. (This step is not essential.)

While colouring, warm the single cream in a saucepan. Add 50 g (2 oz) of the blue cheese and allow to soften. Take care not to overheat the mixture; if boiled, the oils from the cheese will completely separate. Taste for strength: if you prefer a stronger flavour, add the remaining cheese. With the leeks looking braised, having a tinge of golden brown, pour the blue cheese cream across and serve.

Note: *The crumbled blue cheese can be melted over the leeks, simply finishing with a drizzle of warm single cream.*

Serving the leeks straight from the boiling pot, without colouring under the grill, will maintain their rich green and white colours.

The leeks eat very well surrounded by chopped walnuts and parsley, tossed in Nut-brown Butter (page 33) and finished with a squeeze of lemon juice.

Jersey Royals – the Richest New Potato

Serves 4–6

900 g (2 lb) Jersey Royal potatoes or other new potatoes

50 g (2 oz) butter

salt

1 tablespoon chopped fresh flatleaf or curly parsley (optional)

Introduction Jersey Royals are a relatively 'new' new potato, first appearing around 1880. The man responsible was a Jersey farmer, Hugh de la Haye. The story goes that he bought a large seed potato with 16 eyes or sprouts, cut each one out, and planted them in the rich Jersey soil. The result of this little experiment was one of pure pleasure, a crop of tiny, early, kidney-shaped potatoes with a dense, earthy flavour, and a texture not overly waxy. It was a completely new experience in the potato world, thus earning the name of 'Royal Jersey Fluke' (later shortened to Jersey Royal).

Another bonus of these small tubers is that their early harvest means the skins are not set, so they need no peeling, just washing. It's the skin that helps give this potato such a distinctive flavour (perhaps something to do with the seaweed used to fertilize the fields).

The first Jerseys in May are extremely expensive, and they reach their peak in and around August, when size and flavour have both matured to perfection. This recipe is simplicity itself, and treats Royals exactly as they should be – with nothing but honour and respect.

Method Wash and scrub the potatoes under running water rather than sitting them in it so that the tubers do not absorb it. New potatoes should always be cooked in boiling, salted water. Once the Jerseys have been added, return to the boil and cook until tender. Depending on the size of the potatoes, this should take 20–25 minutes. Drain the water from the pan and, if needing to keep them warm before serving, cover with a cloth rather than a lid. This will absorb the steam, retaining the heat, and prevent the steam from condensing and over-moisturizing the potato flesh. Instead, a fluffy, dry, rich filling will be found.

When ready to serve, add the butter, rolling the potatoes to coat, and sprinkle with salt and chopped parsley (if using). Everything this new potato claims to be is there, just waiting to be enjoyed.

Note: *Jersey Royals make a wonderful, warm, sour potato salad. Once cooked, split in half while still warm, season with salt and pepper, add a few tablespoons of soured cream along with a squeeze of lemon juice and 2 tablespoons of chopped fresh chives. The salad is ready to eat.*

Celery with Apples and Walnuts

Serves 4

8 celery sticks (approximately 1 small head)

2 Cox's Orange Pippin apples (Golden Delicious or the sharper Granny Smith can also be used)

1 dessertspoon groundnut oil or walnut oil

25 g (1 oz) butter

8–10 shelled walnut halves, preferably peeled (see introduction) and quartered

1 teaspoon chopped fresh flatleaf parsley

salt and pepper

Introduction The classic combination of flavours here – celery, apples and walnuts – usually comes together in Britain to partner cheese, but here it's offered as a stir-fry vegetable accompaniment. It works very well with roast chicken (page 117), other poultry or game dishes, and pork and veal.

Celery, as we know and buy it today, didn't really appear until the seventeenth and eighteenth centuries, developed by the Italians from wild celery or 'smallage'. Today we have three main types – green, white and celeriac. The green and white are basically the same, but the white is grown out of the light – blanched under polythene or in trenches – to sweeten the rather aggressive flavour. Celeriac is similar in flavour to celery, if more subtle. It is the enlarged base stem, an almost turnip shape, which is eaten, rather than the shoots. Texturally, it is totally different, and makes wonderful soups, and can be puréed, roasted, sautéd or simply grated for salads.

Skinning the walnut halves is not essential but does take away their slight bitterness. Simply cook the nuts in boiling water for 3 minutes, then remove the pan from the heat. Leave them in the hot water, removing just one at a time and scraping while still warm. This takes just a few minutes, leaving you with a more tender component to the dish.

Method Scrub and wash the celery sticks before removing the strings from each. Cut the sticks at an acute angle to make pointed pieces 5–7 cm (2–3 in) long and 2.5 cm (1 in) thick. These pieces can now be cooked in boiling salted water for 2–3 minutes, until tender. Once cooked, drain and keep to one side.

Peel the apples, cutting each into 10–12 wedges and removing the core with a sharp knife. It's best, at this stage, to dry the apple pieces lightly with kitchen paper; this will prevent over-stewing during the cooking process.

Heat a frying pan or wok with the oil. Once hot, add the apple pieces and allow to fry and colour. As this process takes place, the fruits will become tender but retain a slight bite. Now it's time to add the butter, along with the celery. Season with salt and pepper and continue to 'stir-fry' until the celery is heated through, but keeping its natural whiteness. To finish, add the walnuts and chopped parsley.

Note: *At the end of the stir-frying, a good squeeze of lemon juice, a tablespoon of water and a further 25 g (1 oz) of butter can be added to create a butter-sauce finish.*

Slowly Caramelized Lemon Chicory

Serves 4–6

50 g (2 oz) butter

6 chicory heads, halved lengthways and bruised outer leaves removed

a generous pinch of caster sugar

2 tablespoons water

2 tablespoons lemon juice

salt and pepper

Introduction Chicory comes in many colours, shapes and bitter flavours. The predominant three are the curly green endive (more a lettuce than chicory), the Italian red radicchio (used in salads, but braises well too), and the Belgian chicory (eaten raw and braised). This last-named chicory, which is the one to use here, is a firm, cigar-shaped vegetable, white with tinges of yellow at the point (hence the Belgian name *witloof*, meaning 'white leaf'). The story goes that this variety was accidentally discovered by a Belgian grower in 1850. He buried some chicory roots from the salad bed under a deep covering of soil in his cellar, and then noticed that in the warmth and darkness white shoots had begun to appear. These he cut and ate, and a new vegetable – and a new business – was born. When purchasing chicory heads, or 'chicons', you'll often find them wrapped in blue paper; this continues to protect them from light, which encourages bitterness.

The recipe here is very simple to follow, but does take at least 2½ hours to cook. After pan-frying, the chicory heads are slowly braised in a little water and lemon juice, naturally caramelizing, until they are soft and tender throughout. The flavours created work very well as an accompaniment to many of the fish and main-course dishes featured in the book. The chicory is wonderful as a vegetable alone, but you can also purée it to add to Sauce Béarnaise (see Note and page 205).

Method Pre-heat the oven to 150°C/300°F/Gas 2. Melt the butter in a large ovenproof dish. Lay the chicory halves, flat-side down, in the dish with the butter. Cook slowly on a low heat until they have become well coloured, giving a natural caramelized colour. This will take at least 20 minutes. Turn over, increasing the heat, and quickly colour, before turning back on the flat side.

Sprinkle with the sugar. Add the water and lemon juice, before covering with a lid and braising in the pre-heated oven. The chicory will now slowly cook and caramelize for 2–2½ hours, becoming cooked through with a sweet lemon finish. The vegetable becomes so tender it can be carved with a spoon. Season with salt and pepper before serving.

Note: *If following this recipe to provide a purée for Sauce Béarnaise (page 205), the recipe can be halved. Once cooked, place in a sieve to extract excess juices; these are best boiled and reduced to a syrupy consistency. Purée the chicory in a liquidizer, then stir into the Béarnaise sauce. For extra flavour, add a few drops of the chicory syrup to the purée.*

Nutmeg Spring Greens

Serves 4

675 g (1½ lb) spring greens

25 g (1 oz) butter

75 g (3 oz) shallots or onions, sliced

¼ teaspoon freshly grated nutmeg

salt and pepper

Introduction Spring greens are basically young cabbage, with open leaves and a central heart only just beginning to form. Consequently, they have a savoury sweetness with just a hint of bitterness following. Nutmeg is the spice I've used in the English Spinach dish on page 142, but, in this recipe, it gives a slightly different taste. With the spinach the nutmeg is added at the very end of cooking; here, with the spring greens, I'm adding the spice at the beginning, cooking it with some sliced shallots (or onions). In this way the shallots are infused with the spice, and the flavour works into the greens. If you're not a big fan, the nutmeg can of course be omitted; the shallot and spring greens can still be enjoyed.

Method Remove the central stalk from the leaves, rinsing each under cold water. These can now be cut into 1–2 cm (½–¾ in) strips. Melt the butter in a large saucepan and, once bubbling, add the sliced shallots, turning with a spatula until all are coated in the butter. Add the nutmeg and cook on a gentle heat, maintaining the bubbling and cooking for 3–4 minutes until the shallots have begun to tenderize.

While cooking the shallots, boil a large saucepan of salted water. The prepared spring greens can now be blanched for 1–2 minutes until tender to eat. Drain in a colander, gently squeezing away any excess water. This blanching process can be carried out well in advance, and the greens refreshed in iced water. Once drained they can be refrigerated until needed and either quickly blanched again or microwaved to re-heat. If serving immediately, add to the bubbling shallots. Mix everything together, seasoning with salt and pepper. The nutmeg spring greens are ready to serve.

Notes: *When cooking the shallots, 1 cm (½ in) dice of one large Bramley apple can be added, with a teaspoon of demerara sugar. This will give you a classic vegetable dish with savoury, fruit and spice flavours all combining together so well. The finished flavour lends a sweet sharpness to the greens.*

Also, simple buttered spring greens eat beautifully accompanied by Sauce Béarnaise (page 205).

desserts

Warm Whole Lemon and Almond Pudding with Fresh Raspberries

Fills 2 x 450 g (1 lb) loaf tins or 6 individual rings

3 lemons

4 whole eggs

175 g (6 oz) caster sugar

¼ teaspoon baking powder

175 g (6 oz) ground almonds

For the Lemon Syrup (optional)

100 ml (3½ fl oz) lemon juice

100 ml (3½ fl oz) Stock Syrup (page 213)

finely grated zest of ½ lemon

1 vanilla pod, split

50 g (2 oz) caster sugar

For the Raspberry Coulis (optional)

225 g (8 oz) fresh raspberries (tinned can also be used)

3–4 tablespoons Stock Syrup (page 213) or 2–3 teaspoons icing sugar

For the garnishes

caster sugar, for rolling vanilla strips (optional)

2–3 tablespoons Ground Caramel (page 213) or icing sugar, for dusting and glazing (optional)

10 raspberries per portion

6–8 scrolls of clotted or whipped cream (optional)

Introduction Lemons were introduced to Britain in the Middle Ages, and have since contributed to many of the most popular British puddings. Whole lemons appear in the famous Sussex pond pudding, for instance, which is suet pastry steamed around a lemon with lots of soft brown sugar. The dessert here also includes whole lemons, but in a purée form, with the zest, pith and segments all included. Cooking the citrus fruit until tender before blending means no flavour is lost, and this contributes great depths to the pudding's finished flavour.

I'm making the desserts in individual rings, but the mix can be split between two loaf tins for serving in thick slices. A few optional extras are listed to enhance the cake's flavour, among them raspberries, lemon syrup, vanilla and a glazed caramel top on which to sit some clotted cream.

You will need six 8 x 5 cm (3½ × 1¾ in) individual metal rings, well buttered, and a baking tray topped with well-buttered parchment paper, or two 450 g (1 lb) loaf tins, lined with buttered parchment paper (two tins will provide a deeper texture).

Method To cook the lemons, cover with cold water, bring to the simmer and cook for a minimum of 1 hour. Remove from the water, saving 100 ml (3½ fl oz) of the liquor, and cut into quarters, allowing to drain well. Remove the pips and blitz with the saved liquor to a smooth, thick purée in a food processor or liquidizer. Push through a sieve and leave to cool.

Pre-heat the oven to 180°C/350°F/Gas 4. Whisk the eggs and sugar together in an electric mixer to a thick sabayon (similar to lightly whipped cream). This may well take 6–8 minutes to achieve. While this is whisking, add the baking powder to the ground almonds, rubbing the mix between your thumb and forefinger to a smooth texture.

Add the lemon purée to the sabayon, followed by the almonds. Whisk slowly for 1 minute. This will help take some air out of the mix, preventing it from souffléing in the oven.

Spoon into the buttered moulds on a parchment-lined baking tray, filling each three-quarters full, or divide between the papered loaf tins. Place in the pre-heated oven and bake for 30–35 minutes (the loaves will need 45–50 minutes).

Remove from the oven and leave to cool before removing the moulds. The sponges can now be kept in an airtight container for several days until needed. To re-heat, place individual puddings in a microwave for 20–30 seconds until warmed through.

For the lemon syrup, bring all the ingredients to the boil and cook on a rapid simmer to a thick consistency. Remove the vanilla pod and use the syrup as it is, or strain through a sieve to remove the zest. Serve at room temperature.

To make the raspberry coulis, liquidize the fruits with the syrup or sugar, then push through a sieve; the sauce is now ready to use.

To make 'vanilla sticks' to use as a garnish (optional), rinse the split pod removed from the syrup. Press flat with a ruler before cutting with a sharp knife into extra fine strips. These can now be rolled in caster sugar and left to dry.

To finish the dessert, it's best to glaze the puddings on their flat base; this will also provide the perfect platform on which to sit the clotted/whipped cream. The ground caramel or icing sugar (the caramel giving an instant bitter-sweet flavour) can be sprinkled through a tea strainer or sieved on top of the puddings, before glazing with a gas gun or under a pre-heated grill. If using icing sugar for a crunchy top, three layers will be needed. Place each pudding in the centre of a plate. The raspberries can now be positioned in pairs at five spots around the dessert, spooning 2 teaspoons of coulis, if using, on each. Drizzle the syrup around, if using (a squeezy bottle will make this job a lot easier), before finishing with a scroll of clotted cream or whipped cream, if using, on top of each dessert. The fine vanilla stick can now be placed on top of the cream.

Note: *This is quite an extravagant dessert, but also quite an experience too. The raspberry coulis, lemon syrup, vanilla sticks, glazed caramel top and cream are all optional – just the raspberries or syrup being quite enough to accompany the dessert – but they all complement the lemon puddings so well that it would be a shame to leave them out.*

Iced Pear Parfait with Sweet Kirsch Cherries

Serves 6

For the Parfaits

1 x 400 g (14 oz, approx.) tin of pears, drained, saving the syrup

4 egg yolks

50 g (2 oz) caster sugar

3 tablespoons of pear syrup from tin (6 if Poire William liqueur, below, is unavailable)

3 tablespoons Poire William liqueur (see Notes, optional)

250 ml (8 fl oz) whipping cream, whipped to a soft peak

For the Cherries

100 ml (3 fl oz) Kirsch

100 ml (3½ fl oz) pear syrup from tin

150 ml (5 fl oz) water

100 g (4 oz) caster sugar

450 g (1 lb) fresh cherries, stalks removed and pitted

For the Poached Pears

3 fresh pears, preferably Comice, Williams or Conference, peeled and halved

juice of 1 lemon

400 ml (14 fl oz) Stock Syrup (page 213) – 225 g (8 oz) caster sugar and 300 ml (10 fl oz) water will give the quantity required here

caster sugar, to glaze

6 triangles of Caramelized Melba Toast (page 211), to serve

Introduction Pears and cherries make very good partners, having different textures and flavours that complement each other. The pears used to flavour this parfait come from a tin. Drained of their syrupy juices (keep them), the fruits are liquidized to a smooth purée, ready to be added to a sabayon and finished with whipped cream. Fresh pears are not needed at all, but I like to offer a poached half-pear per portion as a garnish. The cherries are cooked with Kirsch, a clear spirit made from cherries (*Kirsch* is actually German for cherry), and syrup, some of it from the tinned pears, so not wasting any of the flavours. The caramelized Melba toasts are not essential, but bring another texture and flavour to the complete dish.

You will need six 8 × 5 cm (3 × 2 in) or 7 × 4 cm (2¾ × 1¾ in) small metal or plastic terrine rings, wrapped in cling film, or a small terrine mould. A round 15–18 cm (6–7 in) flan ring can also be used.

Method Quarter the tinned pear halves and dry on kitchen paper before liquidizing to a smooth purée. This can now be refrigerated until needed. Mix together the egg yolks, sugar, pear syrup and Poire William (if using). Whisk in a bowl over simmering water to a very thick and warm sabayon consistency (similar to whipped cream): an electric hand whisk can be used for this. Transfer the sabayon to an electric mixer and continue to whisk at a medium speed until cool. The pear purée can now be added. Gently fold most of the whipped cream, saving 2 tablespoons to finish the dish, into the pear purée-flavoured sabayon, until completely mixed in.

Divide the mix between the mould(s) before freezing for a few hours until set.

The cherries can be made days or weeks in advance. In fact, as they age, they improve, becoming richer and deeper in flavour. Heat the Kirsch and carefully ignite for 15–20 seconds to burn off the raw alcohol (see Notes). Add the pear syrup, water and sugar and return to the boil. Pour the hot syrup over the cherries, cover and leave to cool. During the cooling, the cherries will become tender. These can now be kept chilled until needed. When serving, 6–7 cherries per portion will be plenty, trickling with a little of the syrup.

For the poached pears, peel and halve the pears, carefully cutting through the stalk: this creates a whole pear look to the finished cut. The central cores of the pears can be removed (not essential) with a round potato scoop (parisienne/noisette cutter). The vein of stalk running from the centre to the top of the pear can also be removed, by cutting diagonally either side of the vein. Roll in the lemon juice before placing, with the juice, in a small saucepan. Add the stock syrup. Cover with greaseproof paper and bring to a gentle simmer, poaching in the liquor for 1–2 minutes. Cover with a side plate to hold the pears beneath the syrup. Remove from the heat and leave to cool. Once cooled, the pears will have become tender. These can now be kept refrigerated until needed.

To caramelize before serving, remove the pears from the syrup and dry well on kitchen paper. Sprinkle 2–3 tablespoons of caster sugar on a side plate and dip the pears flat-side down into the sugar. These can now be caramelized under a pre-heated grill or with a gas gun (see General Information, page 13), allowing little tinges of the sugar to almost burn. The sugar-topping process might need to be repeated for the best caramelization.

The pears can be presented flat-side up, almost standing up, by cutting a small slice from near the base of the fruit. An angle of 45 degrees will give the poached fruit a perfect sitting position.

Before serving any frozen dessert, it's best to pre-chill or freeze the plates, also dusting the spot on which the pudding sits with icing sugar to prevent it from sliding about. Meanwhile, remove the parfaits from the freezer and allow to sit for a few minutes before pushing out of the moulds. (It might help to run a small warm knife around the edges, or you can warm the metal containers with a gas gun.) It's then best to return the parfaits to the freezer, allowing them to re-set around the sides. Once placed on plates, spoon the saved whipped cream on top of each parfait and top with a Melba toast.

The cherries can be served cold or warmed with their syrup, spooning them next to the parfait with a little of the syrup (see Notes). The glazed pear can now be added to the plate, creating a trio of flavours – iced pear parfait with sweet Kirsch cherries and caramelized pear.

Notes: *Poire William is an eau-de-vie (water of life), which describes any colourless brandy or other spirit distilled from fermented fruit juice. The two most common and popular are Kirsch (cherry) and Framboise (raspberry).*

Igniting Kirsch, or any alcohol, obviously creates a naked flame, so it's important to do this carefully, preferably not in the presence of children. If you prefer not to do any igniting, simply boil the Kirsch with the other ingredients.

A thicker cherry syrup to spoon over the fruits can be made by warming 100–150 ml (3½–5 fl oz) of the cooking syrup with 3–4 heaped tablespoons of black cherry jam. Once the jam has melted, strain through a sieve and the sauce is ready.

Iced Nougat Glacé with Bitter-sweet Kumquats

Serves 6

For the praline

100 g (4 oz) caster sugar

30 ml (2 tablespoons) water

15 g (½ oz) blanched and peeled pistachio nuts

50 g (2 oz) pecan nuts, quartered

50 g (2 oz) nibbed almonds

oil, for greasing

250 ml (9 fl oz) double cream, whipped to a soft peak

For the meringue

50 g (2 oz) clear honey

1 tablespoon lemon juice

finely grated zest of 1 small orange

25 g (1 oz) caster sugar

3 medium egg whites

For the kumquats

5–6 kumquats per portion

300 ml (10 fl oz) Stock Syrup (page 213)

To Serve (optional)

Orange Sorbet (page 161)

Introduction Nougat is a French speciality, possibly with Arabic ancestry. Its name derives from *nux*, the Latin for nut. It is usually found in a soft, chewy form, made from boiled sugar syrup or honey whisked into whipped egg whites, with mixed chopped nuts and glacé fruits. This recipe is taking most of those ideas and flavours, turning them into an iced parfait. Here the nougat is made up of the two classics praline and meringue, but loosened with the whipped double cream, lightening the usual chewy, sweet texture of the nougat. The nuts are set into the praline, then crushed, and the honey flavour works its way into the meringue.

Kumquats, a small, orange-like fruit from China, are stewed until tender in stock syrup and served with the nougat, replacing the glacé fruits of the original.

These quantities will fill six metal or plastic rings 8 cm (3¼ in) in diameter and 5 cm (2 in) deep. If these are unavailable, a small loaf tin or terrine, lined with cling film, can also be used. Another alternative is to freeze the nougat in tea cups. The kumquats can then simply be spooned in a small pile on top of each with a trickle of syrup before serving. Another potential extra is an orange sorbet, which provides a wonderful contrast of textures, or tuile biscuits.

Method Start by cooking the kumquats; place them in a saucepan with the stock syrup, bring to the boil and cook at a fairly rapid simmer for 50 minutes to 1 hour, until completely soft and tender. Remove from the stove and leave to cool. These can now be kept in the syrup until needed. As with most fruit cooked in sugar syrup, the kumquats will have a fairly long shelf life.

To make the praline, boil the sugar and water together to a rich golden-brown colour. While caramelizing the sugar, lightly toast the nuts before adding to the caramel. Pour on to an oiled baking tray and leave to cool and set.

Once set, break into pieces, then place in a food processor and blitz to nibbed almond-sized pieces. This can also be achieved by covering the set caramel with a cloth or cling film and hitting it with a rolling pin.

For the meringue, warm together the honey, lemon juice, orange zest and sugar. This process will loosen the honey. Bring to the boil and reduce back to a clear honey consistency. Remove from the heat and leave to cool for 2 minutes. Meanwhile, whisk the egg whites to a soft peak. The honey can now be very slowly drizzled into the whites while whisking. (It's best to use an electric mixer for this.) Once all the honey has been added, continue to whisk until the mix and bowl are cold.

The caramel praline can now be folded into the whipped cream, followed by the meringue. Cover the base of the individual moulds, if using, with cling film, before spooning and spreading the nougat glacé mix between all. This can now be placed in the freezer for several hours to set and freeze.

To serve, use a warm, small knife or gas gun to warm the metal rings and remove the nougats from their moulds. These can now be placed in bowls or on plates and surrounded with the kumquats.

Note: *If serving the orange sorbet, I suggest putting a small scroll on top of each nougat just before serving.*

Orange Sorbet

Makes 800 ml (27 fl oz)

100 g (4 oz) caster sugar

finely grated zest from 3–4 of the juiced oranges

600 ml (1 pint) fresh orange juice, strained

juice of 1 lemon, strained

Introduction A sorbet is often served as a light dessert, but in classic menu-planning was more likely to be found after the fish course, helping to clean the palate ready for the main course. This recipe can be used for either, or as an accompaniment to a dessert, such as the Iced Nougat Glacé with Bitter-sweet Kumquats (page 160).

Method Boil together the sugar, orange zest and 100 ml (3½ fl oz) of water. Reduce to a gentle simmer and continue to cook for 8 minutes. Remove from the heat, adding the orange and lemon juices. Once cool, the mix can be finished in an ice-cream maker and churned for 20–25 minutes to a smooth consistency. Freeze until firm.

Note: *A quick alternative is to whisk icing sugar into the orange juice until sweetened to taste. This can now be churned as described above, before freezing. Freshly squeezed carton orange juice can also be used.*

Lemon sorbet can be made by mixing 300 ml (10 fl oz) of lemon juice with 300 ml (10 fl oz) of Stock Syrup (page 213) and churning as described previously.

Desserts were developed to a fine art for the purpose of keeping girls and young women and children at table to join in family colloquies.

Antoine Carême

Rich Summer-fruit Pavlovas

Serves 6–8

4 egg whites

1 teaspoon lemon juice

200 g (7 oz) caster sugar

2 teaspoons cornflour

pinch of salt

For the Fruits and Fruit Coulis

225 g (8 oz) blackberries

225 g (8 oz) strawberries, hulled and halved

225 g (8 oz) raspberries

225 g (8 oz) mixed blackcurrants and redcurrants

150 ml (5 fl oz) Stock Syrup (page 213) or alternative (see Notes)

juice of ½ lemon

For the Crème Fraîche Ice-cream (optional)

4 egg yolks

100 g (4 oz) caster sugar

300 ml (10 fl oz) milk

300 ml (10 fl oz) crème fraîche

Introduction The meringue, pavlova, was named in honour of the Russian ballerina Anna Pavlova after she visited the antipodes in the 1920s. Both Australia and New Zealand claim to have created it, but the strongest claims belong to the pavlova itself, as one of the tastiest meringues you could experience. It has a crisp outside, like the best traditional meringue, but the centre is gooey, soft and marshmallowy in texture. This is created by the addition of cornflour and vinegar or lemon juice to the egg white and sugar.

A mixture of fresh summer berries makes a perfect accompaniment for this home-made pavlova. Choose raspberries, strawberries and blackberries, or blackcurrants, redcurrants, loganberries and blueberries – whatever is in season. An optional extra that works well with this dish is a scroll of crème fraîche ice-cream. Its simple flavour helps balance the richness shared by the meringue and summer berries.

Method Make the meringue first. Pre-heat the oven to 150°C/300°F/Gas 2.

Using a clean bowl, whisk the egg whites and lemon juice with a pinch of salt to soft peaks. Sprinkle in the sugar and cornflour, continuing to whisk until thick, creamy and at stiff peaks. It's important to continue the whisking until it is at this stage. This particular meringue will have a much creamier and glossy look and consistency than a basic egg-white-and-sugar recipe. The meringue can now be spooned on to a baking sheet lined with baking parchment, creating 6–8 puff-ball shapes. These can also be piped, using a 1.5 cm (⅝ in) plain tube, to form peaked pavlovas. To help keep a regular shape, spoon or pipe the mixture into a large ring dipped first in hot water. Bake the meringues in the pre-heated oven for 40–50 minutes, by which time the outside should be uncoloured but crispy and the centre marshmallow-textured.

These can now be left to cool. They are best eaten fresh on the day but can also be kept in an airtight container for 24–48 hours.

To make the coulis, take half the quantity of each fruit and purée in a liquidizer with the stock syrup and lemon juice until smooth. Taste for sharpness: if a sweeter flavour is preferred, add icing sugar to taste, blitzing again before straining through a sieve. This can now be kept cling-filmed and refrigerated until needed. Pick and rinse the remaining fruits, leaving a little bunch of blackcurrants or redcurrants on a stalk, to decorate, if you wish.

If you want to make the crème fraîche ice-cream, whisk together the egg yolks and sugar until pale and light. Boil the milk and whisk into the egg-yolk mixture. Cook in a bowl over a pan of simmering water to prevent the eggs scrambling. Stir constantly until thickened. Remove from the heat and leave to cool before whisking in the crème fraîche. The mix is now ready to churn in an ice-cream machine for 15–20 minutes, until it is becoming thick and creamy. It's important to remove it and place in the freezer at this point to prevent a grainy finish.

To serve the dessert, mix the cleaned berries with 6–8 tablespoons of the fruit coulis, adding more if necessary to loosen. Crack a small well in the top of each meringue before spooning over the fruits. Extra sauce can now also be spooned over and around the meringues. Finish with a scoop of ice-cream (if using) on top or beside each serving.

Notes: *Coulis is a French culinary term meaning 'sieved', which is what is done to the fruit purée. If you prefer not to use stock syrup, the alternative is to liquidize the fruits with 50 g (2 oz) of caster sugar or icing sugar and the lemon juice until smooth. If too tart, add another 50 g (2 oz) of sugar and continue to blitz before straining. To increase the flavour, a few tablespoons of fruit liqueur, such as* crème de framboise *or* fraise, *can be added.*

The remaining fruits can be softened before being served. This is best done before making the coulis. Place the blackberries in the stock syrup and bring to the simmer, cooking for a minute before adding the strawberries, raspberries and currants. Cover, remove from the heat and leave to cool. The syrup can now be strained and used to make the coulis, leaving very tender summer fruits.

Here are a couple of quick alternatives to making crème fraîche ice-cream:

- *Whisk 300 ml (10 fl oz) of crème fraîche into 300 ml (10 fl oz) of tinned or carton custard, adding a squeeze of lemon juice before churning as above. A sprinkling of icing sugar can be added to sweeten.*
- *Whisk 150 ml (5 fl oz) of crème fraîche into 150 ml (5 fl oz) of tinned custard. Whip 150 ml (5 fl oz) of double cream with 20 g (¾ oz) of caster sugar and fold into the mix. Transfer to an airtight container and freeze until set.*

Frozen White Chocolate Mousse with Port-wine Figs

Serves 4

4 egg yolks

50 g (2 oz) caster sugar

2–3 tablespoons Cointreau (optional)

finely grated zest of ½ orange (optional)

100 g (4 oz) white chocolate, chopped

300 ml (10 fl oz) double cream

For the figs

450 ml (¾ pint) port

75 g (3 oz) caster sugar

3 strips of orange zest, cleaned of all pith

6 fresh figs, halved

For the Spicy Red-wine Sauce (optional)

300 ml (10 fl oz) red wine

150 ml (5 fl oz) port liquor, from figs

50 g (2 oz) caster sugar

½ cinnamon stick

2 cloves

4 black peppercorns

1 star anise

For the Honey Wafers

5 g (1 oz) butter

25 g (1 oz) icing sugar

50 g (2 oz) honey

40 g (1½ oz) plain flour

pinch of ground cinnamon

Introduction The main frozen feature in this recipe is the white chocolate mousse, which is a rich, iced parfait that just melts in the mouth. If figs are not one of your favourite fruits, they can be replaced with Sweet Kirsch Cherries (page 158) or fresh raspberries and raspberry coulis (page 156).

The figs are poached in port wine flavoured with orange peel and are best steeped for 24 hours. The port can now be served, if wished, as an accompanying drink to go with the dessert or cooked with red wine and spices into a sauce to drizzle around. The quantity of ingredients here will fill 4–6 individual moulds, or a large square or round cake or flan ring measuring 15–18 × 2–4 cm (6–7 × 1–1½ in). Using a square tin will provide four square portions, while the ring can produce 4–6 wedges. The mousse ingredients can also be doubled, which will fill a 25 cm (10 in) mould or Le Creuset terrine.

To add extra texture, honey wafers, similar to tuile biscuits, are included in the recipe. These can also be used as containers for serving ice-creams or sorbets, and are often served as *petits fours*. They can be made in almost any shape – curved discs, triangles, squares, twists and many more. To cut a stencil for the wafers, draw and cut the shape of your choice from the plastic lid of an ice-cream box. Simply cut a stencil that will cover the size and shape of the portions being served.

Method To make the mousse, whisk together the egg yolks, sugar, Cointreau (if using) and orange zest (if using) over a pan of simmering water to a thick, creamy sabayon. Transfer to an electric mixer and whisk vigorously for 4–5 minutes. Meanwhile, the white chocolate can be melted in a bowl over gently simmering water, stirring from time to time and not allowing it to get too hot, or the chocolate becomes very grainy.

Once melted, remove from the heat and leave to cool for a few minutes before adding to the sabayon. Whip the double cream to soft peaks, whisking in a quarter to the chocolate mix. The remaining whipped cream can now be gently folded in. Cover the base of the mould(s) being used with cling film before placing on a tray and filling with the white chocolate mousse. Spread the top(s) smooth for an even finish. Place in the freezer to set: this will take 2–3 hours.

To cook the figs, boil together the port, sugar and orange zest. Once boiling, add the figs and return to a simmer. Remove from the heat immediately, cover with a lid and leave to cool. For maximum flavour, refrigerate and steep for up to 24 hours. Once steeped, remove the figs and strain the port through a fine sieve. This is now ready to serve in port glasses as an accompaniment, or can be used in the following sauce.

Place all the red-wine sauce ingredients in a pan and bring to the boil. Cook on a rapid simmer until reduced by at least two-thirds and at a sauce consistency. Strain and leave to cool.

To make the wafers, pre-heat the oven to 180°C/350°F/Gas 4. Whisk together the butter, sugar and honey until light and creamy. Sift the flour and cinnamon together before beating into the honey mix. Place the stencil on to a baking-parchment-topped or non-stick baking tray. Spread the wafer mix across the stencil to create the wafer shape. Repeat until 8 shapes are spread (this may need two trays). Cook in the pre-heated oven for 5–7 minutes, until golden. Remove from the oven and leave to cool before removing from the tray. It's best to cook any remaining wafer mix; once refrigerated, it becomes too thick to spread. The wafers can now be kept in an airtight container. These will last for at least 48 hours.

To present the dessert, remove the mousse from the freezer, releasing it from the ring or mould with a warm sharp knife, or warming with a gas gun. It's now best to return the mousse to the freezer for 10–15 minutes to re-set the edges before cutting into the required shapes. Carefully place each one on a wafer base before topping with another. Use a spatula or fish slice to place each portion in the centre of a plate, before topping with three pieces of the steeped port-wine figs. To finish, trickle around each with the spicy red-wine sauce, if using; this can be easily achieved using a squeezy bottle. The dish is ready to serve.

Toasted 'Spicy' Breadcrumbed Gooseberry Crumble

Serves 6

900 g (2 lb) gooseberries, topped and tailed

100 g–175 g (4–6 oz) caster sugar (100 g/ 4 oz will give a sharper bite)

For the Crumble

175 g (6 oz) butter

100 g (4 oz) fresh white breadcrumbs

¼ teaspoon finely chopped fresh rosemary (½ teaspoon if rosemary sugar is unavailable)

100 g (4 oz) rosemary sugar (see introduction) or caster sugar

175 g (6 oz) plain flour

Introduction It's said that the fruit crumble didn't appear in our culinary curriculum until the Second World War, although it seems so traditionally British. The topping is basically a pastry mix, but it omits the water. When cooked, it maintains its crumbly finish, hence the name 'crumble'.

One of the recipe's ingredients is 'spiced' sugar, which is flavoured with herbs rather than spice. When first created, in the nineteenth century, rosemary and lavender were commonly used. Here I'm using rosemary. The sweet acidic flavour of the gooseberries eats very well with the slight herby flavour behind. If you want to make rosemary sugar, store a few sprigs of the herb in an airtight container with caster sugar. One week will give a mild flavour.

For me, one of the best features of a crumble is the fruit syrup created in the dish, which works its way to the top edges and caramelizes – very sticky and very moreish. Apple, rhubarb and gooseberry are the fruits most commonly used in crumbles, and so they should be, all cooking with enough body and tartness to excite the tastebuds.

Method Pre-heat the oven to 200°C/400°F/ Gas 6.

Melt 50 g (2 oz) of the butter in a frying-pan. Add the breadcrumbs and cook on a medium heat, stirring continuously, until golden brown and crisp. Add the chopped rosemary and remove from the heat. Leave to cool.

Place the gooseberries in a buttered 1.5 litre (2½ pint) ovenproof dish and sprinkle with the caster sugar. Rub the remaining butter into the plain flour to a breadcrumb consistency. Add the rosemary or caster sugar and combine well, creating rough crumbs. This can be achieved in seconds using a food processor.

Once the fried rosemary crumbs are cold, add to the mix and sprinkle over the gooseberries. Bake in the middle of the pre-heated oven for 30–40 minutes. The crumble will now have a crispy, golden-brown topping, hopefully with sweet, sharp gooseberry juices seeping through the top. This crumble, with its herby edge, eats beautifully with thick cream or ice-cream.

If, after 20 minutes, the crumble has received a good golden-brown colour, reduce the oven temperature to 180°C/350°F/Gas 4.

Notes: *The rosemary can be omitted from this recipe.*

The caster sugar in the crumble topping can be replaced with light soft brown sugar.

A good pinch of ground mixed spice can also be added to the crumble topping.

Fresh Cream-tea Custards with Home-made Digestive Biscuits

Serves 4–5

300 ml (10 fl oz) double cream

1 tablespoon jasmine tea leaves

4 egg yolks

25 g (1 oz) caster sugar

icing sugar or demerara sugar, to glaze

Home-made Digestive Biscuits (page 212), to serve (optional)

Introduction Tea and biscuits are very much part of the British heritage, classic accompaniments to one another. The fresh cream tea is a British tradition I feel we can definitely claim as totally ours, and we can be very proud of its influence and acceptance across the whole world. This dessert, however, was actually inspired by Alain Chapel, a French chef who I believe was one of the greatest of our time. Sadly, he is no longer with us, but his eponymous restaurant, based in Mionnay, close to Lyons, was where chefs and the public alike flocked to experience and taste the work of this consummate artist. One of his desserts was a jasmine custard, cousin to *crème brûlée*, but infused with the aroma of jasmine tea. This is my version, and it has a very British home-made biscuit as its accompaniment. Today, many flavoured teas are available, most of which could work equally well with this dish. If you prefer a natural tea flavour, perhaps Darjeeling, the champagne of teas, will be the one for you.

This recipe can easily be doubled to make 8–10 portions.

Method Pre-heat the oven to 150°C/300°F/Gas 2. You will need 7.5 cm (3 in) diameter ramekins or other similarly sized pots.

Bring the double cream to the boil and remove from the heat. Stir in the tea leaves, cover and leave to infuse for 15 minutes.

Whisk together the egg yolks and caster sugar, until creamy. Strain the cream on to the yolks, whisking well.

Divide the custard between the dishes. Sit these in a roasting tin and add warm water until it comes two-thirds up the sides of the dishes. Bake in the pre-heated oven until just setting: this will take 40–50 minutes. To test, remove one of the dishes from the water after 30 minutes and shake gently. There should be a slight movement in the centre of the custard. If still runny, return to the oven and continue to cook, checking every 5 minutes until at the right soft but set stage. Remove from the oven and tray and allow to cool. I believe *crème brûlée* should be eaten at room temperature rather than chilled. Refrigerating will set the custard firmly, leaving a cakey, mousse-like texture, and cold tea has never been one of my favourites.

If glazing the custards with demerara, it will first need to be ground in an electric coffee grinder for a much finer texture. Sprinkle it, or the icing sugar, fairly liberally on top of the custards and glaze until golden brown under a pre-heated grill or using a gas gun. Repeat this process, once more with demerara and twice with icing sugar, not allowing it to over-burn or caramelize as this will mask the jasmine tea flavour. *Crème brûlée* of any variety can be glazed up to 1 hour before serving, then kept in a cool, dry spot (too much humidity will dissolve the sugar).

The fresh cream-tea custards will eat perfectly on their own, but always welcome a home-made digestive biscuit.

Note: *Double the recipe to serve 8–10.*

Caramelized Dutch Apple Steamed Pudding

Serves 6

50 g (2 oz) unsalted butter, softened

50 g (2 oz) dark or light soft brown sugar

450 g (1 lb) Bramley cooking apples, peeled, cored and quartered

450 g (1 lb) eating apples, peeled, cored and quartered

knob of butter

50 g (2 oz) fresh white breadcrumbs

2 tablespoons golden syrup

finely grated zest of 2 lemons

generous pinch of ground cinnamon

100 g (4 oz) raisins

For the Suet Pastry

300 g (10 oz) self-raising flour

pinch of salt

150 g (5 oz) beef or vegetable suet

200 ml (7 fl oz) water or milk

Introduction Apple pie is the most famous of apple desserts, and is very British, although the variety totally encased in pastry is said to have come to us from America. The variation of Dutch apple pie is one of the first desserts you encounter when attending a cookery school or college. This is baked in a cake tin: the apples mixed with cinnamon, cloves, lemon and sultanas sitting comfortably in the centre. These basic flavours are not changing too much here, but there is one significant difference, and that's the pastry. In place of the sweet shortcrust, I'm using suet paste, hence the steaming rather than baking.

The 'caramelized' of the recipe title is achieved by buttering the pudding basin and then generously dusting it with light or dark soft brown sugar. Once the pud is turned out, the caramel colour and flavour appear. The apples used for the filling are half cooking and half eating. The balance between the two, one with a sharp bite, the other with a firmer and sweeter finish, bind together well, resulting in a more balanced finish.

Method Make the pastry first. Sift together the flour and salt. Add the suet, stirring in the water or milk. The dough can now be worked and mixed, creating a smooth consistency. Wrap and rest for 20 minutes.

Spread the softened butter around the inside of a 1.2 litre (2 pint) pudding basin. The soft brown sugar can now be sprinkled on to coat the inside completely.

Roll the suet pastry into a circle, cutting away a triangle equal to one-third of the dough. This can now be re-shaped and used to make a 'lid'. The remaining two-thirds will now form a cone shape when the cut edges are brought together. Place this in the basin; the pastry will fit perfectly without creating 'pleats', which so often leave an uneven finish.

Cut all the quarters of the eating apples in half once more, creating eight wedges per apple. The larger Bramley quarters can be sliced into three, creating 12 wedges per apple. Melt the knob of butter in a large saucepan and, once bubbling, add the apples. Cook for a few minutes, until just beginning to soften. Remove from the pan and leave to cool. Mix all the remaining ingredients with the apples and pack into the lined base, making a domed top. The suet pastry lid can now be placed on top, pressing around the border and sealing the edges well. Trim away any excess and cover with folded greaseproof paper or foil, tied with string if necessary.

Steam over boiling water for 1¼–1½ hours, topping up with water if necessary. Once cooked, remove from the steamer and carefully turn out. The caramelized Dutch apple pudding is now ready to serve. Fresh custard, thick cream or vanilla ice-cream (or perhaps all three) will be tasty accompaniments.

Hot Chocolate Soufflé with Chocolate Sauce

Serves 4–6

50 g (2 oz) caster sugar

20 g (¾ oz) plain flour

20 g (¾ oz) cornflour

25 g (1 oz) cocoa powder

50 g (2 oz) plain bitter chocolate, finely grated

300 ml (10 fl oz) milk

extra caster sugar or finely grated chocolate, for coating

butter, for greasing

8 large egg whites

4 heaped tablespoons caster sugar

For the Chocolate Sauce

200 ml (7 fl oz) milk

100–175 g (4–6 oz) plain dark chocolate, finely chopped

100 ml (3½ fl oz) whipping or single cream

25 g (1 oz) butter (optional)

Introduction This hot 'puffed-up' (the English translation of 'soufflé') dessert was not with us until the late eighteenth century, introduced from France. Most sweet soufflé recipes start with a pastry cream base to which flavours are added before the whisked egg whites are folded in. This recipe is similar, but instead of a custard base, we have a fairly quick chocolate mix that is finished with the whites before baking in the soufflé dishes. I've always been successful with this particular recipe: there's a texture within the soufflé, and it doesn't become too light and fluffy, with no substance. The base can be made well in advance and refrigerated until needed. If so, make sure it has time to return to room temperature, and beat it back to its former consistency before using. Individual soufflé dishes of approximately 10 cm (4 in) in diameter are being used here, but if using smaller ramekins, this recipe will give you 6–8 portions. Sweet soufflé dishes must always be well buttered and sugared, but here they can be buttered and lined with finely grated chocolate as an alternative, to increase the chocolate finish. Simple pouring cream can be offered with this dessert, but I have given a chocolate sauce recipe for real chocoholics. Here are a few points to remember when making sweet soufflés:

- The bowl and whisk must be scrupulously clean.
- A quarter of the whites must be whisked into the base before folding in the remainder.
- The soufflé dish must be well buttered and sugared right up to and including the top of the rim to ensure the soufflé will not stick.

Method Pre-heat the oven to 230°C/450°F/ Gas 8.

Mix together the caster sugar, plain flour, cornflour and cocoa powder.

Add the chocolate to the milk and bring to the boil. Pour and whisk slowly into the dry ingredients and return to the stove. Cook for 5–6 minutes on a medium heat, whisking continuously until very thick and the whisk will almost stand on its own. Pour into a bowl, cover with cling film and leave to cool.

Butter the soufflé dishes generously, sprinkling with caster sugar or grated chocolate.

Whisk the egg whites in an electric mixer or by hand until half risen. Add the caster sugar and continue to whisk to a soft peak. Whisk a quarter of this mix into the chocolate base. Now gently fold in the rest, dividing between the dishes. Smooth over the top with a palette knife, slightly releasing the mix around the border with the tip of a small sharp knife. Bake in the pre-heated oven for 12–15 minutes, until risen and set, but still maintaining a moist centre. The soufflés are ready to serve.

To make the sauce, heat the milk in a saucepan bringing to boiling point. Remove from the stove and add the chocolate (175 g/6 oz will give you a thicker and richer finish), whisking in until melted. Add the cream of your choice and the sauce is made. For a silky finish, whisk in the butter and serve.

Notes: *A strip of greaseproof paper can be stapled around the moulds, standing 5–6 cm (2–2½ in) above the rim. This can also be buttered and sugared before spooning in the mix. This guarantees that the soufflé can rise in only one direction. Once cooked, carefully peel away.*

It's best to use a chocolate with 70 per cent cocoa solids.

When serving sauces with soufflés, make an incision in the top of the soufflé before pouring in the hot sauce. This almost 're-soufflés' the dessert and it now holds the pleasure of two recipes in one.

Classic Rum Baba

Serves 6–8

3 tablespoons lukewarm milk

2 teaspoons dried yeast or a 7 g packet of dried, fast-action yeast

225 g (8 oz) plain flour

1 tablespoon caster sugar

pinch of salt

3 eggs, lightly beaten

75 g (3 oz) butter, softened

4 heaped tablespoons apricot jam, to glaze

For the Rum Syrup

450 ml (15 fl oz) water

325 g (11 oz) caster sugar

250 ml (9 fl oz) rum (or more)

peeled zest and juice of 1 lemon

4 tablespoons water

For the Whipped Vanilla Cream (8 portions)

150 ml (5 fl oz) double cream

150 ml (5 fl oz) whipping cream

25 g (1 oz) icing sugar

1 vanilla pod

Introduction Baba is thought to have originated in Poland, and was a bread at first, rather like a *kugelhopf*, not the gentle, soaked dessert of today. Its present form was, as with so many other dishes, developed by the French at the beginning of the nineteenth century. Early babas were made as small, individual cakes, brioche-like in texture, then soaked in a lemon syrup before being drizzled with aged rum. I remember the dish from the 1960s and 1970s, with its glacé fruit and angelica but without the rum.

In this recipe, I'm going back to the original form, making a syrup flavoured with lemon peel and rum, ready for soaking the hot buns in. Another favourite idea of mine is to finish them with an apricot glaze. This gives the babas quite a sticky edge, eating so well with the softly whipped vanilla cream.

This recipe will fill six 150 ml (5 fl oz) metal moulds or eight classic rum baba darioles (12 savarin rings can also be used).

Method To make the babas, pour the lukewarm water into a bowl. Sprinkle over the yeast and leave for a few minutes to dissolve. Sift the flour, sugar and salt together into a mixing bowl. Add the yeast and milk to the flour mix and stir in. Then add the eggs, working for a few minutes until a smooth dough is reached. Dot the dough with nuggets of the butter, cover the bowl with a damp cloth and leave to rise in a warm place for 45 minutes. Meanwhile, butter the moulds and refrigerate.

At the end of the rising time the butter will have started to work its way into the dough. Knead the dough back to a smooth texture. Butter the moulds again, then divide the dough between them, filling just halfway up. Place on a baking tray, cover with a cloth and leave to rise in a warm place for 15–20 minutes. Meanwhile, pre-heat the oven to 200ºC/400ºF/Gas 6.

Bake the babas for 10–15 minutes, until golden brown. Remove from the oven and leave to stand in the moulds for a further 10 minutes before turning out.

Meanwhile, boil all the syrup ingredients together and simmer for a few minutes. Remove from the heat and leave for the lemon zest to infuse its flavour into the syrup. When just warm, remove the lemon zest and place the babas in the syrup to soak for a few minutes, allowing them time to absorb the rich rum flavour.

Bring the apricot jam and water to the boil and, if lumpy, pass through a sieve. Leave to one side.

Now make the vanilla cream. The double and whipping creams are a good combination, the result being neither too heavy and thick nor too loose and airy. It's important that the creams are well chilled before whipping and that an ice-cold bowl is used to whisk in.

Mix the two creams and the icing sugar together. Slit the vanilla pod and scrape the seeds into the cream mix. Whip by hand to a soft creamy peak. This is best done just before serving to ensure a creamy finish. Refrigerated whipped cream sets, leaving a cakey finish.

Remove the babas from the syrup and allow to drain and cool. Before serving, boil the apricot glaze and brush over each. Serve in bowls with a little syrup and the thick whipped vanilla cream.

Toasted Apricots on Warm Sugared Custard Toasts

Serves 4

knob of butter

10–12 apricots, halved, with stones removed (5–6 pieces per portion)

2 tablespoons light soft brown sugar or demerara sugar

juice of ½ lemon

For the Toasts

4 eggs

4 tablespoons caster sugar

4 tablespoons double cream

1 vanilla pod (optional)

4 thick slices of brioche or white bread

50 g (2 oz) butter

Introduction Apricots are the fruit with the velvety skin holding the rich golden colour of the sun and a sweet flesh that explodes with delight when bitten into. Chinese in origin, it first appeared in Britain in the sixteenth century, although it has never been a major fruit crop here. Its name comes from the Latin word *praecox*, 'precocious', because apricot trees flower early. It's important to buy apricots when fully ripe because, unlike many other fruits, they do not ripen well off the tree; in fact, if picked and shipped too early, they will be dry and woolly inside rather than soft and juicy. In this recipe, though, the fruits are softly caramelized to add an extra sweetness and moisture, replacing any the apricots might lack.

The custard toasts are very simple to make, being dipped in a sugar, egg and cream mixture – all the basic flavours of a home-made custard – before being shallow-fried in butter. A spoonful of crème fraîche or extra thick soured cream (with a hint of lemon) melting on top of the apricots makes a good optional addition.

Method Heat a large frying pan with the knob of butter. On a medium heat, place the apricots in the pan, cut-side down. Fry for 5 minutes until becoming golden brown with tinges of burnt. Sprinkle in the sugar and, once beginning to melt, add the lemon juice and 5 tablespoons of water. This will instantly create a syrup, which can be spooned over the fruits. Turn the apricots over and continue to cook for a few minutes. Remove from the heat. The fruits are almost ready but can be left to cool and re-heated under a pre-heated grill; hence the 'toasted' in the title. With this quantity, they may need to be fried in two separate lots.

Whisk together the eggs, sugar and double cream. A vanilla pod can be scraped into the mix for a fresh vanilla custard finish. Place the brioche or bread slices in the custard, steeping for 2–3 minutes. There will probably be excess custard, but this can be refrigerated for 24–48 hours to re-use.

On a low heat, melt the butter. Once melted, gently lift the soaked brioche or bread (using a fish slice) and place in the pan. Some custard will begin to bleed into the pan; this can be trimmed away once cooked. Fry the bread for 3–4 minutes on each side; this gives enough time for the custard inside it to warm and thicken.
If the breads are browning quickly, remove the slices once coloured on both sides, and place in a pre-heated oven 180°C/350°F/ Gas 4, and cook for 5–6 minutes.

While the breads are frying, place the apricots on a baking tray and slide under a hot grill; cook for 3–4 minutes until becoming sticky and caramelized on top. Heat the frying pan with all its syrup. If too thick, add a few more tablespoons of water.

To serve, place the toasts on plates, sitting 5–6 pieces of apricot on top. Finish by drizzling with the apricot syrup.

Note: *Almost any other fruit can be prepared and served in this way. Plums, in particular, work very well, as do apples and rhubarb.*

Warm Mini Dundee Cakes with Whisky Sabayon

Makes 12–14 mini cakes (2 per portion), or 1 large cake

175 g (6 oz) butter

175 g (6 oz) caster sugar

3 large eggs, beaten

225 g (8 oz) plain flour, sifted

1 teaspoon baking powder

½ teaspoon ground mixed spice

2 tablespoons ground almonds

175 g (6 oz) currants

175 g (6 oz) sultanas

50 g (2 oz) glacé cherries, chopped

50 g (2 oz) chopped mixed peel

finely grated zest and juice of 1 lemon and 1 orange

3–4 tablespoons whisky

milk, if necessary

50 g (2 oz) whole blanched almonds, to decorate (optional)

For the Sabayon (makes about 600 ml /1 pint)

4 egg yolks

75 g (3 oz) caster sugar

100 ml (3½ fl oz) whisky

50 ml (2 fl oz) water

For the Whisky Raisin Syrup (optional)

100 g (4 oz) raisins

75 g (3 oz) caster sugar

100 ml (3½ fl oz) water

100 ml (3½ fl oz) whisky

Introduction Dundee cake, a rich fruit cake decorated with whole almonds, was created in the city of Dundee at some point during the nineteenth century. For many years it was made only by Keiller's, the famous marmalade company, which then introduced citrus fruits to a cake. This made Dundee cake quite different from standard fruit cakes. Sadly, the recipe was copied, and altered, and many ready-made Dundee cakes these days have moved quite far from the original. This recipe, however, keeps as close as possible to the very earliest versions. The one major difference I've made is in including whisky instead of brandy or sherry. I'm also making mini individual puddings, but the quantity here will make one large cake, which has the advantage of keeping for many weeks.

This is a fun dessert, with the thick, sweet whisky sabayon adding an extra pleasure to the whole experience. It's like the lightest of custards without the milk or cream.

Method Pre-heat the oven to 170°C/325°F/ Gas 3 and butter and flour all the tin(s): 12–14 plain or fluted round cake tins measuring 6 × 3 cm (2½ × 1¼ in), or muffin trays, or one large, deep cake tin 20 cm (8 in) in diameter.

The first stage can be reached a lot more quickly if an electric mixer is used. Beat together the butter and sugar until light and creamy. Break and beat the eggs into a jug, then add just a little at a time to the butter mixture until everything has emulsified. If at any time it appears to be separating, just add a sprinkling of the flour. The flour, baking powder and mixed spice can now all be folded in carefully. Also fold in the ground almonds, all the fruits and mixed peel, along with the lemon and orange zest, juice and whisky. The mix needs to be of a good, soft, dropping consistency; if not, add just enough milk to reach that stage. The mixture can now be spooned into the prepared cake tin(s) and smoothed over evenly.

If making one large cake, place the blanched almonds gently around the top of the cake, not pressing them into the mix or the almonds will sink. The individual cakes can be topped with just one almond, if you like.

The whole Dundee cake will take 2–2½ hours to bake in the pre-heated oven, and the individual cakes 20–25 minutes. If, after 1 hour, the cake top is well coloured, cover with a double piece of greaseproof paper or foil. After 2 hours, pierce the cake with a small, sharp knife; the blade should come away clean. If not, continue to cook for the last 30 minutes, checking every 10 minutes.

Once cooked, remove from the oven and allow to cool in the tin(s) before turning out. The whole Dundee cake can now be wrapped in greaseproof paper and stored in an airtight tin. The small Dundees can also be kept until needed.

Here are some extra points that will achieve better results.

All dried fruits in cakes remain dry, not giving the moist finish expected from them. To achieve a stickier finish to this cake, or any other fruitcake, mix and place all the currants, sultanas, cherries and mixed peel in a braising dish. Cover with foil and warm, in a slow oven (130°C/250°F/Gas 1) for 20–25 minutes, stirring once or twice with a fork. The fruits will now be quite sticky. Remove from the oven and allow to cool completely before using. This is best done a few hours before making the cake.

The whisky raisin syrup is an optional extra that can be served with or instead of the sabayon. It moistens the cakes, adding yet another edge to an already exciting dessert. Boil all ingredients together; simmer for 10 minutes before liquidizing and straining through a sieve. The syrup is now ready. If too thin, simply boil and reduce to a thicker consistency before pouring over the warm cakes.

The small Dundees are best served warm. This can be achieved by placing in a medium oven for 5–10 minutes or microwaving just to warm through the centre.

Make the sabayon in a bowl sitting over a pan of gently simmering water. Whisk all the ingredients until at least doubled in volume, holding thick ribbons. The sabayon is now ready to use, but for an extra thick and creamy finish, transfer to an electric mixer or use an electric hand whisk and continue whisking until almost mousse-like in consistency. The sabayon is now ready to spoon over the warm cakes.

Bitter-sweet Strawberry Tart with Mascarpone Cheesecake Cream

Serves 8–12

butter, for greasing

flour, for rolling pastry

1 quantity Sweet Shortcrust Pastry (page 212), flavoured with grated lemon zest (optional)

225 g (8 oz) mascarpone cheese

150 ml (5 fl oz) natural yoghurt

25–50 g (1–2 oz) caster sugar or icing sugar

1 vanilla pod (optional)

150 ml (5 fl oz) double or whipping cream (whipped to a soft peak)

450–675 g (1–1½ lb) fresh, ripe strawberries, preferably small (or halved if large), to decorate

100 g (4 oz) strawberry jam, to glaze (optional)

sifted icing sugar, to decorate (optional)

Introduction Mascarpone is the famous Italian fresh cheese, originally made in Lombardy and Tuscany. It is rich and creamy in texture, and forms the base for the classic 'pick-me-up' dessert from Venice, *tiramisu*. The cream cheese base here also contains natural yoghurt; this is not essential but does add an extra sharpness to the cream, preventing it from becoming over-sweet. I prefer the pastry case to be over-cooked, which lends a crunchy bitterness to the finished dessert.

Method Butter a 25 cm (10 in) flan ring. Roll out the sweet pastry (not too thin, or it will lose the good biscuity texture to work with the mascarpone cream) and line the flan ring. It's best to leave any excess pastry hanging over the edge; once the tart is cooked, this can be trimmed away, leaving a perfectly neat finish. Prick the base of the pastry and refrigerate for 30 minutes. Pre-heat the oven to 190°C/375°F/Gas 5.

Line the pastry case with greaseproof paper and baking beans or rice before placing in the pre-heated oven and cooking for 35–45 minutes. After 35 minutes, remove the greaseproof paper and beans, returning the paper to seal the base for a further 10 minutes. The edges are best deep in colour because this will provide the bitterness. Once cooked, remove from the oven and cool before trimming away the excess pastry.

While the pastry case is baking, the cheesecake cream can be made. Mix together the mascarpone and yoghurt with 25 g (1 oz) of the sugar. If using, split the vanilla pod and scrape the seeds into the mix. Beat to a smooth consistency, preferably in a food processor or electric mixer. Taste for sweetness, adding more sugar, if needed, before folding in the whipped cream. The mixture can be whisked, if necessary, to a thicker consistency. Spoon and spread into the pastry case. Pick and rinse the strawberries, leaving some with stalks on for a more rustic look. Place on top of the mascarpone cream. The tart is now ready to serve.

If glazing the fruit, warm the strawberry jam and loosen with water. Strain through a sieve, then brush over the strawberries. A light sprinkling of icing sugar can be dusted around the tart before serving.

Notes: *Raspberries or mixed summer fruits can also be used in this recipe.*

The pastry can be flavoured with the zest of a couple of lemons, lemon being a great friend of the English strawberry.

savouries

Home-made Baked Beans on Toast

Serves 6 as a savoury, 4 as a snack

350 g (12 oz) white haricot beans, or 2 x 400 g (14 oz) cans of cooked white haricot beans

4–6 thick slices of white or bread

butter, for spreading (optional)

For the Sauce

2 tablespoons olive oil

2 large shallots or 1 large onion, very finely chopped

2 garlic cloves, crushed

2 tablespoons red-wine vinegar

1 teaspoon caster sugar

300 ml (10 fl oz) passata

3–4 tomatoes, blanched (page 209) and cut into 5 mm (¼ in) dice

1–2 tablespoons bought ready-made tomato ketchup

salt and pepper

150–300 ml (5–6 fl oz) water or liquor from boiling beans

Introduction Beans cooked with bacon or ham was an early British classic. The Pilgrim Fathers took the dish with them to the New World, and it is the American version of our dish that has survived and become part of our present heritage as Boston baked beans. The Boston version cooks beans with molasses and spices in the oven. Over the years, after the advent of canning, the sauce developed into a spicy tomato sauce, and today everybody considers beans a store-cupboard basic. I love baked beans in tomato sauce, which are hard, in fact almost impossible, to match or beat. So here I'm not trying to compete, but it's always nice to offer something home-made. And I also like the idea of telling your guests that their next course is baked beans on toast! Canned varieties of dried beans can be used instead of boiling dried ones. If so, drain and rinse before adding to the tomato sauce. Using the canned will obviously cut back on cooking time.

Method It's important to check the date on dried white haricot beans. Once out of date, or close to it, the bean has become so dry that it crumbles rather than softens. Place the beans, carrots, onion and celery in a saucepan covered with lots of water. Bring to the boil and simmer for 2–2½ hours, making sure the beans are always covered with water (the maximum cooking time for a dried bean is 3 hours). Once tender, drain in a colander and bake the cooking liquor, which will have a vegetable-stock flavour. The liquor can be used instead of water to loosen the beans later.

Meanwhile, make the sauce. Warm the olive oil in a saucepan. Add the chopped shallots or onions and garlic and cook for 6–7 minutes, without colouring, until softened. Add the red-wine vinegar and cook until almost dry. Stir in the sugar before adding the passata and 150 ml (5 fl oz) water or liquor from the beans. Bring to the simmer and cook for 10 minutes before adding 1 tablespoon of the ketchup. Continue to simmer for a further 5 minutes. Season with salt and pepper, adding the remaining tablespoon of ketchup for a stronger tomato finish, if preferred.

Add the cooked beans and tomato dice to the sauce. Continue to simmer gently for a few minutes. The sauce will begin to thicken. To loosen, simply add the remaining 150 ml (5 fl oz) of water or liquor.

Meanwhile, toast the bread, then butter it, if you wish. Now spoon the beans on to the warm toasts and serve.

Note: *The beans can be made several hours in advance and left to stand and absorb the tomato flavour. To loosen the sauce, add a little more water and re-season with salt and pepper.*

Twice-baked Cheese Soufflés

Serves 6

25 g (1 oz) butter, plus extra for greasing

25 g (1 oz) flour

150 ml (5 fl oz) milk, warmed

100–175 g (4–6 oz) cheese, such as goat's, Cheddar or Roquefort, grated or chopped

3 egg yolks

grated Parmesan or fresh white breadcrumbs, for coating

4 egg whites

squeeze of lemon juice

salt and pepper

For the Sauce

50–75 g butter

1 shallot, roughly chopped

celery trimmings, roughly chopped

6 grapes, halved

300 ml (10 fl oz) dry cider

150 ml (5 fl oz) Vegetable Stock (page 204) or alternative, or water

4 tablespoons crème fraîche or single cream

salt and pepper

For the Garnishes

2 celery sticks, peeled and cut into small dice (approx. 5 mm/¼ in)

5–6 seedless grapes, per portion, peeled and halved

1 heaped tablespoon chopped fresh parsley (optional)

Introduction 'Puffed up' (a translation of soufflé) dishes can often become a nightmare with the timing having to be just right, and hoping they will actually work. With twice-baked soufflés you can have them all cooked before your guests arrive, finishing them minutes before the course is due. This double-cooking method will only really apply to a savoury soufflé; sweet fruit and chocolate need total lightness for their perfection (Hot Chocolate Soufflé, page 174). Once cooked and risen, the soufflés are removed from the oven and after a few minutes they are removed from their moulds and allowed to cool. To re-heat simply place on trays and within minutes they're warmed through. So this soufflé is the perfect alternative savoury cheese course.

I've included a recipe for celery and grape sauce to partner the soufflé, both perfect accompaniments to cheese. This is a vegetarian savoury, the recipe filling 6 individual ramekin dishes.

Method To make the soufflés, pre-heat the oven to 190°C/375°F/Gas 5. Melt the butter in a saucepan, adding the flour and stirring to a roux. Cook on a low heat for 5–6 minutes before slowly adding the warm milk. Once all the milk has been stirred in, continue to cook for a few minutes before sprinkling and melting the cheese into the mix. Season with salt and pepper and remove from the heat. Transfer to a bowl, straining through a sieve if required, and cool slightly before adding the egg yolks.

The ramekin dishes can now be buttered and chilled, repeating the process three times. On the last occasion, line the moulds with an even layer of the grated Parmesan cheese or white breadcrumbs.

Whisk the egg whites to a soft peak, adding a squeeze of lemon juice. A quarter of the white can now be whisked into the cheese base, followed by gently folding in the remainder. Fill each of the moulds to the top of the paper collar, and smooth with a palette knife.

Place into a roasting dish filled with enough hot water to come a third of the way up the side of the ramekins. Bake in the pre-heated oven for 12–15 minutes: the soufflés will have risen, still maintaining a moist interior. Remove from the oven and leave to cool slightly before turning out of the moulds and keeping presentation-side up. The soufflés can now be kept on a greased baking tray until needed.

To re-heat, return to the oven and cook for 4–5 minutes until warmed through.

To make the sauce, melt a small knob of butter, adding the chopped shallot, celery trimmings and 6 halved, unpeeled grapes. Cook, colouring slightly, for 6–7 minutes until softening. Add the cider and bring to the boil, reducing by three-quarters. Pour in the vegetable stock, also boiling and reducing by one-third. The cream can now be whisked in and, once simmering, the remaining butter, saving a little to cook the garnishes. Season with salt and pepper and strain through a sieve. Once re-heated, the sauce can be blitzed with an electric hand blender for a smoother and lighter finish.

To cook the garnishes, melt the remaining knob of butter in a saucepan and, once bubbling, add the diced celery. Cook, without colouring, for a few minutes, until softening. Meanwhile, re-heat the soufflés in the oven for 4–5 minutes until warmed. To finish the dish, add the grapes to the celery, stirring for 1–2 minutes before pouring in the warmed sauce. Finish with the chopped parsley, if using, before spooning around the soufflés presented on plates or in bowls.

Open Smoked Haddock Lasagne

Serves 4

4 × 100 g (4 oz) natural smoked haddock portions

8 fresh pasta sheets (page 208) or fresh or dried bought ready-made lasagne

½ quantity English Spinach (page 142), or 1 quantity for spinach lovers

For the Sauce

1 small onion, sliced

2 star anise

1 bay leaf

150 ml (5 fl oz) white wine

100 ml (3½ fl oz) double or whipping cream

25 g (1 oz) butter

salt, pepper and a squeeze of lemon juice

Introduction Although this dish is one of my favourite savouries, I also serve it as a starter or supper dish. The 'open' of the recipe title simply means that the pasta is not multi-layered with several sauces or other ingredients. Instead, there are just two sheets of pasta per portion, one for the base and one on top. The fish is cooked in the sauce liquor, which is then finished with cream and butter. English spinach serves as a base for the haddock, which eats extremely well with the pasta, but there are possible alternatives: finely shredded fennel gently cooked in butter and sauce liquor can replace the spinach, or you can leave the haddock on its own under the pasta, surrounded with sweet peas in a cream sauce. To make this recipe even more special, place a warm poached egg on top of the fish before topping with the pasta and sauce. Cutting through and seeing the egg yolks trickle into the dish immediately activates your tastebuds.

Method Place the onion, star anise and bay leaf in a saucepan and cover with the white wine and 150 ml (5 fl oz) of water. Bring to the simmer and cook for 6–7 minutes. Return to the boil and pour over the smoked haddock fillets laid in an ovenproof pan. Cover and leave to stand for 5–6 minutes. Remove the fillets and keep warm.

Boil the flavoured water and reduce by two-thirds, before adding the cream. Return to the simmer, cook for a few minutes and strain through a sieve.

While the sauce is being made, the pasta sheets can be cooked. Fresh sheets will take only 2 minutes in boiling, salted water, with dried taking 4–5 minutes.

Add the butter to the sauce, whisking it in vigorously. Season with salt, pepper and a squeeze of lemon juice. This sauce can now be blitzed with an electric hand blender to create a frothy, milkshake consistency.

Once the pasta sheets have been removed from the water, season with salt and pepper, placing the base sheets on plates. Divide and spoon the cooked spinach (which can be pre-cooked and microwaved or heated in butter when needed) between the four pasta bases. The warm smoked haddock fillets can now be placed on top, spooning a tablespoon of sauce over each before placing the remaining pasta sheet on top. Finish spooning the frothy sauce over each and serve.

Notes: *Fresh mixed herbs, such as parsley, chervil, chives and tarragon, can be added to the sauce before serving.*

A quick lemon oil (a teaspoon of juice to a tablespoon of olive oil) can also be made to dot around the plates before serving.

Soft-boiled Eggs with Spinach and Parmesan Cheese

Serves 4

4 eggs

25 g (1 oz) butter

350–450 g (12 oz–1 lb) spinach, picked and washed

4–6 tablespoons crème fraîche

1–2 tablespoons freshly grated Parmesan cheese

salt, pepper and freshly ground nutmeg

Introduction Boiled eggs became part of the Great British Breakfast in Victorian times. This recipe isn't actually a breakfast dish, although it could perhaps be served as a more savoury alternative to the classic boiled egg and toast soldiers. It really does eat well, though, as a savoury course, either instead of or as well as dessert. Having said that, it would also eat very nicely as a starter or lunch/supper dish on its own.

There's an art to boiling eggs to the right stage. First, always have your eggs at room temperature. A cold egg cooked straight from the fridge will experience such a change in pressure that it will almost certainly crack. This then releases some albumen (the egg white), which creates uneven cooking. Second, boil the egg in simmering water, not boiling; the latter will create turbulence, juggling the eggs around so that they could quite easily crack into one another.

To complete the dish, we have some spinach and a cheese cream. When you break into the succulent soft eggs with their Parmesan cream topping, the runny warm yolk trickles over the rich spinach.

Method To soft-boil eggs, bring your saucepan of water to a gentle simmer. Using a tablespoon, carefully lower the eggs into the water. Once the water has returned to the same simmering point, cook for 3–5 minutes – rare or medium. Or you can sit the eggs in a saucepan of cold water, bring to a fast simmer and then lift the pan from the heat. Place a lid on the pot and leave the eggs standing in the hot water for 4–5 minutes (a minute longer for very large eggs). Alternatively, you can place the eggs in simmering water and cook for 1 minute. Remove from the stove and complete as for the cold-water method, leaving the eggs standing in the pot with a lid on.

Once cooked, allow to cool for a minute before carefully shelling. The eggs can now be kept warm in a bowl, covered with cling film.

To finish the dish, warm a large pan and melt the butter. Once bubbling, add the spinach, cooking and stirring for a few minutes until the leaves have wilted and become tender. Season with salt, pepper and nutmeg. Warm the crème fraîche and add the Parmesan cheese, making sure the mixtre does not boil. Squeeze any excess water from the spinach and divide between four bowls or plates.

Place a boiled egg on top of each, spooning the Parmesan crème fraîche over. The dish is now ready to serve.

Notes: *Olive oil, flavoured with chopped parsley, tarragon or both, can be trickled over each egg for an extra flavour.*

Chopped, fried bacon pieces added to the spinach will also bring a new flavour.

Onion and Fromage Blanc Tarts

Serves 6–8 as a savoury, 4–6 (with a green salad) as a starter

butter, for greasing

flour, for rolling pastry

225 g (8 oz) Shortcrust or Puff Pastry (page 211 or 212) or bought ready-made puff pastry

2 tablespoons olive oil

3–4 onions, sliced

100 g (4 oz) fromage blanc or fromage frais

150 ml (5 fl oz) whipping cream

2 eggs

salt and pepper

For the Double Parsley Dressing

2–3 garlic cloves, roasted (if using raw, one large clove will be sufficient)

4 tablespoons olive oil

squeeze of lemon juice

1 teaspoon chopped fresh flatleaf parsley

1 teaspoon chopped curly parsley

salt and pepper

Introduction These simple tarts suit the savoury course perfectly. The soft, unripened cheese works wonderfully with the slightly bitter-sweet onions, both surrounded by the light, crisp shortcrust pastry. There are very few ingredients here, but lots of flavours. I also suggest a garlic and double parsley oil, which you can drizzle over the tarts just before eating.

There's often argument about fromage blanc and fromage frais. Are they one and the same, or totally different products? The answer is quite simple. Fromage blanc is made from cow's milk with the curds lightly drained, which keeps the texture moist and milky. This, once beaten to a smooth purée, becomes fromage frais.

The parsley dressing combines English curly and Continental flat varieties, both adding their own texture and strength of flavour. The garlic can simply be crushed and mixed with the other ingredients, but does give a slightly raw finish, I prefer to roast garlic cloves in their skins while the pastry case is baking. During this cooking time, the garlic softens and mellows in its overall flavour; also, once peeled, it purées instantly.

Method Butter 4–6 tartlet tins 10 cm (4 in) in diameter, or a 20 cm (8 in) flan tin, 2.5 cm (1 in) deep. Roll out the pastry and line the tin(s), leaving any excess hanging over. Refrigerate for 20 minutes. Meanwhile, pre-heat the oven to 200°C/400°F/Gas 6.

Line the pastry case(s) with greaseproof paper, rice or baking beans and cook in the pre-heated oven for 20–25 minutes. Remove from the oven, take out the paper and rice or beans and leave to cool. The excess pastry can now be trimmed away, preferably with a serrated knife, leaving a neat, even finish.

Heat the olive oil in a frying-pan, adding the sliced onions. Cook on a medium heat until softened, 6–7 minutes, increasing the heat for a few more minutes to give a good golden brown, with tinges of caramelized finish. Remove from the pan and leave to cool.

Whisk together the fromage blanc or frais, whipping cream and eggs, add the onions and season with salt and pepper. Spoon into the pastry cases and bake at the same temperature, 15–20 minutes for the large tin and 10–12 for the individuals, until just beginning to set. Remove from the oven and leave to rest for 10 minutes before removing from the flan tin(s) and serving warm.

To make the dressing, peel the roasted garlics and squash to a purée; if using raw, crush to a smooth purée. Whisk the olive oil into the garlic, add a squeeze of lemon and season with salt and pepper. The chopped parsleys should be added just before serving to prevent them from losing colour due to the acidity of the juice.

Notes: *For a 'warmer' dressing, a quarter to half a teaspoon of Dijon mustard can also be added.*

Another accompaniment that eats well with the tart is a simple tomato and basil salad drizzled with olive oil.

Twice-cooked Poached Eggs with Red-wine Sauce

Serves 4

1 tablespoon olive oil

large knob of butter

4 or 8 Poached Eggs (page 209)

salt and pepper

4 muffin halves or slices of bread

For the Red-wine Sauce

300 ml (10 fl oz) red wine

300 ml (10 fl oz) Vegetable Stock (page 204), or alternative

100 ml (3½ fl oz) double cream

50 g (2 oz) cold butter, diced (optional)

salt and pepper

For the Butter

40 g (1½ oz) butter

1 teaspoon Dijon mustard

1 teaspoon chopped fresh chives

pinch of salt

Introduction Whenever serving poached eggs for dinner parties, I recommend that they are pre-poached, trimmed (see page 209) and then re-heated in simmering water for a minute. By doing this, the dish becomes stress-free, and you don't have to worry about the eggs over-cooking in a pot of cloudy water at the last minute. The twice-cooked eggs here follow that theory but have a different finish. They are re-heated by being pan-fried in butter, which gives a lovely nutty edge to the whites. Whether serving this vegetarian dish as a savoury or starter, the quantity of eggs per portion, one or two, is up to you.

As a base for the eggs, toasted bread or muffin halves can be used. They can be spread with a little mustard and chive butter, which is not essential, but very tasty; plain butter can also be used.

The red-wine sauce is a simple reduction of wine and vegetable stock, finished with a dot of cream, and butter if a richer, silkier finish is preferred. If the reduction of wine and stock is too bitter, add a sugar cube to sweeten the finish.

Method Start by making the sauce. Pour the wine and vegetable stock into a saucepan, bring to the boil and reduce by three-quarters. This will now hold quite an intense flavour. Add the double cream and cook for a few minutes, seasoning with salt and pepper. An extra twist of pepper, giving a warm bite to the sauce, works very well with this dish. For a silkier finish, whisk the butter into the simmering sauce just before serving.

To make the butter, simply mix with the mustard and chives, seasoning with a pinch of salt.

To finish the eggs, heat a frying pan with the olive oil and knob of butter. Make sure the eggs have been gently patted dry before placing in the pan once the butter is bubbling. Pan-fry for 2 minutes, turning the eggs to achieve a coloured edge. The heat of the pan should be hot enough to allow the butter to reach nut-brown stage. This will provide the nutty flavour.

Toast the muffins or bread and spread with the mustard and chive butter; if using toasts, cut diagonally in two pieces, stacking one on top of the other in different directions. Place the eggs on top and spoon over the red-wine sauce.

Notes: *Some of the nut-brown butter can also be spooned over the eggs.*

A teaspoon of strong red-wine vinegar can be added to the sauce for a piquant finish.

Watercress dressed in red-wine vinegar dressing (page 204) can be used as garnish for the eggs.

Dressed Crab Salad

Serves 4–6

½ quantity *Court Bouillon* (page 201)

500–600 g (1 lb 2 oz–1 lb 10 oz) live crab

1–2 tablespoons Mayonnaise (page 207) or bought ready-made mayonnaise, for the brown crab meat, if using

squeeze of lemon juice

salt and pepper

To Finish

mixed salad leaves (sold in bags, usually containing baby spinach, lamb's lettuce, rocket and curly endive)

3–4 spring onions, shredded

For the Salad Vinaigrette

3 x 7-minute hard-boiled eggs (page 31)

200 ml (7 fl oz) groundnut oil

1 teaspoon Dijon mustard

1 dessertspoon white-wine vinegar

25 g (1 oz) capers, chopped

25 g (1 oz) gherkins, finely diced

1 heaped teaspoon snipped fresh parsley

1 heaped teaspoon snipped fresh chives

1 teaspoon snipped fresh tarragon

salt and pepper

Introduction Seafood has been part of the British diet since time immemorial, and excavations of prehistoric and Roman sites have unearthed many mussel, scallop and oyster shells. Lobsters, scallops and langoustines have become expensive delicacies today, but many people class the crab and its sweet meat above them. The most common crab in British waters is the large brown crab, although many different varieties are found and appreciated around the world. Whenever buying crab, it's important to make sure it's heavy in weight, and that, when its shell is tapped, it does not sound hollow.

There are many ways of killing a crab. If you want to present it whole, it's best to put it in cold water, and bring up from cold to hot (this prevents it from shedding its claws). Sometimes the crab is cooked from the start in boiling water; here I've used a boiling *court bouillon*, which adds nothing but flavour. However, it's not essential to cook your own crab for this recipe. Fresh white crab meat, of which you need 225–275 g (8–10 oz), and occasionally brown (which can be omitted from the recipe), can be found in most fishmongers and supermarkets.

The classic dressed crab is cooked crab re-dressed in its cleaned shell and then garnished with chopped hard-boiled egg white and yolk and chopped parsley. It's traditionally served with brown bread and butter. I'm going to change that a little, but I keep all of those flavours, turning them into a fresh salad to finish (or start) your meal with.

Method To cook the crab, bring the *court bouillon* or salted water to the boil. Add the crab and boil for 12 minutes. Remove the pan from the stove. I now like to leave the crabs to sit in the *bouillon* until just at a warm stage. This continues and finishes the cooking of the crab. (If you are cooking another crab dish for which you need the liquor, continue to boil the crab for another 3–5 minutes, making the complete cooking time 15–17 minutes.)

To open a just-boiled and piping hot crab, first run under cold water to calm the fierce heat. To remove the body from the shell, hold the crab firmly and give its back underside a heavy thump. This will release the body and legs. The next stage is to stand the crab on its head and push the underbody with your thumbs. Lever away the shell with your fingers. Now the body is loose on the shell, it can be pulled away completely, with the legs. The intestines will now either still be attached to the base of the shell or to the body. Whichever, pull away and discard, first gently forking away any brown meat attached. Scoop any other brown meat from either side of the shell. On the body flesh itself, you will find grey gills, known as 'dead man's fingers'. Contrary to common belief, these are inedible rather than poisonous, so simply pull off and discard. Remove all the legs and claws; this will reveal white meat in the body. With a heavy knife, make two cuts either side of the centre in a V-shape, cutting the meat into three. The middle part is not needed. Using a skewer, remove the white meat from the other two pieces. Crack open the claws with the back of a large knife or hammer; the meat can now be easily removed from them. Shred, removing any shell, and mix with the white body meat. Season with salt, pepper and lemon juice.

If used, the brown crab meat is, classically, sieved. This can make it very pasty. I prefer to chop through the meat with a knife before mixing with enough mayonnaise to help hold the texture. Season with salt and pepper and a squeeze of lemon juice.

To make the dressing, peel the hard-boiled eggs and separate the yolks from the whites. The yolks can now be crushed to a fine paste. Slowly add half the oil, mixing well to emulsify with the yolks. The vinegar and mustard can now be added, followed by the remaining oil. Roughly chop 1½–2 of the egg whites and add to the mix, along with the capers, gherkins and herbs. The remaining egg white will not be needed. Season with salt and pepper and the dressing is ready.

To assemble the salad, spoon the brown crab meat mayonnaise (if using) into the centre of the plates in a circular fashion. Mix three-quarters of the white crab meat with the salad leaves and spring onions (the onions can also be sprinkled around the plate), adding 4 tablespoons of the dressing. This can now be piled on top of the brown crab meat. Sprinkle the remaining white crab meat around the plates, drizzling with more dressing. The dressed crab meat salads are now ready to serve.

Notes: *Although this recipe looks awfully long for a simple savoury dish, it provides essential information about preparing and cooking crabs that can be applied to any other crab recipe. As stated in the introduction, the dish can be simplified by purchasing cooked white crab meat (checking over it for any shell), omitting the brown crab meat mayonnaise, then making just the dressing and adding the salad leaves. The whole process will then take just minutes.*

Here are one or two extra ideas for more flavours to be included in this dish.

- *Peel (with a swivel potato peeler) half a sweet red pepper and cut into small dice before adding to the dressing. The sweet flavour and red colour give the dish another edge.*
- *Shallot rings can be used in place of the spring onions. Thinly sliced radishes also eat well in the salad.*
- *The brown crab meat mayonnaise can be served on warm round toasts with the salad completed on top, for another texture.*

Sardines on Toast

Serves 4

4 slices of 'uncut', white, brown or granary bread

olive oil and butter for brushing

8 sardines, scaled and filleted (16 fillets)

salt and pepper (preferably sea salt)

For the Sauce Rémoulade

100 ml (3½ fl oz) Mayonnaise (page 207) or bought ready-made mayonnaise

1 teaspoon finely chopped gherkin

1 teaspoon finely chopped capers

1 teaspoon Dijon mustard

1 heaped teaspoon mixed chopped fresh herbs e.g. parsley, tarragon and chervil

1 small anchovy fillet, finely chopped

squeeze of lemon juice

salt and pepper (coarse sea salt can be used)

Optional Extras

green salad leaves e.g. rocket, baby spinach and watercress

2 tablespoons olive oil

2 teaspoons red-wine vinegar

salt and pepper

Introduction Sardines, which belong to the herring family, are among the tastiest of small fish. They also kindly offer us the pleasure of their big brothers, pilchards. People often say they love one and not the other; however, they are basically the same fish, the pilchard simply the larger of the two. Tinned or fresh sardines on toast are a traditional savoury dating from Victorian times, but they also eat well as a starter or supper snack.

Here, fresh fish fillets are sitting on toast that's also carrying a spread of *sauce rémoulade*. This is made from a mildly mustard-flavoured mayonnaise, helped along by the addition of gherkins, capers, fresh herbs and a sardine relative, anchovy. I like to grill the fillets, sitting them head to tail on the spread toasts. As the fish cooks, the sauce begins to melt into the toasts, with the edges of the bread burning to a slight bitterness that contributes incredibly to the overall flavour of the dish.

The fresh sardines need to be scaled, gutted and filleted. Your fishmonger can do this, but it's reasonably easy to do at home. Run the fish under cold water while you push the scales off and away. The head should now be removed, which will then show you exactly where to sit the blade of a sharp filleting knife. Cut along the bone confidently and the fillet will come away in one movement. Turn the fish over and repeat the same cut. Scrape away the gut and bones, rinse and pat dry. Any fine pin bones will virtually disintegrate during the cooking, becoming very tender to eat.

Method To make the sauce, add all of the ingredients to the mayonnaise, seasoning with salt and pepper, if necessary. Brush the bread rectangles with olive oil before toasting to a light golden brown. Spread each slice generously with the *sauce rémoulade*.

Place the fillets, four per portion, top to tail on a greased baking sheet and brush with butter. Season with sea salt and pepper before placing under the pre-heated hot grill. The fillets will now take only 4–5 minutes, even less if particularly small, to cook and crisp.

While the fish is cooking, the salad leaves, if using, can be arranged in small bundles at the top of the plates. Mix together the olive oil and vinegar, season and drizzle just a teaspoon over the leaves.

Place the sardine portions on the toasts, transfer to plates and spoon any remaining dressing on top or around.

Notes: *Any of the flavours (mustard, anchovy, gherkin, etc.) can be omitted from the* sauce rémoulade, *leaving you with a simple lemon and fresh herb mayonnaise, which also works very well.*

Another alternative is to omit the sauce completely and dress the toasts with slices of tomato, thin shallot rings and herbs and trickle with the red-wine vinegar dressing.

Classic Savoury Mince Pies

Serve 6

butter, for greasing

flour, for rolling pastry

350 g (12 oz) Puff Pastry (page 212) or bought ready-made puff pastry

50 g (2 oz) raisins

50 g (2 oz) currants or sultanas

good pinch of ground mixed spice

1 clove

25 g (1 oz) soft brown sugar

juice of 1 lemon

1 medium carrot, cut into 5 mm (¼ in) dice

225 g (8 oz) tail ends of beef fillet, cut into small dice

¼ teaspoon freshly grated nutmeg

pinch of ground cinnamon

knob of butter

1 teaspoon finely grated orange zest, blanched until tender

2 tablespoons brandy

salt and pepper

To serve

3 tablespoons olive oil

1 teaspoon red-wine vinegar

1–2 bunches of watercress, picked into sprigs

knob of butter

Introduction The mince pie was so christened because it did originally contain cooked and minced beef (mincemeat). Slowly the meat was to disappear, with beef suet taking its place, and this is still with us today.

I have been keen for some time to offer my friends the original version, but obviously with a new edge and finish to the dish. So here it is. I'm using raw beef fillet tails, which are inexpensive, especially when you need only 225 g (8 oz). The dried fruit is steeped with spices, lemon juice and a touch of sugar. Other flavours I'm including are carrots (to represent the candied orange peel) and grated orange zest; I usually put both in my Christmas puddings, so they are very familiar with spicy flavours. Basically my modern version of the classic mince pie is a small stir-fry served in a puff pastry tartlet case with a little watercress topping. An optional extra is to spoon mashed potatoes into the base of each tartlet; this helps create a creamy finish, and absorbs a lot of the savoury liquor from the finished dressing.

Method Pre-heat the oven to 200°C/400°F/Gas 6 and butter six tartlet tins 7 cm (3 in) in diameter.

Roll the puff pastry thinly, then use to line the tartlet tins, leaving any excess hanging over the edge. This will guarantee no shrinking during the cooking process. Line the pastry cases with greaseproof paper and baking beans or rice, then bake in the pre-heated oven for 25–30 minutes. Remove the greaseproof paper and beans, and if the pastry is not quite cooked and crispy, return to the oven for a few more minutes. Leave to cool before trimming away the excess pastry.

Place the raisins, currants or sultanas, mixed spice, clove, sugar, lemon juice and 150 ml (5 fl oz) of water in a saucepan. Bring to the simmer and cook gently for 10–15 minutes. Remove from the heat and leave to stand for a further 15 minutes. Drain the fruits through a sieve, saving the spicy liquor. The liquor can now be re-boiled and reduced by half. Leave to one side.

Place the diced carrot in a saucepan and cover with cold water. Bring to the simmer and cook until tender. Strain through a sieve and leave to cool.

Season the beef with salt, pepper, nutmeg and cinnamon. Heat a wok or frying-pan and, once hot, add a knob of butter. On the point of it turning to nut brown, add the beef. Toss in the pan for 10–15 seconds before adding the carrots. Continue to cook for a further 30–40 seconds before adding the fruits and orange zest. Season and flambé with the brandy. The beef is now cooked, taking no more than 1½–2 minutes. Some liquor will have been created with the fruits and brandy. Spoon between the tartlet cases, presenting them on plates or in bowls. If adding mashed potatoes, as mentioned in the introduction, simply pipe or spoon into the tartlet before adding the mince.

Whisk together the olive oil, reduced fruit liquor (approximately 2 tablespoons) and the red-wine vinegar, seasoning with salt and pepper. Sit small bunches of watercress on top of each mince pie. Spoon over some of the dressing and drizzle a little more around.

Note: *An alternative way of using the mashed potato is to pipe it on top of the mince, brush with butter and gratinate under a hot grill, creating shepherd's mince pies.*

Mushroom Toasts with Melting Swiss Cheese

Serves 4

4 × 1.5–2 cm (⅔–¾ in) thick slices of bread, brushed with olive oil

½ garlic clove

8 cup or large flat mushrooms, wiped clean and stalks trimmed

knob of butter, melted

4 thick slices of Gruyère cheese (8 for a cheesier finish), soaked in milk

salt and pepper

For the Dressing

1 tablespoon pine nuts

100 ml (3½ fl oz) olive oil

1 large garlic clove or 2 small

bunch of fresh basil, picked

salt and pepper

Introduction These toasts make a very moreish vegetarian savoury, but they would also be good as a starter, snack or supper dish.

The best mushrooms to use are the cups or the large flat variety, which provide a very meaty, almost steak-like texture, holding all the mushroom juices. These sit on garlic toasts, which are slices of bread (country white, wholemeal or nutty-flavoured granary) brushed with olive oil and baked in the oven until golden. Raw garlic is then rubbed on to the warm slices, which results in a totally different flavour, quite a lot fuller and fresher. If the bread is rubbed with garlic before cooking, the garlic flavour can be lost, or might struggle to let you know it's there. Garlic is also used to flavour the dressing, which is, in fact, a mild, loose pesto sauce. The predominant flavour of a classic Genovese pesto is basil, helped along by toasted pine kernels, garlic, olive oil and grated Parmesan. These flavours eat very well with the mushrooms and the Swiss Gruyère melted across the top just before serving.

Method Pre-heat the oven to 190°C/375°F/Gas 5.

Make the dressing first. Lightly toast or fry the pine nuts in a little of the olive oil to a golden brown. This will increase their nutty flavour. Leave to cool. Place all of the ingredients, bar the basil, in a food processor or liquidizer and blitz to a puréed dressing. Add the basil leaves and continue to blitz until finely chopped. Season with salt and pepper.

A crunchier version can be made by simply chopping the pine nuts and mixing with crushed garlic, chopped basil leaves and olive oil.

For the toasts, place the breads in the pre-heated oven and cook until crisp and golden brown. This will take 10–15 minutes (20 maximum). Once removed from the oven, rub each on the presentation side with the half garlic clove.

While the toasts are cooking, brush the mushrooms with butter and season with salt and pepper. Place on a baking tray, top-side down and cook under a pre-heated grill. They can be left unturned and cooked for 8–10 minutes until tender, or be turned halfway through their cooking time.

To serve, place two mushrooms, either way up, on each toast, top with the Swiss cheese and melt under the grill. Arrange on plates and spoon the dressing over and around. The savoury is ready to serve.

Note: *A selection of green salad leaves can be used to garnish the plates before serving.*

Soft Herring Roes on Toast

Serves 4

pinch of salt and cayenne pepper

1–2 tablespoons plain flour

350–450 g (12–16 oz) fresh soft herring roes (canned roes can also be used)

4 thick round slices of bread

olive oil, for frying

25 g (1 oz) butter

4 wedges of lemon, to serve

Introduction The male and female herring both contain roe, but it is the male that produces soft roe, a very special delicacy. Also known as milt, soft roe carries a creaminess that, when fried in butter and served warm on toast, is quite sublime. The hard female roe is also edible, but lacks that rich, creamy finish.

Cod's roe with bacon used to be a popular breakfast dish in the south-west of England and in Ireland, while herring roes were eaten for breakfast, high tea and as a classic savoury finish to a meal. In this recipe they are simply pan-fried in butter and flavoured with just a hint of cayenne pepper to spice them up. Sit them on toasts with a wedge of lemon and you have a savoury snack which is also good as a starter.

Method Mix the salt and cayenne pepper with the plain flour and lightly dust the herring roes. Heat a frying-pan with the olive oil and butter. Once bubbling, place the roes in the pan and fry for a few minutes, turning until golden brown.

Toast the bread slices, or pan-fry in butter for a richer flavour. Places the roes on them and serve with the wedges of lemon.

Notes: *Here are a few alternative ideas for this recipe.*

- *Once the herring roes are on the toasts, add a few chopped shallots, capers, parsley and a squeeze of lemon juice to the pan before spooning the flavoured bubbling butter over the roes.*
- *Make the red-wine sauce on page 85, pouring it over and around the toasts to create red-wine herring-roe toasts.*
- *A quick lemon butter can be made by boiling the juice of 1 lemon and 2 tablespoons of water together, before whisking in 50 g (2 oz) of cold, diced butter. Once seasoned, drizzle the sauce around the plate. Fresh herbs, such as parsley, chervil, tarragon or sorrel, can all be added to the sauce.*
- *Omit the cayenne from the flour and make a spicy chilli butter to melt over the roes. Simply blitz together 100 g (4 oz) softened butter, 1 teaspoon clear honey or golden syrup, 1 teaspoon mild chilli sauce or a few dashes of Tabasco sauce and 2 teaspoons lime juice. Roll into a cylinder shape in cling film. This can now be frozen until needed. To serve, cut into discs and melt on top of the roes before serving.*
- *Chopped mint or parsley can be added to the chilli butter, creating a herby, spicy finish.*

Oatmeal Fried Salmon Slice on Toast with a Lemon Butter Whisky Dressing

Seves 4

25 g (1 oz) pinhead oatmeal

25 g (1 oz) fresh white breadcrumbs

flour, for dusting

4 × 75–100 g (3–4 oz) slices of salmon fillet, skinned

1 egg, beaten

1 tablespoon olive oil

knob of butter

salt and pepper

For the Dressing

2 tablespoons whisky

1–2 tablespoons lemon juice

4 tablespoons olive oil

large knob of butter

salt and pepper

To serve

4 slices of rectangular brown bread (about 1 cm/½ in thick)

handful of young spinach leaves

Introduction Oatmeal and salmon are two classic Scottish ingredients. The dressing, made with whisky, adds another Scottish dimension, and gives warmth to the finished dish. I also like to top the toasts with young spinach leaves before sitting the hot salmon on top. The wilted greens add a fresh touch to the finished dish.

Method To make the dressing, boil and reduce the whisky by half. Add the lemon juice before whisking in the olive oil. The butter can now be either just melted and added or heated to a nut-brown stage before straining through a sieve and adding to the dressing. Season with salt and pepper, adding more lemon juice (and whisky) if needed.

The bread slices can be simply toasted or pan-fried in bubbling butter until golden.

Mix together the oatmeal and breadcrumbs, seasoning with salt and pepper. Season and brush with the beaten egg before pressing into the oatmeal crumbs.

Heat the olive oil in a frying-pan, adding a knob of butter. Once bubbling, place the salmon in, presentation-side down, and pan-fry for 3–4 minutes until golden brown. Turn the fish over and continue cooking for a further few minutes until just beginning to firm. An alternative method is to drizzle the fillets with butter before cooking under a pre-heated grill, presentation-side only, for 6–7 minutes.

To serve, place the toasts on plates, sprinkling the fresh spinach leaves over each. Spoon the dressing over, before topping with the salmon fillet portions.

Notes: *Chopped fresh herbs, such as parsley, chervil or tarragon, can be added to the oats or dressing.*

A teaspoon of very finely chopped shallot can also be added to the oatmeal topping.

For an extra-crispy finish, re-dip the fillets into egg and press again into the crumbs.

Many's the long night I've dreamed of cheese – toasted mainly.

Treasure Island, R.L. Stevenson

Cheese

Author Clifton Fadiman describes cheese as *'milk's leap toward immortality'.*

The cheese course in Britain comes at the end of the meal as the last course to be enjoyed, whereas in France it is served between that of the main and dessert. Why? In France it's said the cheese has always been served after the main course, and used as a means to polish off the red wine. We all know how greatly French wine is appreciated, and quite rightly so – they produce some of the finest in the world. *Guide de Fromages* (*Guide to Cheeses*) contains a question and answer that reads like this.

If I do not drink wine, may I drink water with cheese?

Never. *Not even with mild cheeses. Water and cheese together can cause a stomach ache. Better to take no cheese at all if you do not take a drink that is slightly alcoholic. Another possibility is to take the cheese and drink nothing. Man has yet to find a better companion to cheese than wine.*

(ENGLISH EDITION BY AIDAN ELLIS PUBLISHING LTD, 1983)

An interesting thought and argument, but I feel in Britain we have found an equally good companion.

The reason, and it's the only one I can find and think of, we take our cheese as the last course is that we enjoy after-dinner drinks, and one that suits cheese, in particular, our resident classic Stilton, is a good glass of port. I feel a good port is equally good to accompany any cheese, providing the temperature of both is just right. France has one of, if not the, finest selection of cheese in the world. However, British cheese-making over the last 30 years has changed dramatically, with literally hundreds of new varieties and imports from Ireland finding their way on to the shelves of many new cheese shops.

The hardest thing with cheese is not so much buying it – in most shops the seller is also the expert who helps you with your choice – but keeping them at the right temperature to guarantee you'll be enjoying them at their best. In the perfect world we would all be fortunate enough to have a cellar in which to keep our cheeses. Cheeses need a fairly humid atmosphere and, like wine, a temperature between 7–10°C (45–50°F). Sadly, refrigerators and closed boxes do not circulate the air in the same way as cellars to keep the cheeses, creating a sweaty feeling to the cheese and consequently spoiling its flavour. It's best to keep cheese in closest conditions possible to those of a cellar, such as a corner in the garage, but be careful: below 4°C (40°F) will kill off almost all the flavours you're hoping to enjoy.

If you have no other choice but to keep your cheese refrigerated, buy small quantities that can be eaten quickly, remembering to give the cheese plenty of time to return to room temperature. There are endless accompaniments to cheese: from simple cheese crackers to home-made biscuits such as Digestives (page 212), good granary, walnut and raisin breads, French bread and even the breadsticks featured on page 210. Then there's fruit, such as grapes, apples, apricots and other flavours such as celery sticks, red-onion salads, watercress, walnuts, along with chutneys and relishes. A fairly modern way of serving a cheese course is to feature a cooked cheese dish, such as melting goat's cheese and soft cow's milk cheeses over toasts, black pudding, hot cheese soufflés, double-baked soufflés (page 186), Roquefort trifles, Stilton toasties and Caesar salads – just some examples of the amazing repertoire this milk-based product holds.

As far as the cheese course itself is concerned, whether you place it as the last course of the meal, as is the British style, or before the dessert is really up to you. Cheese that stands on its own as a complete meal is also one not to forget.

While each person's cheese board will consist of different flavours and strengths, depending on personal taste, here's a short selection which can be found in good cheese delicatessens, that you might like to try.

Caerphilly
Duckett's – traditional Caerphilly made by three generations of the Duckett family at Walnut farm on the Somerset Levels. Made of unpasteurized cow's milk with vegetarian rennet.

Cheddar
Keen's – classic West Country Cheddar made from unpasteurized cow's milk at Moorhayes Farm near Wincanton in Somerset.

Cheddar
Montgomery's – old-fashioned, dry, fruity Cheddar made at Manor Farm, North Cadbury in Somerset, using unpasteurized cow's milk with vegetarian rennet.

Cheshire
Appleby's – the last, real farm Cheshire cheese, made from unpasteurized milk and vegetarian rennet, and matured in cloth at Abbey Farm, near Whitchurch, since 1949.

Cotherstone
One of the last traditional cheeses from the Pennines, made at Quarryhouse Farm on the banks of the River Tees. A light creamy, crumbly cheese, made from unpasteurized cow's milk with vegetarian rennet.

Cashel Blue
A soft-textured blue cheese made from pasteurized cow's milk and vegetarian rennet, and produced in Tipperary, Southern Ireland.

Stilton
Colston Bassett – made to a traditional recipe, which results in a gentle-flavour, greenish mould and a creamy texture that is at its best. Produced at Colston Bassett Dairy, near the Vale of Belvoir in Nottingham.

Cooleeny
A rich, full-flavoured Camembert-style cheese using unpasteurized cow's milk and vegetarian rennet. Made near Thurles in Tipperary, Southern Ireland.

Elmhirst
A soft Jersey cheese made from full-fat, thermized milk with added cream, using vegetarian rennet. Produced at Sharpham Creamery, near Totnes, Devon.

Gubbeen
Fresh, milky cheese with a smooth, pliable texture. Made in West Cork, Southern Ireland.

Milleens
An exciting cheese made on the Beara penisula, County Cork, Southern Ireland.

Beeleigh Blue
Sweet, full-flavoured sheep's milk blue cheese produced near the River Dart in Devon, using unpasteurized sheep's milk and vegetarian rennet.

appetizers

soups

fish

mains

vegetables

desserts

savouries

basic recipes

menus

basic recipes

Fish Stock

Makes about 2 litres (3½ pints)

1 large onion, sliced

1 leek, sliced

2 celery sticks, sliced

50 g (2 oz) unsalted butter

few fresh parsley stalks

1 bay leaf

6 black peppercorns

1 kg (2 lb) turbot or sole bones, washed

300 ml (10 fl oz) dry white wine

2.25 litres (4 pints) water

salt

Introduction To make a good fish stock, white fish bones – turbot and sole in particular – should always be used. These give a good flavour, a clear, jelly-like finish and do not carry an oily texture. A friendly fishmonger will help you out by providing the bones. This stock is perfect for poaching and for making fish soups and sauces.

Method Sweat the sliced vegetables in the butter, without colouring. Add the parsley stalks, bay leaf and peppercorns. Chop the fish bones, making sure there are no blood clots left on them. Add to the vegetables and continue to cook for a few minutes. Add the wine and reduce until almost dry. Add the water, season with salt and bring to the simmer. Allow to simmer for 20 minutes, then drain through a sieve. The stock is now ready to use, or you can store it for a few days in the fridge, or for up to 3 months in the freezer.

Court Bouillon

Makes 2 litres (3½ pints)

1 carrot, sliced

1 onion sliced

1–2 celery sticks, sliced

1 garlic clove, sliced

15 g (½ oz) fresh root ginger, peeled and sliced

½ teaspoon each fennel seeds and white peppercorns

1 star anise

1 tablespoon sea salt

250 ml (9 fl oz) white wine

2 tablespoons white-wine vinegar

grated zest of 1 orange

bouquet garni of tarragon leaves, bay leaf and thyme, tied in muslin or a strip of leek

2 litres (3½ pints) water

juice of 1 lemon

Introduction Court-bouillion is used mostly for fish, in particular shellfish. It's quite powerful, but when cooking lobsters, crabs (page 192), langoustines and mussels (page 92), it does nothing but add flavour.

The quantities listed above can easily be halved.

Method Place all the ingredients in a suitably sized saucepan and bring to the boil. Cook on a fast simmer for 15–20 minutes.

Remove the pan from the heat and leave to infuse for 2–3 hours before using. The liquid can now be used as it is or strained through a sieve.

Chicken Stock

Makes 2.25 Litres (4 pints)

2 onions, chopped

2 celery sticks, chopped

2 leeks, chopped

25g (1 oz) unsalted butter

1 garlic clove, crushed

1 bay leaf

sprig of thyme

few black peppercorns

1.8 kg (4 lb) chicken carcasses, chopped

3.4 litres (6 pints) water

Introduction Chicken stock is one of the most important bases in the professional and domestic kitchen. It's used for most soups and many cream sauces, the latter because it is pale in colour. (It is often known as 'white' rather than 'brown' stock.) It's very easy to make but you need to use raw chicken bones. Your butcher should be able to supply you with some, or you can take the breasts off a whole chicken, saving then for another dish, and use the carcass for the stock.

Or, if you can find one, cook a whole boiling fowl with vegetables in water and you will have a quick, tasty stock and the bird to eat as well. Chicken wings also give you an equally flavoursome result.

If you do not have a large stockpot, you can easily reduce the quantities listed.

In a large stockpot (minimum 5¾ litre/ 10 pint capacity), lightly soften the vegetables in the butter, without colouring. Add the garlic, bay leaf, thyme, peppercorns and chopped carcasses. Cover with the cold water and bring to the simmer, skimming all the time. Allow the stock to simmer for 2-3 hours, then drain through a sieve. The stock is now ready to use and will keep well chilled or frozen.

Game stock

Makes 1.2 litres (2 pints)

1 tablespoon cooking oil

3 wood pigeons, chopped into small pieces

1 large onion or 2 shallots, roughly chopped

1 large carrot, roughly chopped

2 celery sticks, roughly chopped

4–5 mushrooms, quartered

bottle of red wine

1 garlic clove, chopped

sprig of thyme

5 juniper berries, crushed

few black peppercorns

2–3 tomatoes, chopped

1.2 litres (2 pints) Chicken, Veal or Beef Stock (pages 201 or 203)

Introduction For this stock, I'm using wild (wood) pigeons. If you are going to be roasting pigeons, use the carcasses for stock, removing the backbone and legs before roasting the breasts on the bone. For this recipe, I suggest you buy frozen birds. These don't give you the fullest flavour, but the whole birds will be used, so a good stock can be made. This stock includes red wine, giving a good all-round flavour, but armagnac, cognac, Madeira and port can also be used.

Chicken stock gives you a thin game stock while veal *jus* gives an instant game sauce.

Method Heat the oil in a large frying pan. Add the pigeons and cook on a medium heat until well coloured and caramelized/roasted. This will take about 20 minutes on top of the stove.

Transfer the pigeons to a saucepan. Add the onions, carrot, celery and mushrooms to the frying pan and cook until beginning to soften and colour, but do not let them get too dark as this will create too bitter a finish. Increase the heat and add a third of the red wine to lift the flavours from the base of the pan. Transfer everything to the saucepan with the pigeons. Add the garlic, thyme, juniper berries, black peppercorns and tomatoes. Cook until the tomatoes have reduced into the red wine. Add the rest of the wine, bring to a fast simmer and reduce by three-quarters. Add the stock. Return to the simmer and cook for 1–1½ hours. Strain through a fine sieve and the stock is ready.

Game *Jus*

600–900 ml (1–1½ pints) Veal/Beef *Jus* (page 203)

300 ml (10 fl oz) water

Follow the above method, replacing the stock with the *jus* and water. Simmer for 1 hour before straining through a fine sieve. The *jus* is now ready to use.

Lamb Stock

Makes about 1.2 litres (2 pints)

oil, for frying

450 g (1 lb) chopped lamb bones (ask the butcher to cut quite small)

225 g (8 oz) diced stewing lamb, or trimmings available from butcher (these are not essential but will offer a stronger flavour to the stock)

1 large carrot, cut into rough 1 cm (½ in) dice

1 large onion, cut into rough 1cm (½ in) dice

1 medium leek, roughly diced

fresh rosemary sprig

fresh thyme sprig

2 bay leaves

2 garlic cloves, halved

2–3 over-ripe tomatoes, chopped

300 ml (10 fl oz) white wine

1.8 litres (3 pints) Chicken Stock (page 201) or alternative, or water

Veal or Beef Stock or *Jus*

Introduction Most of the recipes in this book that require lamb stock need only 600 ml (1 pint) maximum, so I suggest you freeze the remainder until needed. Chicken stock is listed, as this will give a good flavoured start to the stock, but water can also be used. If using water, I suggest allowing the stock to cook for an extra 30–45 minutes, to maximize the flavours.

Method Heat the oil in a large frying-pan. Once hot, add the bones and diced stewing lamb. Cook for 10–15 minutes until well coloured. Transfer to a large saucepan. Any excess fats can be left in the pan and used to fry, with just a little colour, the carrots, onions and leek. Cook for 8–10 minutes until beginning to soften before draining and adding to the lamb bones.

The herbs, garlic and tomatoes can now also be added, cooking on a medium heat until the tomatoes have reached a stewing stage. Add the white wine, bring to the boil and allow to reduce by three-quarters. Pour on the stock or water and bring to a simmer, skimming away any impurities. Cook for 1–1½ hours, skimming from time to time and allowing the stock to reduce by one third. Strain through a fine sieve and leave to relax. Any fat content will now be sitting on top of the stock, making it easy to skim away. Once cool, freeze in your preferred quantities.

Makes 4.5–6 litres (8–10 pints) or 600 ml–1.2 litres (1–2 pints) *jus*/gravy

3 onions, halved

2–3 tablespoons water

2.25 kg (5 lb) veal or beef trimmings (from the butcher)

225 g (8 oz) veal or beef bones

225 g (8 oz) carrots, coarsely chopped

3 celery sticks, coarsely chopped

1 leek, chopped

3–4 tomatoes, chopped

1 garlic clove, halved

1 bay leaf

sprig of thyme

salt

Introduction This brown stock takes a long time to achieve, particularly if you make the *jus* after the stock, but it's very satisfying and any left over can be frozen. The stock is best started in the morning so that it can cook throughout the day. Your butcher might be able to supply you with veal or beef trimmings and bones (government bans permitting). Good, ready-made stocks and *jus* gravies can also be brought in supermarkets.

Method Pre-heat the oven to 120°C/250°F/Gas ½. Lay the onion halves flat in a roasting tray with the water. Place in the oven and allow to caramelize slowly for 1–2 hours, until totally softened and coloured.

Pop the onions into a large stockpot and leave on one side. Increase the oven temperature to 200°C/400°F/Gas 6. Place all the trimmings and bones in the tray and roast for about 30 minutes until well coloured. Roast the carrots and celery in another roasting tray (do not add any oil) for about 20 minutes, until lightly coloured. When ready, add to the onions in the pot, along with the leek, tomatoes, garlic, bay leaf and thyme. Fill the pot with cold water – you'll need about 6–7.2 litres (10–12 pints). Bring the stock to the simmer, season with salt and skim off any impurities. Allow to cook for 6–8 hours for maximum flavour. If it reduces too quickly, top up with cold water.

When ready, drain and discard the bones and vegetables. The remaining liquid is your veal stock, which can be cooled and frozen.

Alternatively, make a veal or beef *jus* with stock. Allow the liquid to boil and reduce to 600 ml–1.2 litres (1–2 pints), skimming all the time. The stock should be thick and of a sauce-like consistency. Make sure you taste all the time during reduction. If the sauce tastes right but is too thin, thicken it slightly with cornflour.

Vegetable Stock

Makes about 1.2 litres (2 pints)

225 g (8 oz) carrots (optional)

2 onions

4 celery sticks

2 leeks, white parts only

1 fennel bulb

1–2 courgettes

1 tablespoon vegetable oil

1 bay leaf

sprig of thyme

1 teaspoon coriander seeds

1 teaspoon pink peppercorns

½ lemon, sliced

1.5 litres (2½ pints) water

pinch of salt

Introduction This is a great alternative to chicken and fish stock in many recipes, particularly if making vegetarian soups. This is a basic recipe, but it can be adapted in any number of ways: simply add or substitute other vegetables, or herb flavours for a subtle difference. Never use root vegetables, however, as they will make the stock cloudy.

Method Cut all the vegetables roughly into 1 cm (½ in) dice. Warm the oil in a pan, then add all the diced vegetables, the herbs, coriander seeds, peppercorns and lemon slices. Cook, without colouring, for 8–10 minutes, allowing the vegetables to soften slightly. Add the water with a good pinch of salt and bring to a simmer, then cook without a lid for 30 minutes. The stock can now be strained through a sieve, leaving you with about 1.2 litres (2 pints). If there is more, just boil rapidly to reduce.

Red-wine Fish Gravy

Makes about 400–450 ml (14–15 fl oz)

cooking oil

2 shallots, or 1 onion sliced

2 tablespoons red-wine vinegar

2 tablespoons brandy

2 glasses of red wine

300 ml (10 fl oz) Fish Stock (page 201) or alternative

300 ml (10 fl oz) Veal *Jus* (page 203) or alternative

Introduction This recipe uses both veal *jus* and fish stock, the two working together to give a light fish flavour to the gravy. The sauce is served with the Tunafish Steaks on Bitter Red-wine Onions (page 71), and also works as a good accompaniment to grilled and roasted fish, such as turbot, sea bass and monkfish.

Method Warm a little oil in a saucepan and add the shallots. Cook on a medium heat until at a golden, rich caramel stage. Add the red-wine vinegar and reduce until almost dry. Add the brandy, also reducing by three-quarters, and then add the red wine, repeating the reduction by three-quarters.

Pour in the fish stock, bring to the simmer and reduce by half. The *jus* can now also be added, cooking on a medium heat for 15 minutes. Strain through a sieve, pushing through all the juices. The gravy is now ready.

If you need only half the quantity, simply freeze the remainder.

It's a good idea to freeze these sauces in ice-cube trays. Some recipes require only a trickle of sauce and each cube will give you an individual portion.

Red-wine Dressing

Makes about 150 ml (5 fl oz)

2 teaspoons Dijon mustard

2 tablespoons red-wine vinegar (if using Cabernet Sauvignon, add 1½ teaspoons, adding more once finished if preferred)

1 egg yolk or 1 tablespoon bought ready-made mayonnaise

4 tablespoons walnut oil

4 tablespoons groundnut oil

salt and freshly ground black pepper

mustard

Introduction This dressing can be used to complement many dishes, including salads, the Country Pâté (page 24), and the Grilled Mackerel with Champ Potatoes and Black Pudding (page 22). A Cabernet Sauvignon red-wine vinegar is my preferred variety, as this holds a very rich and complete taste. It is made by a long, slow and gentle process, known as the Orléans method, which makes it more expensive, but also more mature, powerful and full in flavour; consequently, less is needed to enhance the dressing. If using a basic red-wine vinegar (instead of Cabernet Sauvignon), it can be strengthened by the addition of a few tablespoons of reduced red wine. White-wine vinegar can be used in this recipe, but I've found a good-quality red-wine variety gives much the best flavour.

The addition of an egg yolk almost guarantees a creamy emulsion finish, holding the dressing together for a lot longer. Whenever using raw egg yolk, the dressing should be kept refrigerated. If you'd prefer not to include the yolk, it can be replaced by a tablespoon of bought mayonnaise.

Method Whisk together the Dijon mustard, vinegar and egg yolk or mayonnaise. Mix together the two oils, the walnut giving the dressing a nutty finish, and gradually whisk into the mustard and vinegar. Mix very slowly, as you would do when making home-made mayonnaise or hollandaise sauce. This will help the oil to emulsify with the base ingredients. Once all the oil is added, season with salt and pepper and the dressing is ready.

Note: *If using only a red-wine reduction in this dressing, add it as the last ingredient when the reduction has cooled.*

Sauce Béarnaise

Serves 4–6 (about 200 ml/7 fl oz)

2 large shallots, finely chopped

½ teaspoon crushed black peppercorns

1 tablespoon snipped or broken tarragon leaves, stalks chopped and reserved

3 tablespoons white-wine vinegar

2 egg yolks

3 tablespoons cold water

175 g (6 oz) clarified butter (see Simple Hollandaise Sauce, page 206)

squeeze of lemon juice

salt and pepper

Introduction A French classic that accompanies many dishes – grilled steaks, lamb chops, fish fillets and more. I give you the recipe for the standard *béarnaise* here, but within the book you'll find one or two extra flavours have been added to suit the particular dish – such as mustard seed in Pork Mixed Grill Plate with Roasted Apple and Bacon (page 122) or green peppercorns in Tunafish Steaks on Bitter Red-wine Onions (page 71).

Method Combine the chopped shallots, crushed black peppercorns, chopped tarragon stalks and white-wine vinegar in a small saucepan. Boil and reduce by half. Leave to cool. Once cold, mix with the egg yolks and 3 tablespoons of cold water in a bowl over simmering water and whisk until a thick ribbon stage (sabayon) is achieved. Remove the bowl from the pan and ladle in the warm clarified butter very slowly, whisking continuously until all has been added. The mixture will emulsify and thicken. Add a squeeze of lemon juice and season with salt and pepper before straining through a sieve. Add the snipped tarragon leaves and keep warm.

If *béarnaise* sauce is allowed to cool, the butter will set, so when spooned on to anything hot, the sauce will separate. For this reason, do not make the sauce more than 1 hour in advance. Keep it covered with butter paper or cling film and sit in a warm place to retain its temperature.

Note: *Should the sauce become too thick when adding the clarified butter to the sabayon, slightly loosen with warm water before continuing.*

An extra egg yolk will give extra body to the finished sauce.

Basic Butter Sauce

Makes about 150 ml (5 fl oz)

100 g (4 oz) cold butter, diced

1 shallot or ½ small onion, finely chopped

1 bay leaf

½ star anise (optional)

2 cardamom pods (optional)

2 tablespoons white-wine vinegar

4 tablespoons white wine

6 tablespoons Chicken, Fish or Vegetable Stock (page 201, 201 or 204) or alternative, or water

2 tablespoons single cream

salt and pepper

Introduction This sauce is better known among chefs as *beurre blanc* (white butter). It is a simple and buttery sauce that works with many fish, meat or vegetarian dishes. The basic ingredients are normally white-wine vinegar, water, chopped shallots and butter. I have added a few more to add a lot more flavour. I have also given four alternative 'stocks': your choice depends on which dish you are serving the sauce with.

Method Melt a small knob of butter in a pan and add the shallot/onion, the bay leaf, the star anise and cardamom pods, if using, and a twist of black pepper. Cook for a few minutes, without colouring, until softened. Add the vinegar and reduce by three-quarters. Add the wine and reduce by three-quarters. Pour in the stock of your choice and reduce again by half. Add the single cream to emulsify the butter.

Bring the reduction to a simmer and whisk in the remaining butter a few pieces at a time. Season and strain through a sieve. If the sauce is too thick, loosen it with a few drops of water or lemon juice. The basic butter sauce is now ready to use.

Simple Hollandaise Sauce

Makes about 200 ml (7 fl oz)

175g (6 oz) unsalted butter

2 egg yolks

2 tablespoons warm water

juice of 1 lemon

salt and cayenne or ground white pepper

Introduction I'm not sure how this famous butter sauce found its name, but it certainly wasn't from Holland. It's a French classic, and has alos been known as a suace Isigny, named after the home town of France's finest butter. Classically, a white-wine vinegar reduction is made, similar to that in bearnaise sauce, but without the herbs. In this simple version, acidity is provided by lemon juice, which also lends its wonderful fruit flavour.

Method Clarify the butter by melting it until its solids have become separate from the rich yellow oil. Remove from the heat and leave to cool until just warm. The solids will now be at the base of the pan. Any excess solids on top can be skimmed away.

Add the yolk to the water with half the lemon juice. Whisk over a pan of simmering water to a ribbon stage until at least doubled in volume, lighter in colour and almost the consistency of softly whipped cream.

Remove from the heat and slowly add the clarified butter, whisking vigorously. This will emulsify the butter into the egg-yolk mixture. If the sauce seems too thick and almost sticky while adding the butter, loosen slightly with another squeeze of lemon or water. Season with salt and cayenne or white pepper, and add the remaining lemon juice, if needed, to enrich the total flavour. The sauce is now ready to serve. For a guaranteed smooth, silky finish, strain through a sieve once seasoned.

Keep the sauce in a warm bowl and cover with cling film for up to 1 hour before use. If allowed to cool, the butter sets and the sauce separates when reheated, so don't let this happen.

Notes: *Hollandaise sauce can take on a lot more flavours, so here are a few suggestions.*

- *For a sauce mousseline add whipped cream before serving.*
- *Add a teaspoon or two of Dijon mustard for* sauce moutarde.
- *Melt the butter to a nut-brown stage before adding, and this gives you a* sauce noisette.
- *Replace the lemon juice with the juice of 2–3 blood oranges, reduced to a syrupy consistency. The finely grated zest of 1 blood orange can be added to the juices while boiling to tenderize. When added to a basic hollandaise, this creates a classic* sauce maltaise, *perfect for serving with grilled duck, game or fish dishes.*

Mayonnaise

Makes about 450 ml (15 fl oz)

3 egg yolks

1 tablespoon malt or white-wine vinegar

1 teaspoon English or Dijon mustard

300 ml (10 fl oz) olive oil

1 teaspoon hot water

salt, pepper and a few drops of lemon juice (optional)

Introduction Home-made mayonnaise is so easy to make, offering a fuller flavour than many bought varieties.

Method Whisk the egg yolks, vinegar, mustard and seasonings together, then slowly add the olive oil, whisking continuously. When all the oil is added, finish with the water and correct the seasoning. A few drops of lemon juice can be added to enhance the taste. If refrigerated, the mayonnaise will keep for up to 1 week.

Home-made Tomato Ketchup

Makes about 600 ml (1 pint)

1 clove

1 bay leaf

½ teaspoon ground coriander or a few coriander seeds

½ teaspoon ground cinnamon or ½ cinnamon stick (optional)

250 ml (9 fl oz) cider or white-wine vinegar

8 tablespoons demerara or caster sugar

1.5 kg (3 lb) net weight of ripe tomatoes after quartering and seeding

½ teaspoon sea salt

½ teaspoon English mustard powder

1 garlic clove, crushed

dash of Tabasco sauce

1 tablespoon tomato purée

Introduction This ketchup provides the perfect flavouring for the Cocktail Sauce (page 18).

Method Tie the clove, bay leaf, coriander and cinnamon, if using, in a piece of muslin. Place the vinegar and sugar in a heavy-based pan and bring to a simmer. Add all the other ingredients and bring to the boil, stirring to prevent any sticking. Reduce the temperature and simmer, stirring occasionally, for 40 minutes.

Discard the muslin bag, blitz the tomato mixture in a food processor or liquidizer, then push the sauce through a sieve.

If you find the sauce too thin once cold, simply boil again and thicken with a little cornflour or arrowroot mixed to a paste with water, being careful not to make it too starchy. This will prevent the tomato water separating from the sauce. The sauce will keep for up to 1 month if refrigerated.

Tarragon Oil

Makes 150 ml (5 fl oz)

150 ml (5 fl oz) olive oil (50–85 ml/ 2–3 fl oz can be replaced with groundnut oil for a softer olive flavour)

1 bunch of tarragon

Introduction This oil works well with many fish and chicken dishes, as well as being a good base for salad dressings. Once made, it will keep almost indefinitely if refrigerated.

Bunches of tarragon, like most herbs, come in many different sizes. Obviously, a generous bunch, say 50 g (2 oz), will give you a stronger-flavoured oil.

Method Tear the leaves and stalks and place in a small saucepan along with the oil. Bring slowly to the simmer and cook for 1–2 minutes without colouring the tarragon. Remove from the heat, place a lid on the pan and leave for several hours to cool and infuse. When ready, push through a sieve, squeezing every bit of flavour from the tarragon. The oil is now ready and will have taken on a pale green colour with a rich tarragon flavour.

Fresh Pasta

Makes about 400 g (14 oz)

250 g (9 oz) '00' flour (if unavailable, substitute with a pasta flour or fine semolina)

pinch of salt

2 whole eggs

2 large egg yolks

1 tablespoon olive oil

1 tablespoon water

Introduction The Italian word 'pasta' means 'dough', but over the last 50 years it has come to mean the product made from it. A combination of flour and water has been manufactured as food for thousands of years. There is no real record of where and when it originated, but most culinary cultures have some form of pasta or noodle. The first reference to pasta in Britain – a ravioli – appeared in a fourteenth-century cookery book. Over the next few centuries, other types of pasta were introduced, among them macaroni and vermicelli ('little worms'), but it was not until the second half of the twentieth century that it became a staple food in Britain.

Pasta is made with a durum wheat flour or semolina, and there are many conflicting recipes (this probably becoming another), which tell different stories and give different methods and results. The original dough may have been just water mixed with flour, but other ingredients have been added since.

I have found the best flour to use is an Italian wheat flour known as '00'. It is finely milled, giving good results, particularly if making spaghetti, tagliatelli, fettuccine or lasagne. To make special shapes, the flour needs to have its texture reinforced with some semolina. Eggs also help to do this, and the recipe can be made with just whole eggs, but I'm using egg yolks as the main binding agent. This will give a richer flavour and colour to the pasta. For extra flavour, a pinch of saffron can be added to the water. Warm, infuse and cool before squeezing all the flavour from the strands. The deep yellow-orange saffron water is now ready to use.

Method Sift the flour and salt on to a cold surface. Arrange into a volcano shape. Place the eggs in the 'crater' with the olive oil and water. Now slowly work the flour into the centre until a paste has formed. It is now best to knead the dough with clean hands on a freshly floured surface. You may find the dough quite soft, in which case simply work with extra flour. The dough can now be worked for 10 minutes until smooth with a slight elastic texture. Wrap in cling film and leave to rest for 30–40 minutes.

The pasta is now ready to roll into the required shape. Before putting through a pasta-rolling machine, it's best to roll it out 3–4 mm (about ⅛ in) thick. This will now easily pass through the machine, cutting to the size and thickness (1–2 cm/½–¾ in) required. If a pasta machine is unavailable, simply roll to 1–2 cm (½–¾ in) by hand.

Most pasta needs just simmering salted water to cook in. If cooking pasta sheets, add a tablespoon or two of olive oil. It's always best to cook leaving a slight bite in the texture. Fettuccine, tagliatelle and pasta sheets will take 2–3 minutes.

Goat's Cheese and Sweet Pepper Pancakes

Makes 12–15 pancakes

1 egg

150 ml (5 fl oz) milk

125 g (4 oz) self-raising flour

1 tablespoon mashed potato

1 small or ½ medium red pepper, very finely diced

1 heaped tablespoon finely chopped spring onion

1 tablespoon grated Parmesan cheese

75 g (3 oz) goat's cheese, rind removed, diced

salt and pepper

olive oil and butter, for frying

Introduction This recipe is a great way of using up any leftover mashed potatoes. It can be multiplied by many, making the pancakes a complete starter (lovely with a green salad) or savoury dish.

Method Whisk the egg with the milk. Add the flour, mashed potato, finely chopped red pepper and spring onion. The Parmesan and goat's cheese can now be folded in. Season. The mixture should spread slightly when spooned into the pan.

To cook, simply heat a non-stick frying pan with a trickle of olive oil. Divide tablespoons of the mix around the pan and cook on a medium heat for a few minutes until golden brown. Flip over the pancakes and continue to fry, adding a small knob of butter, for a further minute or two. As cooked, the pancakes can be kept warm under a cloth while the process continues. They can be made in advance and warmed gently in the oven, brushing with butter before serving.

To achieve perfectly round cakes, lightly grease a few metal round cutters, spooning the mix into them in the frying pan.

Poached Eggs

Serves 4

4 eggs

water

malt or white-wine vinegar

Introduction There are one or two dishes in this book that require poached eggs. I love their consistency, with the soft yolks, once cut, spilling into the other flavours. But there are also one or two secrets concerning the perfect poached egg, and I'm going to share those secrets with you. A fairly generous quantity of vinegar, up to one-third of the water content, can be added. This helps set the protein of the whites almost instantly around the yolks, without tainting their fresh flavour. Once the water approaches the simmer, whisk it fairly vigorously and crack the egg into the centre. As the liquid turns, it pulls and sets the white around the yolks, leaving a wonderful round shape. It's also very important that the water is deep. This means that the egg will be poaching before reaching the base of the pan and spreading.

Method Fill a saucepan with two-thirds water and one-third vinegar; at the very least add a generous splash of vinegar. Bring to a rapid simmer and whisk vigorously. Crack the egg into the centre and poach for 3–3½ minutes. Serve straight away or plunge into iced water to stop the cooking process. Once all eggs have been poached and cooled, trim off any excess whites to leave perfectly shaped eggs. To re-heat, plunge into rapidly simmering water for 1 minute: the eggs are now ready.

Note: *All four eggs can be poached together, placing one after the other in the centre of the rotating liquid. However, if cooking beforehand and keeping refrigerated in iced water until needed, poach each separately for the perfect cooking times.*

Blanching Tomatoes

Introduction Blanching is a process that can be applied to virtually all vegetables, fruits or meats. The idea is to plunge the particular item briefly into rapidly boiling water, then into ice-cold water to stop the cooking. (A lot of meats require quite the opposite, starting in cold water, then transferring to boiling.) Blanching is used to firm or soften flesh, to maintain colour, to help with skinning, or to remove raw flavour. For tomatoes, we just want to remove the skin.

Method Remove the stalk, then use the point of a small, sharp knife to make a 5 mm (¼ in) incision at the edge of the eye. Cut around and the eye will now become completely free.

If using very firm, or slightly under-ripe tomatoes, I suggest you make a shallow criss-cross cut at the opposite end too; this allows the boiling water to penetrate more efficiently.

Bring a pan of water to the boil, but have a bowl of ice-cold water nearby. When the water has reached a rapid boil, immerse the tomatoes using a slotted spoon. Leave firm tomatoes in the water for 8–10 seconds, very ripe ones for 6–8. Transfer to the iced water. The fruits are now ready to peel, with the skin pulling away easily.

The tomatoes are ready for slicing or quartering. For dicing, I suggest you quarter the tomatoes, remove the seeds and the flesh on kitchen paper. This will absorb excess water, leaving a firmer texture. The flesh can then be diced.

Blanching can be executed up to 24 hours in advance.

Home-made Crunchy Breadsticks

Makes 40–45

450 g (1 lb) plain flour, sifted

1 teaspoon salt

15 g (½ oz) fresh yeast or 7g sachet of dried yeast

250 ml (9 fl oz) warm water

80 ml (generous 3 fl oz) olive oil

flour, for rolling dough

coarse sea salt

Introduction These simple thin sticks of bread dough, baked until crisp and often completely dried through, are known in Italian as *grissini*. They are popular all over central Europe, offered or sold in bars, often with the salt adhering to the outside, which has the effect of stimulating the thirst. Breadsticks are a perfect accompaniment to virtually all soups, many salads and to offer with dips. This quantity of dough makes a lot of sticks, but they are irresistible. Once cool and dry, store in an airtight container for a longer life.

Method Mix the sifted flour and salt in a bowl, making a well in the centre. Crumble the fresh yeast into a separate bowl mixing with half the water until dissolved. Add all but 2 tablespoons of the olive oil to the water and pour into the well of the flour. Work together by hand, transferring to an electric mixer. Using a dough-hook attachment at a slow speed, add the remaining water and mix until a smooth consistency is achieved. If a machine is not available, the dough can be worked by hand for 10–15 minutes, also until smooth.

If using dry yeast, simply add to half the warm water (as for fresh yeast), then mix as described above.

Place the dough in a clean, lightly oiled bowl and cover with cling film, leaving to prove until doubled in volume. This process usually takes between 45 minutes and 1 hour. Pre-heat the oven to 200ºC/400ºF/Gas 6.

Knock back the dough, then break into walnut-sized pieces. Rolled by hand into thin strips 20–25 cm (8–10 in) long. Lay on parchment-lined baking trays, keeping a space between each. Brush the sticks with olive oil, sprinkling a little crunchy sea salt over each. Prove for no more than a further 6–8 minutes before baking for 10–15 minutes, until crispy and golden. Once cooked, remove from the oven and transfer to wire racks to cool. Store in an airtight container. If a crisper finish is preferred, increase the heat to 230ºC/450ºF/Gas 8 and cook for up to 20 minutes, turning the sticks over halfway through the cooking time.

Bread Croûtons for Soup

Serves 6

6 × 1 cm (½ in) thick slices of bread, crusts removed

4 tablespoons olive or groundnut oil

salt

Introduction 'Crouton' (with or without the circumflex) has been accepted in English since the early nineteenth century, the word deriving from the Latin *crusta*, meaning 'shell'. Croûton today means a small cube of bread that is fried or toasted until crisp in texture and golden brown in colour. Almost any bread can be used. Croûtons are served mostly with soup, but also feature in other dishes, in particular the world-famous Caesar salad.

It's best if the bread is 48 hours old: this prevents the pieces from absorbing too much of the oil.

Method Cut each slice into equal cubes, 1 × 1 cm (½ × ½ in). Heat half the oil in a large frying pan. Once hot, sprinkle in half the diced bread. Fry on a fairly high heat, turning the cubes to ensure an even all-round colour. If the pan becomes dry, add a splash more oil. It's important that the cubes are not deep-fried because this will make them greasy. Once totally coloured, spoon from the pan into a colander or on to kitchen paper; sprinkle with salt while still warm. Repeat the same process for the remaining cubes.

Croûtons can be made well before eating and either warmed through in the oven or in an almost dry frying pan.

Notes: *Just before serving, toss all the croûtons together in the frying pan and add 1–2 tablespoons of finely grated Parmesan cheese. This melts and sticks to the crispy bread pieces and eats well with many soups. Other flavours that can be included are crushed garlic and chopped herbs, or you could change the oil flavour to walnut or hazelnut.*

Caramelized Melba Toasts

Makes 4 triangles

1 slice of thin sliced white bread

icing sugar, for dusting

Introduction This is a simple accompaniment to many sweet dishes, such as the Iced Pear Parfait with Sweet Kirsch Cherries (page 158).

Method Toast the bread on both sides, then remove the crusts and cut the slice through the width of the bread. Scrape away the crumbs and cut each piece into two triangles. Dust heavily with icing sugar and sit them at the bottom of a grill on a low setting. The sugar will slowly caramelize. Once it is golden with burnt tinges of sugar, your melbas are ready.

Note: *Ground caramel can also be used instead of the sugar to give a richer flavour.*

Shortcrust Pastry and Sweet Shortcrust Pastry

Makes about 400 g (14 oz) of Shortcrust Pastry and 450 g (1 lb) of Sweet Shortcrust Pastry

225 g (8 oz) plain flour

pinch of salt

50 g (2 oz) butter, diced (or 100 g/4 oz if the lard is omitted)

50 g (2 oz) lard, diced

1 whole egg (optional) or an extra 25–50 ml (1–2 fl oz) water or milk

25 ml (1 fl oz) water or milk

Introduction The earliest pastry to be made in Britain was similar to hot-water crust and not, at first, intended to be eaten. Many more varieties developed over the years, among them shortcrust, which is probably the commonest and easiest to make. However, to guarantee good results, there are one or two golden rules that should be applied.

A straightforward plain flour will always work well. Self-raising is sometimes used but this can create too cakey a texture.

For plain shortcrust, the fat content can be split between butter and lard; the two work well together, giving a good flavour, and the lard really shortens the dough. Sweet shortcrust is best made with butter alone, as lard doesn't help the finished taste.

The fats should be cool before using, but not necessarily refrigerated, as this can make crumbing hard work.

Always rest the finished dough for 20–30 minutes. The gluten content in the flour reacts with the liquid (water or milk), giving a better texture to roll and work with.

Always roll pastry out on a cool and lightly floured surface. Pastry must remain cold, and the flour will prevent the pastry from sticking.

Method Sift the flour with the salt. Rub the butter and lard into the flour until a breadcrumb texture is achieved. Beat the egg with the water and work gently into the crumbs to a smooth dough (if excess crumbs are left in the bowl, add an extra tablespoon of water). Wrap in cling film and relax in the fridge for 20–30 minutes before using.

When needed, remove from the fridge and leave to approach a cool room temperature before rolling.

For the sweet shortcrust pastry, simply add 50–75 g (2–3 oz) of caster sugar or icing sugar to the above recipe once the breadcrrumbed stage has been reached, omit the lard and use all butter. Follow the method above.

Notes: *The pinch of salt can be omitted from the sweet pastry. The scraped seeds from a vanilla pod added to the pastry mix at its crumb stage will add another flavour, which enhances the taste of many fillings.*

Another flavour that works very well in the sweet version is the finely grated zest of one lemon.

Whenever lining a flan case or mould, it's best to leave excess pastry hanging over the edge during the cooking time to prevent it from shrinking into the case. Once removed from the oven, gently trim the excess pastry away leaving a neat finish.

Quick Puff or Flaky Pastry

Makes 750 g (1¾ lb)

300 g (11 oz) butter, chilled

450 g (1 lb) plain flour

1 teaspoon salt

200–250 ml (7–8 fl oz) cold water

Introduction We might think that puff pastry is a French invention, but the British were making rich butter pastes – flour mixed with butter, sugar, rose-water and spices, then interleaved with more butter – in the sixteenth century. It was given the name puff pastry in 1605, and was used mainly in the making of sweet tarts and the precursors of vol-au-vents.

Making puff pastry in the traditional way cannot be beaten. This recipe, however, is a lot quicker and does bring you very close to it. The resultant pastry can be used in any recipe needing puff pastry. Any not used will freeze very well.

Cut the chilled butter into small cubes. Sieve the flour with the salt. Add the butter, gently rubbing into the flour but not totally breaking down. Add the water, mixing to a pliable dough, still with pieces of butter showing.

Turn on to a floured surface and roll as for puff pastry, into a rectangle (approximately 45 × 15 cm/18 × 6 in). Fold in the right-hand one-third and then fold in the left-hand side on top. Leave to rest for 20 minutes. The pastry now needs to be rolled three times in the same fashion, resting it for 20 minutes between each turn.

The pastry is now ready to use.

Note: *A richer version of this pastry can be made with a higher butter content and with the addition of the juice from 1 lemon. Just follow the above recipe, only adding 175–225 ml (6–7 ½ fl oz), 75% of water with the juice.*

Good puff pastry can also be bought.

Home-made Digestive Biscuits

Makes about 24

100 g (4 oz) wholewheat flour

100 g (4 oz) medium oatmeal

50 g (2 oz) soft brown or caster sugar

1 teaspoon baking powder or ½ teaspoon bicarbonate of soda

pinch of salt

100 g (4 oz) butter or margarine

1–2 tablespoons milk

Introduction The word 'biscuit' applies to a huge variety of flour-based items, which are generally small and crisp. The name derives from the Latin *panis biscoctus*, 'bread twice cooked'. The original biscuits were like rusks, slices of bread re-baked to create a crisp finish. In this country, most early biscuits were spicy and sweet, but around the eighteenth century, plain varieties became popular as cheese accompaniments and 'nibbling' extras.

After featuring biscuits in many of my books, the one I've included here is the crumbly digestive biscuit, which is also known as wheatmeal and sweetmeal. It's a perfect accompaniment to the Fresh Cream-tea Custards on page 171, and also has the double pleasure of working well, because it is not over-sweet, with many cheeses, a usage popular in Victorian times. The commercial biscuit is of a finer texture than this home-made one, but you'll still be able to recognize its familiar flavour. For a finer, smoother finish, the wholewheat flour can be replaced with plain flour.

Method Pre-heat the oven to 180°C/350°F/Gas 4. Mix together all the dry ingredients and rub in the butter to make a breadcrumb texture. Now add enough milk to create a moist pastry consistency. Refrigerate for 15 minutes to firm the mix.

This creates a reasonably delicate dough, so it's important to roll between sheets of cling film with great care. When 3mm (⅛ in) thick cut into 6–7 cm (2½–3 in) discs, re-rolling any trimmings.

Place the discs on a lightly greased baking sheet and bake in the pre-heated oven for 15–20 minutes, until lightly browned and firm to the touch. Remove from the oven and leave to rest for 5 minutes before transferring to a wire rack. The digestives are now best kept in an airtight container and eaten within 2–3 days. However, once you've made them, it's very rare they last that long!

Ground Caramel

100 ml (3½ fl oz) water

150 g (5 oz) caster sugar

cooking oil, for greasing

Introduction Used to glaze (and colour) crème brûlée, melba toast (page 211) and more, ground caramel is very easy to make and stores well. It is basically just boiled water and sugar cooked to the caramel stage, before being set and then finely blitzed in a food processor.

Method Pour the water into a saucepan with the caster sugar. Stir with a spoon to mix and then leave on a low heat until the sugar has dissolved. Now turn up the heat and cook the sugar to a golden caramel stage. During this time, you may find some of the sugar crystallizing around the edge of the pan. If so, wash it away with a pastry brush dipped in cold water.

Once at a golden-brown stage (if you have a sugar thermometer, you need to heat the mixture to 150°C/300°F), pour into a lightly oiled tray, and allow to set. Once cool and crisp, break into small pieces before blitzing in a food processor to a caster-sugar consistency. The caramel is now ready to use, and when sprinkled on to melba toast or crème brûlées, simply melt with a gas gun (page 13) or under the grill to finish.

Any dessert item finished with this glaze gives the impression that liquid caramel has been used.

Stock Syrup

Makes about 300 ml (10 fl oz)

150 ml (5 fl oz) water

100 g (4 oz) sugar

Introduction This simple sweet syrup is ideal for poaching fruits and for making coulis and sorbets. The quantities here can be readily multiplied to suit required quantities.

Method Bring the two ingredients to the boil. Simmer for a few minutes until the sugar has completely dissolved and thickened the liquor. Cool and keep refrigerated until needed.

Crème Anglaise (Custard Sauce)

Makes 750 ml (1½ pints)

8 egg yolks

75 g (3 oz) caster sugar

1 vanilla pod, split (optional)

300 ml (10 fl oz) milk

300 ml (10 fl oz) double cream

Introduction This recipe will give you the tastiest of custard flavours.

Method Beat the egg yolks and sugar together in a bowl until well blended. Scrape the insides of the vanilla pod, if using, into the milk and cream in a saucepan, add the pod too, and bring to the boil. Sit the bowl of egg yolks and sugar over a pan of hot water and whisk the cream into the mixture. As the egg yolks cook, the custard will thicken. Keep stirring until it starts to coat the back of a spoon, then remove the bowl from the heat and the vanilla pod from the custard. Serve warm or cold. To prevent a skin forming while cooling, cover the custard with greaseproof paper while it cools, or stir it occasionally.

The custard can be brought back up to heat over a pan of hot water, but it must never boil. If that happens, the sauce will separate.

Redcurrant Jelly

Makes 750–900 g (1½–2 lb)

1.5 kg (3 lb) freshly picked redcurrants

preserving sugar

Introduction Redcurrant jelly is the classic British accompaniment to lamb, mutton and game dishes, its sweetness working and helping with those meats' rich flavours. The jelly is recommended with the Roast Rump of Lamb on page 118, but it will also go very well with the Pigeon and Red-onion Pasty (page 108).

Method Place the picked redcurrants in a saucepan and barely cover with water. Bring to the boil, then reduce the heat and simmer for 25–30 minutes, until the currants have become overcooked and mushy.

Leave to strain naturally through a fine sieve or muslin bag. This will take all the flavour and colour from the fruit. After several hours, when the dripping has stopped, measure the quantity of juice. For every 600 ml (1 pint) of juice, add 450 g (1 lb) of preserving sugar. Boil the sugar with the juices and simmer for 10 minutes. To test for consistency, simply spoon a little on to a side plate and refrigerate. Once at setting point, the jelly is ready. If still too loose, continue to cook and reduce to its 'setting' consistency. The jelly is now ready to pour into sterilized, hot jars. Once cold, the jelly will set.

For a slightly less sweet jelly, use 350 g (12 oz) of preserving sugar. This requires a little more reduction during its cooking time, but still gives a stronger, natural redcurrant flavour.

Note: *To sterilize the jars, place them in a large saucepan, cover with cold water, bring to the boil, and boil for 15 minutes. Carefully remove and leave to dry. Once the jars have been filled, covered and sealed, you can sterilize again: sit the jars on a wire rack or cloth in a large pan and almost cover them with water. Bring to the boil and boil for 15 minutes. Remove from the pan, dry and cool.*

Pumpkin and Date Chutney

Makes 1.8 kg (4 lb)

1.3 kg (3 lb) pumpkin, seeded, peeled and cut into 2.5 cm (1 in) chunks

450 g (1 lb) onions, chopped

225 g (8 oz) dates, stoned and chopped

350 ml white-wine vinegar or malt vinegar

1 teaspoon ground ginger

1 teaspoon ground allspice

1 teaspoon black pepper

450 g (1 lb) light soft brown sugar

juice of 1 orange

juice of 1 lemon

½ teaspoon salt

Introduction Pumpkins are best known in the culinary world as major ingredients in spicy pies and soups, as well as in bread, stews and casseroles. I was given this chutney to try, and have really enjoyed the results. It's a good accompaniment to the Country Pâté on page 24, and eats particularly well with tongue, ham and most cold meats, including roast game and pork pies.

The most common date available in the European market is *Deglet Noor*, which is quite sweet in flavour, with a translucent flesh. One that I prefer and recommend is the *Medjool*, which I have always used in sticky toffee pudding. It's an Indian fruit with a thick, toffee-like flesh packed with flavour.

Method Mix all the ingredients together and leave to marinate for 2–3 hours.

Place everything in a large pan and bring to a simmer, cooking gently for 40–50 minutes until the pumpkin has softened. Once cooked, strain the chutney in a colander, collecting the juices in a suitable saucepan. This can now be placed on a fast heat, reducing the liquor to a syrupy consistency. Once reduced, add the cooked pumpkin mix and the chutney is complete. Place in warm, sterilized jars and seal, storing in a cool dark place until needed.

Note: *To sterilize the jars, place them in a large saucepan, cover with cold water, bring to the boil, and boil for 15 minutes. Carefully remove and leave to dry. Once the jars have been filled, covered and sealed, you can sterilize again: sit the jars on a wire rack or cloth in a large pan and almost cover them with water. Bring to the boil and boil for 15 minutes. Remove from the pan, dry and cool.*

Pumpkin and Date Chutney

menus

Compiling a menu

Entertaining and cooking for friends can be a stressful event, with the workload in the kitchen sometimes becoming too heavy. Consequently, the event isn't fully enjoyed and, quite often, whoever's cooking loses their appetite.

Here are some points to remember when compiling menus. No matter how many dishes you feature, try and stick to these few golden rules. I've followed these with some suggestions for balanced menus, featuring a selection of dishes from this book that you might like to try.

1 Entertaining friends usually means we have to become hosts as well as chefs, but this double role can be played successfully with the right amount of preparation beforehand. If one dish involves a fair bit of work, make sure that the other courses need much less.

2 Always choose the main course first. This is the main feature of the meal, so dishes on either side of it must be balanced and shouldn't over-power it.

3 Break down the tasks for the main course. Does the dish need to be prepared and finished on the day or are there sections of it that can be prepared 2–3 days in advance? If it's the former, assess the workload according to the number of guests being entertained. If you would prefer to have very little last-minute work for the main course, for instance, choose a dish that is simple to finish off. The Turkey Ballotine (page 113), for example, requires much of the work to be done beforehand, and is finished off simply by carving (with no bones to worry about) and serving.

4 To see whether a menu will be feasible for you to carry out, compile a preparation list of the work that needs to be done in advance and just before serving for all the courses.

5 Decide the dessert and/or starter after the main. It's important to balance hot and cold dishes. If you choose a hot dessert, then it's almost essential to go for a cold starter, and vice versa.

6 Having provisionally chosen three courses, look at the ingredients and avoid repeating flavours or main ingredients (except for the bases of dishes, such as wine or stock).

7 Use cooking ingredients that will suit your guests.

8 Pay attention to the strength of flavours. A dominant one, such as heavy garlic, in a starter dish should be followed in the next course by a flavour that matches or even over-rides it.

9 Bear in mind what the textures and consistency of the dishes will be. These will depend partly on the cooking method, so use a different cooking method (steaming, stewing, pot-roasting, pan-frying and so on) for each course. A fillet of steamed salmon, for instance, will give you a totally different texture and flavour to pan-fried salmon, so, if you choose a pan-fried main-course dish, go for a steamed one, say, for a starter. This will help to give a separate 'identity' to each.

10 Create a balance between vegetarian, fish and meat dishes.

11 Weigh up the flavours by looking at the sauces. Don't go for too many cream-based ones. Dressings work well with many starters and fish dishes, and will complement a cream sauce featured in a main course. Obviously a dessert with a custard sauce (crème anglaise) would not be a good follow-up to a previous course that was creamy.

12 Look also at the seasoning of a dish. Other than the basic salt and pepper, there are also spices to consider – they will need to balance the seasoning of the other dishes.

13 Think about the seasons when fresh produce will be available. British cookery, in particular, has too many good flavours to ignore. Here's a guide to the best seasons to buy some of our favourite ingredients:

Asparagus	May–June
Broad beans	May–September
Broccoli	May–June
French Beans	June–September
Leeks	August–May
Peas	May–October
Runner beans	July–October
Tomatoes	March–November
Apples	July–March
Blackberries	July–September
Cherries	June–August
Pears	August–February
Plums	July–October
Raspberries	July–September
Rhubarb	December–June
Strawberries	May–June

Potatoes, cabbages, carrots, cauliflowers and spinach are 'in season' all year round.

Bearing these points in mind, overleaf are some suggested menus you might like to try.

Two courses

Here are a few two-course menu suggestions, which have been created to give a balanced meal without the necessity of a third course. After all, desserts are not everybody's favourite.

Menu 1

Lettuce Soup Finished with French Dressing (page 47)

Roast Monkfish with Crispy Bacon or Parma Ham (page 64)

A 'salad-style' soup, simple to make, with a light, fresh flavour. The main course has a 'meaty' roast feel, without the monkfish becoming too strong and overfilling.

Menu 2

Pork Cutlet Hotpot (page 136)

Dressed Crab Salad (page 192)

A filling and complete main course with onions, potatoes and pork all under one roof. The savoury, which could also be served as a starter, provides the contrast of a crisp, light finish with very distinctive flavours.

Menu 3

Braised Creamy Rice and Poached Egg 'Pie' (page 95)

Marmalade Cream Tart (page 167)

A risotto-based main course, with a rich orange second course. The pastry case provides the 'pie' base.

Menu 4

Soft-boiled Eggs with Spinach and Parmesan Cheese (page 189)

Open Smoked Haddock Lasagne (page 188)

These two courses show the versatility that a menu can have. Both have been chosen from the savouries chapter because they are light dishes but with very distinctive flavours.

Menu 5

Chicken Liver Pâté with Bramley Apple Jelly (page 29)

Flourless Chocolate Slice (page 179)

Both of these are rich dishes, but are appropriate for a lunch or supper. For me, these dishes are ideal for an eating-with-pleasure-and-leisure lifestyle, with no rush – just seconds!

Three courses

Menu 1 – Vegetarian

Two-onion, Two-cheese Potato Tart (page 38)

Aubergine Charlottes with Ratatouille Dressing (page 106)

Nutmeg Spring Greens (page 154)

Glasses of Dark Chocolate Mousse with Icy Frothy Coffee Milkshake (page 178)

This three-course menu holds a great balance of flavours, with the starter containing two cheeses – Gruyère and Parmesan – and the potatoes themselves. The latter cut out the need for a potato accompaniment to the main-course dish. Thinking about accompaniments is so important in menu-planning. There are many dishes that need little help, and quite often 'overloading' a course can almost spoil the meal, certainly the main dish they are accompanying.

You'll also notice that the ingredients are themselves simple and, when put together, pay one another nothing but compliments.

The main-course charlotte is quite an unusual and stunning dish, visually and in terms of the flavours. Ratatouille has a popular flavour, so all tastes are catered for with this dish. Moulding aubergines in individual pudding basins creates a nice surprise for your guests and, when broken into, the slightly spicy-flavoured filling stands up by itself against the previous course.

Vegetables are not essential here, but a plate of nutmeg greens (or English Spinach, page 142) is fresh and clean enough not to interfere with the ratatouille dressing flavours. A big bonus when making this dish is that it can be prepared well in advance (up to 48 hours ahead) and microwaved when needed.

On to the dessert. The rich, dark chocolate mousse works in a similar fashion to the ratatouille, with flavours strong enough to hold up against the previous course. The mousse is set in the fridge, with just the frothy coffee milkshakes to top and finish the dish.

Menu 2 – Fish

Country Pâté (page 24)

Roast Sea Bass with Glazed Crab Mashed Potatoes (page 63)

'Braised' Blue Cheese Leeks (page 146)

Toasted Apricots on Warm Sugared Custard Toasts (page 176)

Country pâté needs 2–3 days' maturing to acquire its full flavour, so it can be made well in advance. The suggested tartare dressing connects with the main course because tartare is normally served with fish. The dressing does eat well with the pâté, and when eating this, I always find my tastebuds telling me they are expecting some form of fish course to follow.

Sea bass is a superb fish to cook and eat. It is quite expensive, but certainly worth paying for. Other fish, such as cod, salmon or sole, can be used in its place. The dish is clean in its flavours, without being over-saucy. The fish is always best cooked at the last moment so you can appreciate all its freshness. The mashed potato can be made one or two hours before the meal, re-heated and the crab meat added after the first course. The sauce has a base that comes straight from a tin, but it has a little magic about it for this very reason: it tastes as if you've spent hours making a crab bisque.

Leeks, always a perfect accompaniment to fish, eat well with the bass and crab flavours, just buttered and without the blue cheese.

The apricot dessert takes British fruit sponges and custards and turns them into quite a sensational dish. The sponge and custard come from the steeped brioche slice, which is pan-fried and topped with apricots. The apricots can be prepared and cooked to their first stage before the meal, and warmed while the sponges are frying. Food provides talking points, and this dessert will certainly do that with its surprise of hidden custard.

Menu 3 – Meat

Warm Sole Salad '*Belle Vapeur*' (page 20)

Beef Goulash with Sweet Red Pepper and Parsley Gnocchi (page 126)

Fresh Cream-tea Custards with Home-made Digestive Biscuits (page 171)

The beef goulash is quite a rich and filling dish, accompanied simply by the buttered gnocchi. Comforting main-course dishes like this immediately create a relaxed, homely atmosphere at the table. Like a pâté, it will improve if made up to 24 hours in advance. Allow the meat to relax and take on all the flavours, ready for re-heating. The gnocchi can also be cooked in advance and finished after the first course. Because of its rich flavours, the goulash must be balanced by the courses before and after it.

The steamed sole salad is very light, crisp and fresh in texture. The sole fingers offer a succulence to accompany the leaves and garnishes. Everything can be prepared earlier and the last-minute job of layering the leaves can be done while the sole steams.

The cream-tea custards are based on crème brûlée (burnt cream), a favourite with everyone. It always eats well after a rich main course. The jasmine tea flavour is not over-powered by the paprika-flavoured meat, and it gives this custard cream a very British feel, with the home-made biscuits becoming the tea's natural accompaniment.

No vegetables have been mentioned here, but if required I suggest the Red-wine Baby Carrots (page 150) or the English Spinach (page 142).

Four courses

table d'hôte

Menu 1

Poached Eggs Benedict (page 34)

Fillets of John Dory Poached in Shiraz Wine on Creamed Celeriac and Cabbage (page 82)

Chicken Sauté with Mushrooms and Tarragon (page 120)

Bitter-sweet Strawberry Tart with Mascarpone Cheesecake Cream (page 182)

Each of the first three courses has its own distinctive flavour and sauce: the poached egg with a buttery béarnaise sauce, the John Dory in the red-wine sauce, and the chicken with a creamy finish.

Obviously only half the portions of John Dory will be needed for a second course. The general flavour of the dish is not 'over-saucy' and the red-wine poaching liquor produces a good, all-round flavour. This menu also offers a red wine in the fish dish and a white wine in the chicken dish.

Chicken, mushrooms and tarragon are classic flavours that can afford to take on others. Roast onions (page 144) therefore fit in very well with everything else on the plate. If a potato dish is also required (it's not essential), I suggest the *Pommes Macaire* on page 141. It can be prepared well in advance and finished in the oven quite quickly.

A strawberry dessert is usually a firm favourite with most people. The tart base provides a pastry element to the menu, and its soft mascarpone cream offers a contrast of textures to the other dishes.

None of these dishes is too filling, so a good balance can be found, all with different presentations and flavours.

Menu 2

Seared Sea Trout with Fennel-flavoured, Tender Sauerkraut and a Red-wine Sauce (page 86)

Roast Rump of Lamb with Redcurrant Jelly and Lyonnaise Potatoes (page 118) and Red-pepper Potatoes (page 112)

Iced Nougat Glacé with Bitter-sweet Kumquats (page 160)

A plate of British cheeses (page 198)

Two hot and two cold courses. The sea trout is featured within the book as a main course. Simply halve the ingredients for a starter. Sea trout has its own distinctive flavour that is complemented by the soft piquancy of the fennel sauerkraut. The red-wine dressing should be lightly drizzled around the fish to enhance its flavour rather than overpower it. The tender, roasted rump of lamb is accompanied perfectly by the redcurrant jelly. The two rich flavours together are lifted and complemented by the savoury sautéed potatoes and onions.

This menu is balanced by the iced dessert that follows. Nougat glacé has a sweet caramel flavour that could become oversweet but for the cheese course afterwards. However, the bitter-sweetness of the kumquats checks and prepares the palate for the savoury to follow.

A plate of cheese needs no introduction. It offers choice for the guests, with various textures and flavours to suit all palates.

Six Courses

Marinated Vegetables with Soft Cauliflower Cream (page 27)

Fresh Herb Broth (page 54)

Pan-fried Sea Bass with Blackberry Shallots and Creamy Hollandaise Sauce (page 76)

Crusted Lamb with Creamy Ham and Red-pepper Potatoes (page 112)

English Spinach (page 142)

Iced Pear Parfait with Sweet Kirsch Cherries (page 158)

Onion and Fromage Blanc Tart (page 190) or cheese and biscuits

The thoughts behind this six-courser are first concerned with the flavours not over-powering one another, then with the various cooking methods and the advance preparation that can be done. Although it sounds overwhelming, the menu can be executed quite easily with some planning.

Although the vegetables are marinated in a dressing that's quite powerful, they are 'calmed' nicely by the addition of a smooth cream. They can also be prepared, peeled, trimmed and so on 24 hours in advance, ready to be blanched/cooked on the day before marinating. The cauliflower can be cut into florets the day before, again ready to be cooked and creamed. Once all are made, they simply need to be presented on a plate. There is no last-minute cooking.

The fresh herb broth has few components. The soup relies on the fresh, natural herb flavours. The base is best made on the morning of the day required, needing only to be warmed and the herbs added. This will allow a good 8–10 minute rest period between the first two courses. With the herbs all snipped before the meal, there's little to worry about.

The blackberry shallots hold the bonus of maturing like a good wine. These can be cooked up to 48 hours in advance, which allows them to mature and results in a very rich, balanced flavour. The Sauce Mousseline (page 206) is also included but, as mentioned in the recipe, it can be made up to 1 hour before the meal, and finished with the whipped cream when the dish is served. The sea bass, the main feature of the course, is best cooked at the last minute.

Lamb is a very popular meat, a favourite among many people. Here it's a roasted dish, providing a contrast to the pan-fried fish course and marinated vegetables of the first. The beauty of this particular lamb dish is that its first stage of roasting, before it's topped with the crust, can be executed during the fish course. This gives you plenty of time, once you've finished the fish, to top with the already pressed crusts. Finish by baking in the oven and it's ready to serve.

The accompaniments – mashed potatoes and spinach – can both be cooked in advance. The spinach can even be cooked in the morning, buttered, seasoned and microwaved when needed, or cooked at the last minute.

The components of the dessert can be prepared at least several days in advance. The crisp, iced parfait can be made 2–3 days ahead, the cherries can be steeped in Kirsch literally weeks before needed and the poached pears also have a long fridge life. This is a sumptuous dessert and stress-free.

For a sixth course, cheese, biscuits and good port or red wine provide the easiest of answers. However, the onion and fromage blanc tart is a wonderful alternative, allowing you to show off your cookery skills, and also helping to balance the menu by including a pastry dish. As you'll notice from the ingredients list, it needs very little but offers an awful lot.

Index